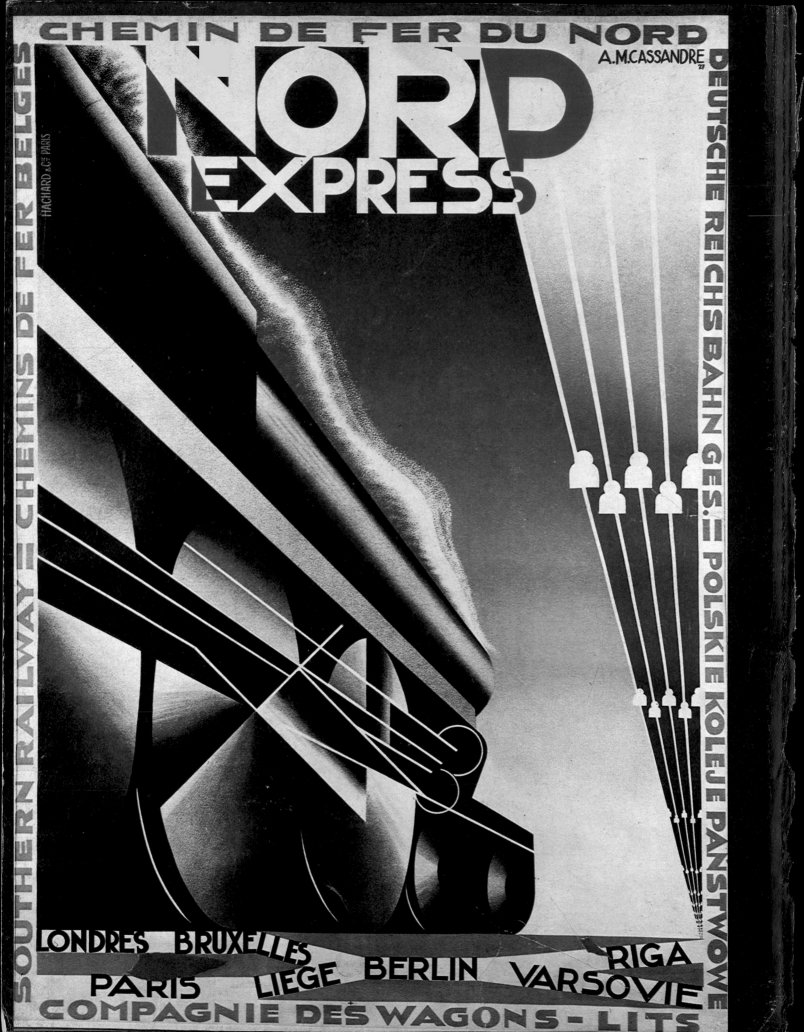

THE LANGUAGE OF
GRAPHICS

by Edward Booth-Clibborn
and Daniele Baroni

Harry N. Abrams, Inc., Publishers, New York

Frontispiece: Adolph Mouron Cassandre, *Nord Express*, 1927

Captions and Chapter 8 translated from the Italian by Anna Harper

Library of Congress Cataloging in Publication Data

Booth-Clibborn, Edward.
   The language of graphics.

   Translation of Il linguaggio della grafica.
   Bibliography: p.
   Includes index.
   1. Graphic arts. 2. Communication in art.
3. Commercial art. I. Baroni, Daniele, joint author.
II. Title.
NC997.B5513   741.6   80–10984
ISBN 0–8109–1252-X

Library of Congress Catalogue Card Number: 80–10984

The illustrative material of this book is based on the seven-volume series *Graphic Design of the World* originally published by Kodansha Ltd, Tokyo, 1974–76.

Published in 1980 by Harry N. Abrams, Incorporated, New York

Printed and bound in Italy by Officine Grafiche di Arnoldo Mondadori Editore, Verona

CONTENTS

FOREWORD

The term "graphic art" is used to denote all activities connected with the technique of writing; yet this term seems too generic to represent such a specific research area as the design and creation of an image. The term, moreover, sometimes causes confusion by implying an association between activities that actually have no interaction with each other. Graphics in art, which means a limited and exclusive production, is quite separate from the treatment of various aspects of graphic design and visual communication, which is intended instead for a wider audience and which is the subject of this book. What distinguishes the graphics examined here from other graphic activities is that the former are communicated through a medium, that is, through a channel of communication that is far reaching, such as the press (the most traditional channel), television, cinema, commercial activity, or even the street, which in the language of graphics is understood as exhibition space for visual messages.

The fundamental principle governing the process of graphic communication is derived from the mathematical theory of information, which establishes that communication always takes place between those units that transmit information and those that receive it; the process requires a means of explanation. And since the transmission of a coded message occurs between man and man or between man and machine, graphic design and visual communication find their natural diffusion through the instruments of the mass media, or at least through the techniques of picture reproduction.

Graphic art is thus a creative technique at the disposal of anyone who would devise a message intended for a wide audience. The successful communication of any message requires a visualization that is based not only on the application of graphic techniques but also on the expression of meaningful values, and to achieve this, graphic artists must make use of the valuable contributions of other disciplines, such as psychology, symbology, and iconography. In this book we have grouped into sections the most distinctive applications of graphic art, showing—through themes, analogies, and examples—the various works by visual artists, designers, and art directors as seen in their own context and defined accordingly.

The Introductory chapter examines the significance of the sign, and puts forth, in a nonsystematic way, a few examples of historical symbols that have formed a pictorial apparatus through the years and are now considered a universal heritage. Iconography owes much to the esoteric, symbolic representations peculiar to the cabala, theosophy, the Rosicrucians, masonry,

oriental philosophies, and, of course, the Christian world. All symbolic communications, even the contemporary trademark, are based on the earliest representations of mystical signs: the cross, the circle, the triangle, particular numbers, such as three (the unity of the trinity), as well as conceptual symbols such as the star, the labyrinth, and the spiral.

The second and third chapters illustrate numerous examples in which the communicative function of graphics services the editorial world, the advertising world, the fields of illustrated news, and also the freer, more escapist newsstand genres. In the advertising field the criterion has been to honour works of art direction and the more creative compositions rather than to pass any specific judgment on the nature of the publicity campaign itself.

The fourth chapter investigates the psychological effects of the graphic sign, in particular when its action is pushed to the limits of perception or when it acts within the sphere of an optical ambiguity.

The fifth chapter probes the use of three-dimensional graphics by large commodities dealers, from the sleek and elegant design of packaging to the equally polished use of games, from origami to the fashion object. The sixth chapter enlarges on this concept as it applies to the environment as a whole. Graphics intervene in interior design, in architecture, in the application of colour within the city, in environmental art, in murals offered as political gestures or simply as decorative props, and in all the other aspects that constitute the phenomenon of supergraphics.

The seventh chapter explores the design of visual communication, that is, illustrations, focusing on their expressive value and the significance that this has in the creation of an image. Concluding the book is an historical review of the development of graphic art from the end of the nineteenth century to the present day, a span of barely a hundred years.

The examinations of these various chapters allow for a general but clear vision of a language devised for signs and visual codes, a language considered to be an integral and relevant part of what is today defined as the cult of the image.

The authors (Edward Booth-Clibborn, who wrote the main text, and Daniele Baroni, who devised the general layout, selected the pictures, and wrote the captions as well as Chapter 8) both work within the field of graphics and design. Each draws a sharp profile of the subject, touching on its fundamental problems, presenting this exciting material in a richly informative way.

1. THE SIGN AND SYMBOL IN GRAPHIC ART

The highest seraph has but
a single image. He seizes as a unity all that his
inferiors regard as manifold.
MEISTER ECKHART

Today signs and symbols can either be highly charged with emotional, political, economic, aesthetic, or religious meaning, or they can be trivial and inconsequential. The materials and technologies for producing signs and symbols are so readily available that creating a significant mark or sign is something that can be done quite casually and does not in itself require much consideration.

In the past, and in simpler societies of the present, a far higher degree of search for and preparation and modification of materials is necessary before a mark can be made. The act of making a mark of any kind takes on a far deeper significance and the mark itself, therefore, takes on a special meaning and power.

It is not surprising then that in all such cultures these highly charged signs deal with the most important of all subjects—the fundamental ordering of the universe—a pattern of meaning which man imposes on the raw input of experience in order to make sense of his world. In making sense, in our own terms, of the signs of other cultures, it is necessary to unravel the whole network of references and meanings that make up the cosmology or world view of the culture in question.

In looking at a sign we can, for analytic purposes, say that it has three aspects. It has form (how it appears), it has objective definition (it is a cross or a dagger), and finally it has significance (a meaning in the particular context in which it appears). A written X, for instance, may have an identical form (it is also called a cross); it may mean an implied rejection (if it is used to mark an answer in an exam paper); or it may mean an acceptance (if it is by a candidate's name on a voting form). In each of these examples the same sign

takes on meaning through its relation to the context in which it appears—an accepted conventional system of meanings in which the sign finds its place. Fundamentally, a sign is a way of modifying the world in which we live. It is part of a system of ordering reality into meaningful units which are all related through a larger system of ideas about the world.

Body paint or tattoos can distinguish one set, sex, or class from another. A stone can be marked to set it apart from other stones. A pot can be marked to identify it as mine, not yours.

It appears to be characteristic of the human mind that it thinks in terms of analogies or metaphors. Thus, some objects are more readily understood in terms of others. The dome of the sky is likened to a bowl. The Milky Way becomes a huge python or a spray of cosmic sperm.

It is out of this metaphorical aspect of human imagination that the symbol is born. The bare mark is elaborated further into a series of meanings. A line of dried clay on a rock represents the moon. The moon (Selene) is the sister of the sun (Helios). In a myth the moon transgressed divine moral law and therefore stands for profane sexuality. So the pattern of meaning spreads out from the clay mark on the rock to stand for a whole series of interrelated cosmic forces. The act of drawing calls on these forces and harnesses their power.

As a word finds its meaning in the context of a sentence, so the symbol finds its meaning in the context of other symbols with which it is associated. The simplest signs have so much meaning encoded in them that a basic symbolic expression (such as a cross or a swastika) is enough to trigger an elaborate train of associations and significances.

In understanding symbols, however, we come across a very real difficulty. The French anthropologist Claude Lévi-Strauss pointed out that the historian and the anthropologist share a similar dilemma. Both are separated from the cultures that they are studying—one by time, the other by space.

So deeply embedded is the symbol within its cultural context that mere translation of the term, or explanation of its meaning, is not enough to understand the true significance of the symbol to that culture. The symbols are part of an actual mode of thought that may be available only to those of that particular culture. An Australian aborigine can explain to a visiting student why a certain mark or sign fills him with dread, but the student will not feel that dread. Conversely, the student might be hard pressed to explain to the aborigine his dread of a sign warning of dangerous radiation levels.

After expressing himself by means of conventional symbols, condensing meaning into pictographs, man made these gradually more complex by changing them into conceptual symbols, until through them he was able to express complete religious, philosophical and scientific systems. Thus, from primitive, simple shapes, such as the cross, the pyramid, the circle, and the square—to which other connotations would later be given—emerged the categories of more complex symbols, such as the sun, the moon, the stars, the labyrinth, the spiral, the tree, the sacred mountain, the tower, and so on. These recurred frequently in iconological studies. In the eighteenth and nineteenth centuries, theorists of sacred societies and brotherhoods, in their search for a universal cosmological order with a

bipolar tension between the human and the divine, were concerned more with symbols bearing profound truths. They created reading codices that were indecipherable to those outside the restricted circle of the initiated.

The universal tree represents the knowledge of good and evil. Designed at the end of the eighteenth century, it is indicative of the questing spirit of the Enlightenment, and reveals two characteristics: the desire to place the irrational within a rational framework, and the search for a mystical explanation. From its strong symbolism emerge references to cabalistic signs of Jewish origin. The left root draws nourishment from the kingdom of heaven (superconsciousness), while the right root remains in hell (subconsciousness). From *Geheime Figuren der Rosenkreuzer*, 1785.

9

Le grant pardon de nostredame de Rains

feu de saincte memoire pape pius second en ampliant et estendant les indulgences naguerres donnees a leglise de reims par le pape nicolas V. a donne a tous vrays crestiens hommes et femmes de toutes les parties du monde Qui

The Cross and the Devil

The cross, a simple shape consisting of two lines in a bipolar tension, gradually became laden with connotation, representing the principal syntagm of the tree seen as universal symbol of, for instance, the male piercing the female, or the appurtenances of a faith, until it acquired for its followers a metaphorical function as the symbol of victory.

Above left: Interpenetration within the cross of the human features of Christ and the instruments of the Passion. Cross of Atzacoalco, Mexico, seventeenth century.

Below left: Detail of a medieval painting portraying the Virgin Mary suffused with light, from whom a lily blooms on which Christ is crucified.

Above: Exemplification of heavenly power, the temporal power of the church, and the kingdom of France. Woodcut, 1498.

Below: The birth of Adonis. The beautiful youth of Greek mythology, who was loved by Aphrodite, was born of a myrrh tree. In the Phoenician language, as in the Jewish cabala, his name means dominator. He is the god of vegetation, born of the tree-mother, which emphasizes the importance attributed to the tree as symbol of fertility. Ceramic plate, now preserved at Urbino, sixteenth century.

lilye blanc.

10

The power of symbols can be demonstrated in an oblique way by the struggles that sometimes occur when cultures clash: symbols are annexed or subverted in order to harness or destroy their power. Thus, one sees that Christianity, when it was first introduced to Bronze Age Europe, found the symbol of the cross already in use as a charm to ward off evil spirits. The Iron Age Whiteleaf Cross, cut into the Chiltern Hills, is a fine example of the symbol being used to curb and contain the baleful influence of the hill-folk or fairies. The use of the cross as a weapon against demonic forces (for example, Dracula) had a much earlier provenance than its Christian meaning. However, its appositeness made it easier for early Christian missionaries to use it as a sign of good against evil.

The depiction of the devil, with horns and tail, shows a more complex development. Originally, Satan was the fallen angel and was often portrayed with angelic wings. In their early missionary work in Europe, however, the Christians found themselves in opposition to local gods, preeminent among whom was the horned man-beast, familiar as Pan in Greek mythology but appearing in many other guises, such as the images in the Paleolithic paintings in the Caverne des Trois Frères in Ariège, France, and other horned deities in India, Mesopotamia, and Egypt. Thus, the horned deity became to the Christians a symbol of dark, anti-Christian forces against which they must struggle. By a simple conversion the fallen angel was transmuted into a horned man with a serpentine tail. The original angelic Satan, with the subtlety of symbolic meaning that that myth contained, was replaced by a bogeyman who once had been a god.

A recurring subject of symbolic systems is the direct relationship of the human body to the cosmos. Perhaps a starting point for this metaphor can be seen in the ambivalent role in which man sees himself vis-à-vis the world he inhabits. He is clearly a part of nature, dependent on it for his very life. At the same time he sees himself as somehow set apart from the natural order. His is a special and unique niche in the universe inasmuch as he alone can conceptualize and invent. He is both a part of nature and able to manipulate the natural world for his own ends. His need to find significance in the world about him and to integrate himself into that pattern of meaning leads to such elaborate and highly symbolized philosophies as palmistry, astrology, alchemy, and acupuncture. Leaving aside the contentious problem of whether these are empirically based sciences or poetic attempts to supply meaning to the world, it is useful to explore the ways in which such approaches to understanding embrace many aspects of experience.

Acupuncture is one of the oldest forms of healing known to mankind and there are many fine illustrations showing the acupuncture spots. It originated in China nearly five thousand years ago. The fact that it is still being practised thousands of years later speaks much for the belief people have in this treatment and in the laws and principles on which it is based. These laws and principles of creation underlie the whole of Chinese culture.

The devil, a fallen angel who retained his wings, assumes animal semblances in medieval iconography in order that his obscure evil power in juxtaposition to the forces of good might be better expressed.
Above: Woodcut from the *Compendium Maleficarum,* fifteenth century.
Left: Medieval woodcut in which two witches sacrifice a cock and a snake in order to produce rain.

Right: A representation of the zodiac. These signs are associated with the corresponding principles in the human body, the most perfect creature in the world. Considered a microcosm of the image of heaven, man reflects himself in the heavenly mirror. From *Les Très Riches Heures du Duc de Berry,* fifteenth century.

Imago Mundi

The cosmos as seen through the fantastical metaphors of medieval man.
Below: The labyrinth has its origins in the mythical experience of Theseus within the underground passages of a sacred cave at Crete. It is the emblem of future destiny, seen as a dark and tortuous path where no way out can be glimpsed.
Below centre: A portrayal of heaven on earth. In the middle is the tree of knowledge. Engraving by Fra Mauro, fifteenth century.
Bottom: The gardens of Semiramis. A naive, intellectualistic representation of artificial nature. From Sebastian Münster's *Cosmographia Universa,* 1550.

Left: The heavenly stairway, which postulates a continuum of existence according to which each material and spiritual thing influences one another, and where the major dominates the minor in every instance. It is the structure on which the basis of astrology is formed. From Raimondo Lullo's *De Nova Logica,* 1512.
Below: The world imagined as a tree. The universal tree joins sky, earth, and subsoil; in its role as axis of the world it symbolizes the protection of a universal god. The earth, which is at the centre of the universe, is surrounded by a snake which personifies life. This view of the universe derives from Scandinavian mythology.

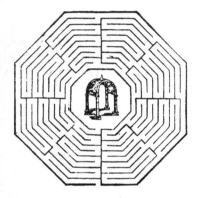

Above: An Egyptian deity, created in the iconography of the ancients of mythology. By the essayist V. Cartari, sixteenth century.
Below: A personification of truth. From Cesare Ripa's *Iconologia*, Rome, 1593.

The application of these principles to the health of the human body first appeared in the book *Nei Ching* in about 400 B.C., a golden age of Chinese thought. These same principles remain the foundation of all Chinese medicine, of which acupuncture is an important part.

The ancient Chinese, learning of life from nature, discovered the law of the five elements—the basic law of acupuncture. The cycle of the five elements, which has been interpreted on many charts, follows this law. Beginning with fire, and moving through earth, metal, water, and wood, it returns to fire. This cycle describes the flow of ch'i energy, the life-force in every human being and in the universe. Nature's very existence is a part of this ch'i energy, which is characterized by its dual aspects of yin/yang. Yin is the passive force—the negative, the night, the moon—and is never separated from yang—the active, the positive, the day, the sun.

The yin/yang is further subdivided into the five elements as a way of classifying and refining the understanding of ch'i energy and the whole of nature. Like yin/yang, the five elements never exist alone. Each one governs and is itself governed by another. Fire creates earth and rules metal. Earth creates metal and rules water. Metal creates water and rules wood. Water creates wood and rules fire, while wood creates fire and rules earth.

Through this matrix of classification, the whole world can be divided into a yin/yang spectrum. On another axis, as it were, the affinity of any object to any one of the elements begins to generate a specific relational situation with the rest of the spiritual and phenomenal universe.

Much of ancient imagery and symbolism in alchemic texts relates to the search, not for the recipe for turning base metals into gold, but for the external truth that underlies all religions. This symbolism attempts to penetrate the secrets of such things as nature, life and death, eternity and infinity. The changing of base metals into gold is an allegorical way of describing the transmutation of everyday objects into higher consciousness. Needless to say, the essence of these texts and illustrations is difficult to follow, and it is intended to be so. Only the dedicated will continue on the path to truth.

Alchemists used pictures not to tell a story to an illiterate audience but to convey what cannot be written. If anything, alchemy demanded the rejection of dogmatic and specific culture. Many cultures—Chinese, Indian, Egyptian, Greek, and Arab, for example—have practised the art of alchemy, but it reached its most developed form in medieval Europe.

The symbolism of colour is particularly important in alchemy. Green is the colour of the beginning or rawness, and red is associated with the goal of the Great Work or sulphur. The emergence of white from black represents the birth of mercury. A white-headed raven, therefore, signifies that black yields up the white. Twin fountains with two waters, one red and the other white, are of sulphur and mercury, respectively. A green lion disgorging a red liquid represents the raw or primordial (green) state from which sulphur is being extracted.

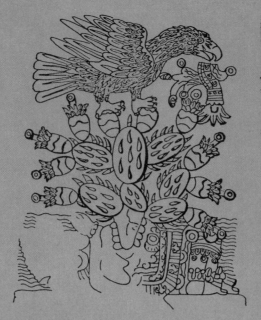

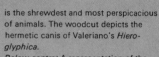

Above centre: From the body of the river goddess Chalchiuhtlicue emerges a prickly pear laden with fruits which symbolize the human heart. The eagle represents the sun.

Above right: In the eighth book of his *Etymologies,* Isidore discusses the origin of the name Hermes and its attributes, explaining that the god is represented by the head of a dog because the dog is the shrewdest and most perspicacious of animals. The woodcut depicts the hermetic canis of Valeriano's *Hieroglyphica.*

Below centre: A representation of the scattered order of the universe. From the alchemical treatise *Trionfo Ermetico (The Hermetic Triumph);* engraving by Limojon de Didier.

Below right: Allegorical panel with harpies. By V. Cartari.

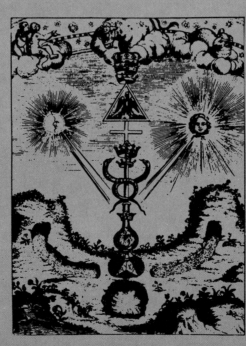

Portrayals of the Fantastic

Old alchemy texts do not just deal with the simple transformation of base metals into gold, but, as with the cabala and astrology, they are concerned mainly with the pursuit of conceptual and religious truth, symbolized by the philosophical stone.

Top left: The snakes which appear in alchemy have various meanings and functions. The three snakes generally represent the elements sulphur, mercury, and salt. When the snake has wings, it represents an element which is not volatile.

Above left: The fundamental symbols of the Christian world are the serpent, the Ouroborous, and the two-headed eagle, together with the seven planets that receive the light of the sun. Here the Ouroborous is crossed by the universal tree. The picture is typical of sixteenth-century alchemy texts.

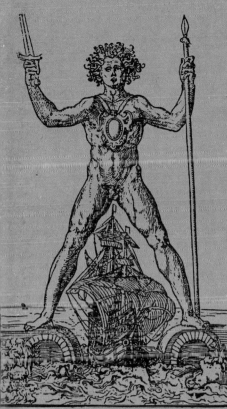

Above: The Colossus of Rhodes. The mirror round the neck and the weapons refer to the solar nature of the Colossus. From André Thevet's *Cosmographie*, 1556.

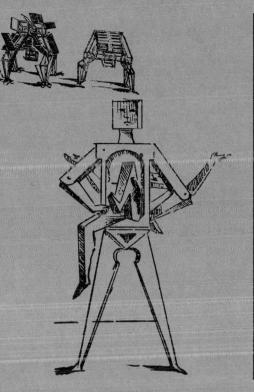

Above centre: The split-up man. These experiences can be placed within the cultural framework of the Italian baroque, in which the existing relations between exact sciences and natural sciences were developed and expanded. From Giovanni Battista Bracelli's *Bizzarrie di Varie Figure*, first half of the seventeenth century.

Above right: The cabalistic symbol of the Zohar. In the holy book of the cabala, *Sefer ha-Zohar (The Book of Splendour)*, the Judaic teaching states: "The tree exists in the seed, in the seed exists the tree." Pictured here is the emanation of the character of God turning in on himself.

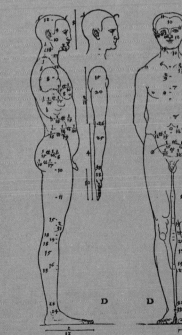

Man as a Measure of Everything

With Renaissance studies, man, even as a physical body, is a "measure of everything." He is viewed in relation to the universe as being the measure for all values of a dimensional and proportional nature.

Above left: The god Neptune in a detail from a picture of Venice. By Jacopo de' Barbari, 1500.

Above centre: Studies on the proportions of the human body. By Albrecht Dürer; from *Vier Bücher von menschlicher Proportion*, 1528.

Right: Bernini's map of Saint Peter's Square, based on the proportions of the human body, which is seen in relation to the universal.

The alchemic illustration of a tree growing from the body of a dead man may be interpreted in the following manner: from death comes new life; while the body remains below, the volatile part rises, just as the human soul or spirit leaves the body when released by death.

Stanislas Klossowski de Rola, in his study *Alchemy,* has aptly defined the alchemist's role: "Alchemists attempt to create models of the universe or of human consciousness in which the opposing complementary forces symbolized by male and female, sulphur and mercury, earth and air, fire and water, attain the perfect synthesis of which gold is the emblem."

A sign that is used almost universally as a symbol is the circle. Although it originally may have been used as a patterning device or a pictogram of the earth, sun, moon, or vagina, the circle began to take on far greater meaning when it was employed to symbolize the concept of a cyclic development. This is an event as significant as the circle's later reinvention as first a wheel and, later still, as zero. The notion of cyclic evolution gave man the means of conceptualizing such notions as the passing of seasons, time, night and day, life and death, the progress of the human spirit. Life could be perceived as a series of patterns—birth, development, death, and rebirth—rather than as a chaotic or a one-way linear progression.

This represents another stage in the development of the symbol. For now the symbol is not merely a representation of a quality or a force but stands for something in itself—it characterizes the notion of circularity. It proclaims, in itself, the possibility of an ever-changing but fundamentally stable pattern of regeneration. Thus, underlying the many uses of the circle in specific cultures is the universal idea of the regenerative pattern of life, a meaning that is not associated with the contextual significance of the sign but is an attribute of the sign itself.

This is a crucial development of the way in which signs are used inasmuch as the figure is no longer a pictographic device, representing some other element in the cosmos, but is a diagrammatic device, demonstrating its own properties as a figure. Thus, a line represents division, a triangle is used to show three aspects of a single figure, and any hollow figure can demonstrate the principle of inclusion and exclusion. The figure itself embodies an underlying principle, which can then be employed within a symbolic system to explain or represent one of the elements therein.

In tantric art, form is composed of complex patterns and images, some of which are iconographic, or assemblages and interpretations of symbolic imagery and myths. They are not meant to be understood instantly; the viewer must be drawn into the subtle inner meanings gradually, until, according to Madhu Khanna and Ajit Moorkerjee in *The Tantric Way,* "one enters into its circumference to grasp the wholeness it enshrines."

Perhaps the most powerful systems of abstract symbols are letters and numbers. As Marshall McLuhan has pointed out, a set of symbols, like a painting, can convey a total message at once; whereas the act of writing imposes a linear progression on experience. Each element must be given a before-or-after relationship with the other elements of the mes-

Geographic and Astrological Visualization

Imagines cœli Meridionales.

With the creation of the first geographical maps by the great explorers, a process of formalizing a new language got under way, made up of increasingly complex symbols and, in recent times, carried out with greater technical sophistication.

Above left: The author's fantastic interpretation anticipates sea monsters and gorgons in this woodcut, as in the case of the maelstrom portrayed in the centre. By the cartographer Olaus Magnus, 1539

Above right: One of the first maps of the sky in an engraving showing the traditional representations that form the constellations. By Albrecht Dürer with the help of two astronomers.

Below left: A map of Ptolemy's geocentric world. 1482.
Below right: The celestial sphere according to Ptolemy. Medieval engraving, Venice, 1496.

17

Figure d'un Botuan.

Above: Tree-letters with an expressive function. The letter A of Yasuno Mitsumasa's alphabet, an impossible picture produced by means of an optical illusion, and the letter B in a tree-trunk design, an example of applied art inspired by naturalism.

Below: Example of a moon tree, which appears frequently in alchemy. The tree ends at the roots with the features of a woman's and a man's face—the characteristics peculiar to an hermaphrodite.

The shape of the tree is a symbol that has been portrayed everywhere throughout the ages. Its timeless appeal is due, according to different iconographies, to its many meaningful values, but it is important above all for the intrinsic sense of immortality it evokes, through the development of a circular path that brings it back to the seed that will regenerate it. The tree of life exists, as do the cosmic tree, the tree of fertility, and the trees of sacrifice, knowledge, psyche, and history.

Above: Print depicting a family tree of the Jesuit order. Eighteenth century.

Left: A Maya human sacrifice. A tree grows out of the sacrificial victim, whose heart has been removed.

Below: A process of metamorphosis whereby a tree becomes a young girl, taking up the traditional Greek idea of the absolute reign of the unconscious in the vegetable kingdom. From Francesco Colonna's *Il Sogno di Polifilo,* fifteenth century.

Top right: Picture of a botuan. From Ludwig von Holberg's *Voyage de Nicolas Klimius dans le monde souterrain,* 1753.

Centre right: Hebrew mythological picture relating to the Creation, in which another sex, in the shape of a tree, sprouts forth from Adam as he is pierced by Mercury's arrow. Its meaning is probably linked to the original sin of Adam and Eve, which brought the tree among us.

Right: The tree of time. By Rajasthan, India, eighteenth century.

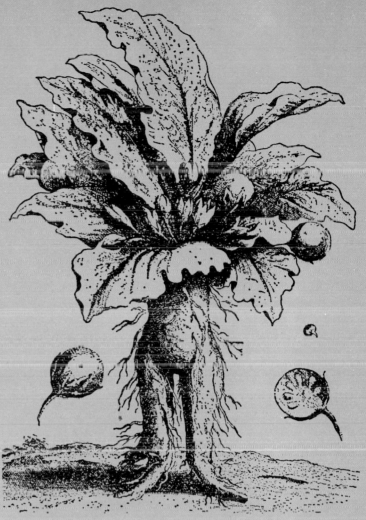

Above, left and right: Two illustrations depicting the anthropomorphism of a medicinal plant. In the Middle Ages the mandrake was considered a mysterious and magical plant with particular human-vegetable characteristics. Alchemists have always attached particular importance to it for its divinatory powers.
Below left: The snake curled up in the universal tree.

Below right: Family tree of the Bonapartes. Since the second half of the Middle Ages, genealogy has been the symbolic expression of the authority of each dynasty.

Expressiveness in Script

As these pages illustrate, writing—according to a dichotomous value—represents the expression of a concept and its visualization, undergoing a process of code-cracking that leads from the symbol to its description.

Above: The outline of an Islamic temple in Turkey, produced by a double Kufic inscription.
Below: Two Arabic monograms realized according to Kufic writing and the nasuhi style.

Left: In the *Ramayana* of Hindu literature, the design that symbolizes the monkey-god Hanumat is outlined with various sentences (mantra) that tell the story of his life. Usually, all these figures fly. At the Hanumat's feet are gathered his followers.

Top: Fantastic composition in Gothic-like calligraphy. From Paul Franck's *The Treasure Chest,* 1601.
Above: Mazelike construction of calligrams in a German Renaissance composition.

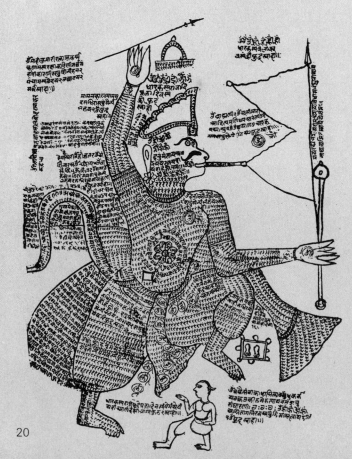

Above: Mural decoration used by Turkish priests; in one part of the composition can be read: "The lion of God, countenance of God, the victor Ali." For Islamites, the lion and the tiger represent the strength of Allah. Nineteenth century.

Right: An elephant composed of Urdu letters in such a way as to form sentences exalting the moral and material gifts of a soldier. Nineteenth century.

20

Right: A calligram depicting the figure of Perseus bearing Medusa's head. From the Greek poet Aratus di Soli's *Phenomena*, which describes all the celestial bodies and their positions, and includes twenty five exceptional astronomical calligrams.

Above: Winding construction of a German eighteenth-century script, styled in Gothic lettering.

Left: Drawing of Jonah and the whale, composed using the text of Hebrew mythology.

Left: Digital elaboration of a face created by means of an electronic calculator.
Bottom left: A portrait, achieved manually by means of six different print strengths, obtained by making ideograms with a different number of strokes that correspond to each degree of density. All the Kanji used have a meaning relating to facial expressions. By Kohei Sugiura and Masayoshi Matzuoka.

Right: A portrait of Abraham Lincoln, reproduced by means of words relating episodes from his life.

21

sage. Thus, the act of writing imposes a logical order, which is not an aspect of experience but of the medium through which experience is reported. Only in such languages as Chinese and Japanese, where some content of the original pictograph (word symbol) still remains, is there a dimension of symbolism which complicates—and enriches—the reading of a written message.

While numbers remained a part of the alphabetic system, as they did in Greek and Roman, it was too clumsy a system for much progress to be made in the art of reckoning. It was the introduction of the Arabic positional system that freed numbers from their linear expression and allowed mathematics as a self-enclosed system to develop and flourish.

It is instructive to look, in rather a macroscopic way, at the changeover from medievalism to modern rationality and the fare of the symbol in this development. In the Middle Ages, symbols were the characteristic mode of expression. The world was largely explained in terms of good and evil forces, humours, elements, and so forth, each carrying a rich lode of symbolic meaning. Even writing was embellished with illumination, a way of making the words themselves carry a symbolic force over and above their bare logical meaning.

For a brief period, during the Renaissance, the wealth and power of medieval symbolism was wedded to the new rationality and technology. In almost every European country this marriage of symbolism and rationality produced, in a relatively short time, an incredible outpouring of what remains to this day some of the greatest literature and art of all time.

The seventeenth and eighteenth centuries saw, in broad terms, the withering of symbolism as proponents of rationality and formal classicism sought to reduce the world to numerical and logical order. Aesthetics itself became the subject of measurement and formula. Yet, while rationality produced many valuable technological studies, the metaphorical, symbolic mode of viewing the world became increasingly devalued.

Long before Sigmund Freud and Carl Gustav Jung sought to retrace the link between symbolism and science, poets and writers such as Blake and Ruskin were attempting to reinstate the power of the symbol in the Western consciousness.

The vogue of Gothic romance in Blake's time later unfolded into a serious aesthetic with Ruskin and the French symbolists. This Gothic taste, trite and ridiculous as it first appeared to serious people, was yet a confirmation of Blake's diagnosis of the defects and needs of his age and his subsequent quest for a unified mode of perception. In *Modern Painters* Ruskin states the matter in a way that entirely dissociates Gothic medievalism from any historical concern about the Middle Ages. He states the matter in a way that won him the serious interest of Arthur Rimbaud and Marcel Proust:

A fine grotesque is the expression, in a moment, by a series of symbols thrown together in bold and fearless connection, of truths which would have

Above left: French silk merchant's seal. Eighteenth century.
Above: Monogram making up the name of Charlemagne.
Below: Trademark of Aldus Manutius's sons, printers in Venice. 1547.

taken a long time to express in any verbal way, and of which the connection is left for the beholder to work out for himself; the gaps, left or overleaped by the haste of the imagination, forming the grotesque character.

For Ruskin, Gothic appeared as an indispensable means of breaking open the closed system of perception that Blake spent his life describing and fighting. Ruskin championed Gothic grotesque as the best way of ending the regime of Renaissance perspective with its limited vision of realism:

It is with a view (not the least important among many others bearing upon art) to the reopening of this great field of human intelligence, long entirely closed, that I am striving to introduce Gothic architecture into daily domestic use; and to revive the art of illumination, properly so called; not the art of miniature painting in books, or on vellum, which has ridiculously been confused with it; but of making "writing," simple writing, beautiful to the eye, by investing it with the great chord of perfect colour, blue, purple, scarlet, white and gold, and in that chord of colour,

Some examples of Italian bookplates, all created during the first two decades of this century. A personal symbol intended to represent ownership of books with a sign of identification and recognition, the ex libris has become an interesting element as applied by

graphic artists with an innate sense of literature, among whom Adolfo de Carolis stands out in particular. The iconographic representations that recur most frequently—such as the light, the fountain, and the oak tree—symbolize, above all, the auspices of a long life, as

well as the will to conquer and overcome almost insurmountable obstacles.
Below right: A letterhead for book pages, illustrating Roman ruins. Engraving by Giovanni Battista Piranesi.

permitting the continual play of the fancy of the writer in every species of grotesque imagination, carefully excluding shadow; the distinctive difference between illumination and painting proper being that illumination admits no shadows, but only gradations of pure colour.

Therefore, when looking at symbols—marks, signs, or pictographs—it is important to remember that they are a product of a symbolic mode of thought. It is a different way of communicating experience from the logical or numerical modes of expression. It is, in a sense, the antithetical mode. For whereas language and numbers define and separate, symbols are suggestive of the similarities, the common identity, of phenomena.

It is not that one mode of expression is superior to another. Even in pure science the symbolic mode is important in providing the sudden flashes of insight and the resolution of seeming opposites that offer a new dimension of understanding. Jung cites the celebrated example of the nineteenth-century German chemist August Kekule von Stradonitz. Having tried in vain, by applied reason, to deduce the structure of benzene,

Kekule was confronted in a dream by the vision of Ouroborous, the mythical serpent that continually grows by feeding on its own tail, thus maintaining a constant size. Returning to his problem with this symbol, Kekule was able to demonstrate that the structure of benzene is a closed carbon ring. The intuitive image, apprehended in a dream, had supplied him with the solution his rational mind could not reach.

Although it was a common belief in the eighteenth and nineteenth centuries that rationality had superseded the more primitive perceptions of symbolism, Freud and Jung were able to show that symbolism—the collapsing of one meaning into another—is a constant part of daily life. Rationality, for all its valuable deductive power, seems to impose a strain on the human mind which the symbolic mode can release. The way forward is, as it was for the men of the Renaissance, to achieve a balance between rationality and symbolism, to become aware that there is a fundamental contradiction in all that we experience, and that everything is at once truly unique and at the same time simply one facet of an undifferentiated unity.

23

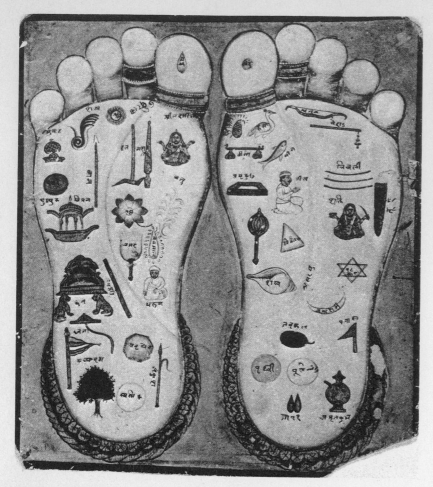

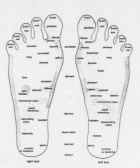

Far left: The soles of Vishnu's feet, signs that point to the function of the cosmic man. Rajasthan, India, eighteenth century.

Left: The sole of Buddha's foot in nirvana, of Thai origin.
Below: The feet according to the tantra yoga.
Below centre: Buddha's feet, according to a Japanese school, with symbolic representations of the master's various strengths.

The Interpretation of the Cosmological Order

Signs with a naturalistic bent and primary geometric shapes (the circle as continuity; the triangle as synthesis of the one and the trine; the square) contribute, in Eastern mystical philosophies, to the constitution of symbols that express metaphysical concepts.

Below: An illustration of various kinds of yantra (tantric diagrams which back up meditation). Through the symbols, they denote a development toward a very ardent faith. From a hand-made book, Nepal, seventeenth century.

Below: Two pictures depicting formal and dimensional values. From Claude Bragdon's *The Beautiful Necessity*, 1922. The "beautiful necessity" of the title is an intimate system of harmonious correlations within the laws of both art and nature, the basis of which, according to Bragdon, is to create organically, conforming with the cosmic scheme, while rationally and rhythmically heading toward predetermined ends.

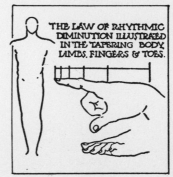

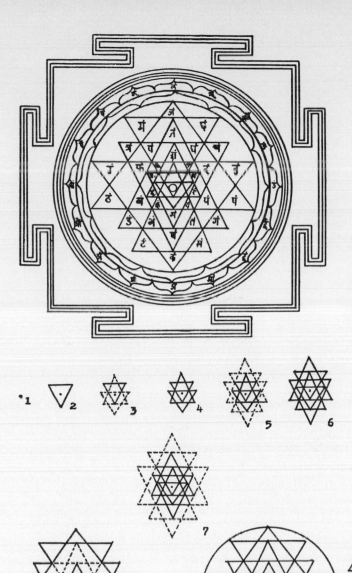

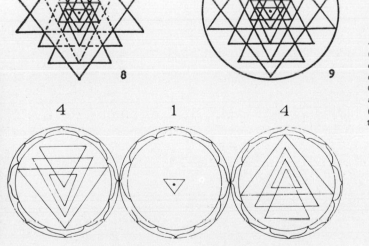

Examples of the use of the circular shape in oriental symbolism.

Top: Image of the ceremonial fire of purification, which serves as a symbol of the proper conduct of life

Above: A yantra with a divine figure in the centre. Initially the yantra was a design traced on the ground; afterward there was a universal meaning of the mandala in a circle. During the period of transition from the yantra to the mandala, efforts were made to make the figure in the centre divine. The mandala is thus a magic circle.

Above: Some representations of the goma (sacred fire) altar hearths, the concept of which includes Kofu Gunsa, to defeat the opponent (top); Socusai Gunsa, for life to proceed well (centre); and Zeki Gunsa, the increase of vitality (bottom). The picture of the hearth serves to reinforce the concept.

Above: Yin and yang correspond to the principles of negative and positive (female and male), through which, according to ancient Chinese philosophy, the perfect balance could be attained.

Above: A yantra and the analysis of the intersection of the triangular shapes that make up the structure of its central part. This geometric portrayal, which is obviously symbolic and which hints at complex metaphysical meanings, is comprised within a circular shape, in which a line portrays lotus petals by stylizing them. The yantra is the most important concentration of primary forces and abstract design to be created by ancient Eastern culture. The kind of yantra shown here suggests a picture of arcane geometry.

The French Revolution brought an increasingly wider diffusion of both printed political news and a popular kind of iconography with an historical flavour, which, for the first time, portrayed the new social levels that had come to the fore, and were themselves destined to take part in history. The political prints also constituted the sole source to which the poor and the illiterate had access. Portrayed in this detail from a print is a public assembly held at the Palais-Royal on July 12, 1789, in which Camille Desmoulins is seen intervening with a motion.

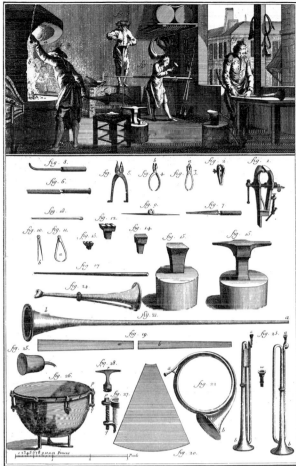

Far left, above: Picture of the family of the duke of Saxe-Weimar visiting Goethe. The silhouette technique was a popular means of graphic expression in the eighteenth century.
Far left, below: An explanatory picture in which the pattern of movement and dance steps are seen in relation to the musical notes of a minuet. From a book printed in London and intended for dance teachers.

Left: Plate from the monumental *Encyclopédie,* published in Paris between 1751 and 1772. Its treatment of a culture as seen through illustrations of its materials produced a veritable philosophy of objects; through its criteria, characterized by rationalization, and through the continuity of the sign, the *Encyclopédie* became a sort of bible of the Enlightenment, an expression of the essential and concrete vision of human doing which would later lead—albeit indirectly—to the French Revolution.
Below: A print drawn and engraved that revives an ancient Italian game played with dice. The print reproduces the various combinations of three dice. Eighteenth century.

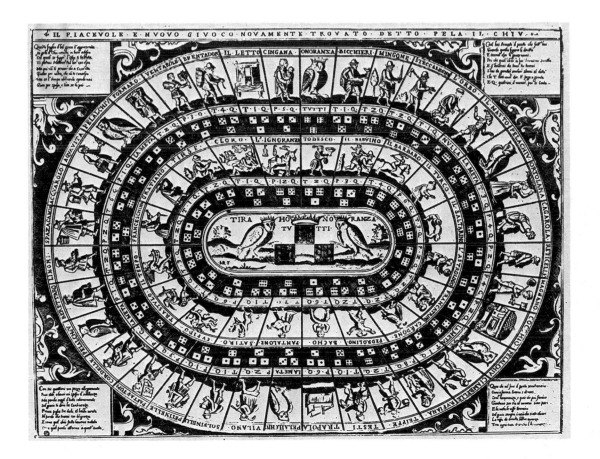

Above: Puzzle label for a box of confectionery. French engraving, nineteenth century.

The Popular Image

It is not difficult, even with popular prints, to come across complex symbolical values or mystical-mythological references that go beyond a mere description of contents. The history of iconography is, after all, made of these popular prints, of playing cards, and of all the imagery that comes under the classification of minor art and that all too often has been regarded as inferior.

Above: A series of personified numbers and a detail (above right), emphasizing the comic posture of arithmetical units. This kind of visualization of the alphabet was practised for amusement, but also provided children with an easier, mnemonic way of remembering their numbers. Plate, eighteenth century.

Left: The various parts that make up the figure of a harlequin, ready to be cut out, assembled, and held by strings to make it into a puppet. Italian print, nineteenth century.
Below left: Popular calendar laid out as a picture, with clear references to good auspices for a year without troubles.
Below: Structure of a symbolic poem, entitled "Teapot and Cup," within the outlines of a precise representation, a forerunner of modern visual poetry. Amsterdam, 1708.

Left: Eighteenth-century French playing cards, the result of a pictorial expression of popular taste.

Right: Instructive cards by Murner with masonic symbols; they represent "le deux de supposition et l'as d'appellation." Sixteenth–seventeenth century.

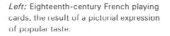
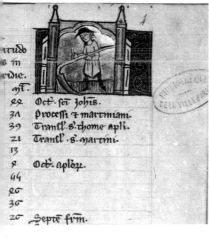

DEGRÉS DES AGES.

Left: The months of the year. From a manuscript page of the Vaast Psalter, fourteenth century.
Right: One of the famous Épinal popular prints, describing the scale of human life. C. 1840.

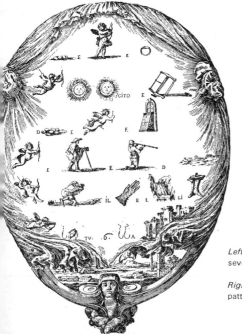

РАЧИТЕЛЬНОЕ ДОМОВОДСТВО.

Left: Puzzle. By Stefano della Bella, seventeenth century.

Right: Popular Russian print with augural patterns. Nineteenth century.

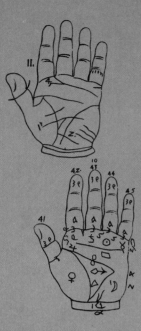

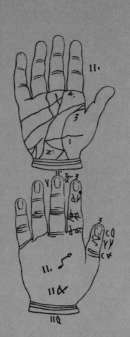

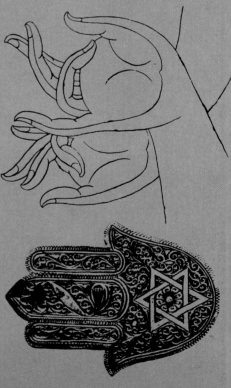

Hand Language

Above: A picture with outlines for the interpretation of palm reading. 1733.

Left: The lines of fate imprinted on a chimpanzee's hand.

Below: Three hands (reading clockwise from top left) include model of a hand according to the typical configuration of modern man, each part showing the

characteristic imprints for interpretation; hand with symbols, a story-cum-riddle of French origin; the hand of Gian Pero, a fortune-teller who read hand signs.

Top: In early times, fortune-tellers saw in the lines of the palm a reflection of the line of the universe. This drawing shows various representations of the destiny of a whole life.
Above: The hand is portrayed according to the soothsayer who picks up its celestial signs.

Below: The hand in the picture of a Tibetan seal.
Bottom: Cabalistic symbols contained within a hand.

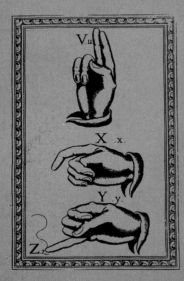

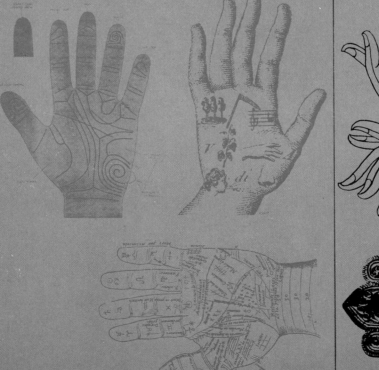

Above: Visualization of some letters in the deaf-and-dumb alphabet. Spanish engraving, seventeenth century.

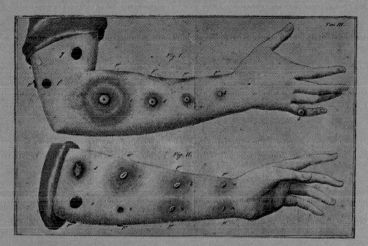

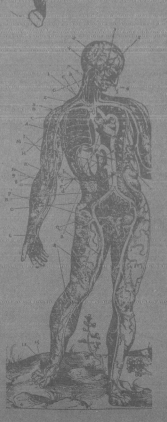

Scientific Illustration

Above: Didactic illustration of the cutaneous effects of smallpox vaccination. From a medical treatise, nineteenth century.
Below: Pictorial view, according to Wilder Graves Penfield, of the various parts of the human brain. Each part of the body has been given a size relative to the sizes of the various areas of feeling in the cerebral hemispheres. Drawing by Gallardo.
Bottom left: One of the classic Rorschach marks which in psychology may be translated into different interpretations, depending on the subjects.
Above right: The cerebral functions described in a humorous way. Print, nineteenth century.

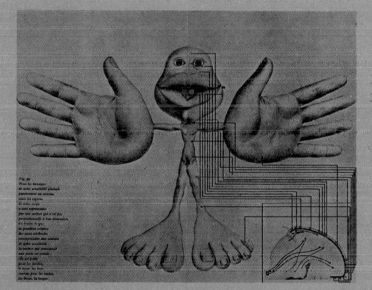

Above: German illustration showing arthritic deformities.
Below: During the edo period in Japan the relation between the two points marked for contact and piercing in the practice of acupuncture was established.
Right: Anatomical chart. Sixteenth century.

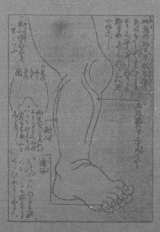

2. THE ONTOLOGY OF COMMUNICATION

On Friday, August 13, 1965, the first issue of a new weekly paper, *The Berkeley Barb,* hit the streets of Berkeley, California. Its lead story reported the previous day's demonstration at Berkeley's Santa Fe station, where Vietnam Day Committee supporters tried to stop a twenty-car train carrying Vietnam-bound troops. The *Barb*'s founder and editor Max Scherr later went on record with his definition of the paper's function: "The community saw itself reflected in the paper and went out to act in the way it was encouraged to act by seeing it had done something of substance. That's what a newspaper does."

Communication builds the social environment in which we set ourselves. Indeed, communication is the social environment: The processes of communication shape each individual's personality and through such processes the individual affects the world. A conversation between parent and child, interjections at a trade union meeting, a television broadcast by a head of state, a printed page from the Bible, or a letter notifying call-up into the armed forces all confirm the reality of the social universe at the same time as they convey their particular messages.

Communication, with its various levels of meaning, defines the social world each individual perceives. Some find that the socially constructed universe potentially includes all human experience and accepts all human beings as equal; others encounter a comparatively limited and hierarchical synthesis. In one example of limited vision, Europeans making their early forays into the Americas held that the Indians they slaughtered were less than human, as they could not possibly be descended from Adam and Eve. In another, more recent example, American soldiers, by referring to both North and South Vietnamese as "gooks," reduced their chances of relating to the hearts and minds of their ostensibly equal allies.

Even the seemingly insignificant contributes to a certain perception of the world. *The Blue Book of Etiquette for Men,* written in 1904, devoted a section to calling cards: "The card should be of unglazed white board. The name in full is engraved in small, plain type, with the prefix Mr., except in the case of men with titles. The card of a young man living at home should bear the number of his house and the street in the right hand corner." *The Blue Book,* written for "the man who desires to regulate his life after the manner of gentlemen," went on to explain how and when these cards

should be handed out. The type specification for a few words on a piece of pasteboard conjures up the idea of a world in which gentlemen went calling in the afternoon, in which others might acquire the appurtenances of genthood, and in which still others laboured twelve-hour shifts seven days a week to make all this possible.

Although all communication has the basic effect of making real the social world, people and groups within that world vary in their awareness of how this happens. The social, communicative world is the lived experience of the individual. The system of representations and messages that permeates that lived-in world appears to some as the framework of everyday life; others make the analytical jump of comprehending these representations and messages as the processes that perpetuate everyday life within a more complex system, which is the actual social universe. These attitudes lead to the potential opposition between accepting the world as it is and believing that change is possible, an opposition that affects all aspects of communication and that is latent in every image.

An advertisement on a roadside billboard seems to have a single function—to sell the product—and in other respects appears to be a neutral factor within the landscape. Yet the very existence of that billboard reveals a society that encourages this kind of commercial activity and is rich enough to make it worthwhile. People who travel from Times Square or Piccadilly Circus to city centres devoid of advertisements realize immediately that something has changed, even if they cannot say what.

An advertisement, too, may stir reactions far removed from the intended "I must buy that." The advertiser presents an image as an attention-getting device; other viewers may discover in that image implications that are offensive, for example, a negative representation of the position of women in society. In 1978 a British soft-drinks firm ran a national poster campaign of a number of exaggeratedly stereotypical orange-juice drinkers in holiday mood with the slogan "Juicy, Fruity, Fresh, and Cheap." A number of women's organizations and individual men and women complained to the Advertising Standards Authority about one poster that featured an illustration of a woman in a bikini above the slogan. The British Code of Advertising Practice, the basis for the self-regulatory system adopted by the Authority, condemned advertisements that were "offensive to the standards of decency prevailing among those who are likely to be exposed to them." The complainants considered the poster to be offensive because it degraded women. The Authority (whose slogan is "Legal, Decent, Honest, Truthful") decided against upholding the complaint.

Communication, within the world that it itself constructs, has many aims. Single messages or representations, and even more so the systems that disseminate

The arms race and the disturbing production of nuclear weapons, particularly between the two superpowers during the Cold War, have in the past decades provoked the formation of civil-protest committees, as well as the staging of numerous demonstrations, all over the world. Various opportunities have arisen for artists and graphic designers to voice their support of such anti-war activities with messages of social commitment. This poster succeeds in dramatically evoking the monstrous danger of atomic destruction through its use of primitive shapes. By Ben Shahn.

The Call to Patriotic Sacrifice

Below: One of the posters circulated in Britain at the beginning of World War I in order to sensitize the public—by playing on conscience and self-respect—into subscribing to enlistment. By S. Lumley.

Right and opposite, far right: The imperious call to male citizens was successfully employed during World War I by all countries engaged in the conflict. The most famous and undoubtedly the most effective of these posters are the British one by Alfred Leete and the American one by James Montgomery Flagg.

Below: Poster exalting the dynamism of flight according to some futurist schemes; it inspired Winston Churchill with the new symbol for the Royal Air Force. By E. McKnight Kauffer.

Opposite, above left and below left: Poster for a British military organization and one for a Paris exhibition. By Abram Games, 1940.

I WANT YOU
FOR U.S. ARMY
NEAREST RECRUITING STATION

KEEP 'EM ROLLING!

Above: Propaganda poster for the American troops. It is an example of the use of such new techniques as photomontage and abstract composition. These are the first effective results of the teaching of schools like the Bauhaus and some of its more outstanding teachers who, having abandoned Nazi Germany, continued their work of proselytism in the United States. By Leo Lionni, 1941.

JOIN THE
ATS

K FOR INFORMATION AT THE NEAREST EMPLOYMENT EXCHANGE OR AT ANY ARMY OR ATS RECRUITING CENTRE

EXPOSITION
DES ARMEES BRITANNIQUES
INAUGURATION LE 25 MAI, ANNEXE DU GRAND PALAIS

War : Death and Destruction

Opposite, above left: Protest poster against the Vietnam War, within which lies a double meaning: by tearing off the benevolent face of Uncle Sam, the true face of war appears. A caustic satire of James Montgomery Flagg's famous World War I poster.
Opposite, below left: British anti-nuclear campaign, inspired by the ideas of Bertrand Russell. By F. H. K. Henrion, mid-1960s.
Opposite right, above and below: Spanish posters created during the civil war. The first protests the invasion of Italian volunteer troops; the second, by Cervignon, advocates evacuation of the cities.

them, take on many functions. One significant role is contact with others. A conversation between friends provides the most obvious form of social contact, but a picture postcard sent home during the holidays makes its contribution. Even the most apparently impersonal of publications carries some notion, however minimal, of human beings coming into relationship with each other. Take, for example, the posters pinned on a crowded college noticeboard. Perhaps one shrieks "Stop H-bomb tests!" The demand is clear enough, but in a way that poster also says, "We, who oppose H-bomb tests, exist, and you can join us." It implies contact with a movement, with a network of people who derive strength from knowing that others share their convictions. The mere expression of a feeling becomes a potential bond. In another example, almost everyone will agree with the slogan "No More War," or identify with the humanity of the figure sketched in 1924 by Käthe Kollwitz, its mouth open in a desperate cry, its right arm raised in urgent application, reproduced in one of the first posters with just that message.

In an extension of social contact, communication leads to social concern. Appeals for charitable help—from Dr. Barnardo's circulation of photographs of street waifs in late-nineteenth-century Britain, calling attention to his homes for orphaned or abandoned children, to present-day campaigns by the Salvation Army for their work with down-and-outs and children and by Oxfam and other agencies concerned with Third World countries—have relied on making those who have the comforts of home, family, and an income directly aware of the human distress of those who do not. A photograph of a small, nearly naked child, its belly distended with the diseases of protein deficiency, presents an image of vulnerability that may touch the hardest heart.

Communication is essential to the growth of communal interests. For example, consider a poster with this message: "Be all you can be. Read." It has a much wider implication than that of picking up a book to while away an evening. The printed word, however reproduced, locates people in the world in a particular way because of its permanence, its comparability with other values, the range of experience it records, and its availability. Think back to the time of the handwritten book, limited to the libraries of the few who could afford to have them copied. Some were handsomely illustrated, but many were unattractive, poorly copied, difficult to read, and worse. Succeeding copyists compounded each other's errors until the substance of a book became unintelligible and, since comparison with the original was impossible, uncorrectable. In a period in which there might be only a single copy of a manu-

Above: Poster designed for an American association, formed to help Greece at war. The artist abandons the rigid patterns of symbolism to give the figure a more classic interpretation. By E. McKnight Kauffer, 1943.
Below: Political poster with an unequivocal meaning. By Kinkichi Takahashi.

Below and right: Two posters in favour of Nazi propaganda. By Ludwig Hohlwein, one of the major German graphic artists who, in his later years, and even with appropriate signs, lent his talents to the illustration of Hitlerian ideology.

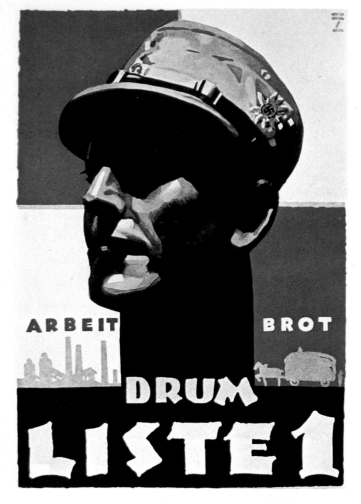

for full employment after the war
REGISTER · VOTE
C I O POLITICAL ACTION COMMITTEE

YESTERDAY'S MEN
(They failed before!)

Above: This poster was commissioned by the Political Action Committee, one of their platforms being full employment after the war. By Ben Shahn, outstanding interpreter of a particular American reality, 1943.

Left: An ironical interpretation of the political poster, printed in England. Employed here are refined techniques of modern advertising; while the artist did not design the poster, he did build the diminutive statues, which were then photographed. Design by Alan Aldridge.

Opposite, below right: One of Ben Shahn's more eloquent posters, demonstrating for peace. Some references to Picasso's art may be noticed in the expressive and dramatic qualities of the picture. 1946.
Opposite, below left: Czech cinema poster on Nazism, realized by means of the montage technique. By Zdenek Ziegler, 1968.

平和は一つ **UNANIMOUS IN WISHES FOR PEACE**
TOUT LE MONDE AU MÊME DÉSIRE POUR LA PAIX
EINSTIMMIG IN WÜNSCHE FÜR DIE FRIEDEN
UNANIME EN DESEOS PARA PAZ سلام کے لیے سب
和平是一个 **BCEM MUP** 평화는하나

国際連合
UNITED NATIONS

John Heartfield

5 Finger hat die Hand
Mit **5** packst Du den Feind!
Wählt Lifte
Kommuniftifche Partei!

241

Gesture of Freedom and Fighting

The unmistakable gestural qualities of the hand have often been codified into symbols of notable expression that can be readily understood.
Above left: A United Nations poster which is read as a sign of peace. Design by Yoshikatsu Shimomoto and Takakazu Yokozawa; art direction by Kuniomi Uematu.
Above: "A hand has five fingers. With five you can repel the enemy! Vote List Five!" Propaganda poster for the German Communist party. By John Heartfield, one of the inventors of political photomontage, 1928.
Left: May 1968 produced a creative stimulus in France even in the renewal of protest pictures, something that had not happened since the years of the partisan fight.
Opposite: Propaganda poster for a plan of economic development in the Soviet Union. The graphic technique is the constructivist one pointed out by El Lissitzky, where the use of photomontage serves to emphasize the reading and the content. By Gustave Klutsis, 1930.

LA LUTTE CONTINUE

1870-1924

Ahead with Revolution

Left: Poster which commemorates the figure of Lenin by sublimating him. By A. Straxov, 1924.
Below left: Poster for the subscription to a war loan in Germany during World War I. By Otto Lehmann.

script volume, burning a person's books for a crime against church or state was more than a symbolic punishment—it could destroy the record of an idea. Multiplicity, the product of the printing press and the copying machine, is its own defence against suppression.

At every stage of social evolution, those who have wanted change favoured the spread of literacy and the supply of materials to feed the desire for knowledge. Look back to fourteenth-century England, when unlettered congregations, unable to read Latin, learned Christianity from the preacher's explanations of pictures painted on the church wall: the seven deadly sins, Saint Michael weighing souls, the Day of Judgment, the mouth of hell, devils at their unhappy work. Followers of the religious reformer John Wycliffe, who proclaimed that the Bible and not the church was the ultimate source of spiritual truth, translated the Old and New Testaments into English to make them more accessible. While these translations remained as manuscript copies, the religious authorities could hope to limit their availability to those who could be trusted. When the printers began work, starting in 1526 with John Tyndale's new translation of the New Testament, the authorities intensified their efforts to retain control. For instance, at one point they banned all women other than noblewomen, artificers, apprentices, journeymen, serving men, husbandmen, and labourers from reading or using the English Bible. But with printed copies pouring into Britain the attempt to prevent people from reading the Bible had to be doomed.

In later centuries, activists of all persuasions, whether religious or political, Methodists, Chartists, trade unionists, and so on, made sure that they and their fellows learned to read; they collected and passed around books associated with their causes, from the Bible to Tom Paine's *Rights of Man*, and arranged access to printing presses where they could produce their own texts, pamphlets, and handbills calling for action. In the strongest possible statement of the reason for pursuing universal literacy, Lenin argued that the illiterate person was excluded from the sphere of politics.

Another function of communication emerges in the development of private interests, in the ways each individual establishes an identity and affirms, "This is me." In choosing which messages and representations to pay attention to, and which to pass on or display, the individual expresses a personality. In the process, small differences can become personally significant. Fashion magazines thrive by providing hints and photographs intended to help those who wish to present themselves as up-to-the-minute socialites, business leaders, holiday-makers, or whatever. When clothes are used as signs for others, even the label becomes important: for a few fleeting weeks the label on a pair of fashionable jeans or the flashy silk-screened image on a T-shirt can reveal that the wearer is alive to the

STÜTZT UNSRE FELDGRAUEN

ZEREISST ENGLANDS MACHT ~ZEICHNET

CONSELLERIA DE TREBALL

ALLISTEU-VOS per al TREBALL VOLUNTARI

SINDICAT de DIBUIXANTS PROFESSIONALS. U.G.T.

TODA LA JUVENTUD UNIDA POR LA PATRIA

JSU
SECRETARIADO DE PROPAGANDA
VALENCIA

Above: Two posters designed to organize and defend the Spanish Republic from the threat of civil war. By Cervignon and Marti Bass, 1937.

Below: "We are the power." Proletarian poster created after the great strikes of 1968 in France

nous sommes le pouvoir

Above left: Anti-American poster that sets out to shake public opinion, with the effect of a blow to the stomach, in this case because of U.S. interference in Vietnam. By the well-known satirical artist Tomi Ungerer.
Above right: In this poster, Ungerer synthesizes the ruthless fight between whites and blacks in America in the late 1960s.
Left: Another poster against the military power of the United States. By Makoto Wada, 1968.
Below: One of the posters of the French student movement, circulated after May 1968.
Opposite left: Cinema poster for the film *Exodus,* which recalls the setting up of the state of Israel. By Saul Bass.
Opposite right: The British campaign to help the Jews who survived the Nazi persecutions. By Abram Games.

OTTO PREMINGER PRESENTS PAUL NEWMAN, EVA MARIE SAINT, RALPH RICHARDSON, PETER LAWFORD, LEE J. COBB, SAL MINEO, JOHN DEREK, HUGH GRIFFITH, GREGORY RATOFF, FELIX AYLMER, DAVID OPATOSHU, JILL HAWORTH IN "EXODUS." SCREENPLAY BY DALTON TRUMBO. BASED ON THE NOVEL, BY LEON URIS. MUSIC BY ERNEST GOLD. PHOTOGRAPHED IN SUPER PANAVISION 70, TECHNICOLOR® BY SAM LEAVITT. TODD AO STEREOPHONIC SOUND. A UNITED ARTISTS RELEASE. PRODUCED AND DIRECTED BY OTTO PREMINGER.

tiniest nuances of a particular in-world. In another, yet similar, area, a teenager may use the act of cutting photographs from a rock magazine and sticking them to the bedroom wall as a symbol of autonomy, a test of parental understanding and control in the teenager's increasing urge for independence. Yet though these choices distinguish one person from another, they do so in relation to the shared background of the society in which both live. The person who buys a poster of Che Guevara may be hinting at a belief in the need for revolutionary change, indulging romantic notions of life as a lonely hero, or may be simply accepting a commercial culture that has developed its own methods of diffusing fantasies of liberation.

Communication provides entertainment, too, a joyful uplift of the spirit, a way of passing the time, of adding spice to the business of life. As one small example, consider the range of birthday cards drawn around Charles M. Schulz's *Peanuts* characters, Snoopy, Lucy, and Charlie Brown. A birthday card conveys a basic message: "You are remembered." The joke that comes with the *Peanuts* card is a pure extra, inessential but adding the gift of a moment's amusement.

Providing information, passing on an explanation, finding out what is known, or putting across a point of view are significant aspects of communication. In public life this ranges from the simple direction arrow on a road sign to the complicated rules of the code of law, from the step-by-step diagrams of a handicraft book to the equations of quantum physics, from the plans for an urban development to the day-by-day proceedings recorded in the *Congressional Record* or parliamentary speeches recorded in *Hansard*.

Access to information has always been an important factor in social struggles. Some of the tensions that ultimately led to the French Revolution were manifested previously in a tussle over the publication of the monumental *Encyclopédie* compiled by Denis Diderot. The content of the *Encyclopédie* hardly seems controversial today, but, as with all aspects of communication significant in social change, it was the differences from the prevailing context that mattered. In presenting its information the *Encyclopédie* took for granted the justice of religious tolerance and the right to speculate freely on religious and political ideas; it held that a government should be concerned for the welfare of the common people of the nation; and it accepted the growth of scientific inquiry and of manufacturing industry. This was considered seditious by the court, the church, and the military, and in 1759 the work was banned, although Diderot later received permission to continue publication.

Many governments and other central authorities have tried to limit and control the flow of information. The publishers of the earliest news-sheets in Britain, which began circulating about 1620, found it prudent to report solely on happenings abroad; none of them attempted to describe the activities of the English government. Later governments, of all political colours throughout the world, have continued to manipulate the availability of information regarding their own activities, whether by controlling the publication through presenting their own versions or by censoring and suppressing other sources. Other bodies, too—local authorities, political parties, business and commercial organizations, trade unions, pressure groups and their critics or opponents—have an interest in the ways in which information is presented.

In the political world at large, where the actions of governments and the decisions of groups and individuals may be influenced by public opinion, any technique that can affect that opinion becomes significant. Photographs and drawings, cartoons and caricatures, posters, advertisements, layouts in magazines and newspapers all come into play.

Layout has the double role of calling attention to a message and making it accessible. An advertisement for the post of art editor on a British women's magazine called for a person "who can create pages with real stopping power." This aim applies to every publication that wishes to make itself noticeable amid a flood of visual blandishments. The layout that calls attention to itself also has the task of displaying pictures and text so that they will make their point, and this may impose its own logic. One of the minor ironies of World War II was the similarity in layout between the illustrated magazines *Signal* and *Picture Post*, the one German, the other British. A typical page from 1942 carries a photograph of a German panzer grenadier crouched in a foxhole on the Russian front. With a few changes in the caption that page could have come from either publication. In fact it appeared in *Picture Post*.

Left: In this poster, which was displayed at a world conference against the use of nuclear bombs, the horrors of the bombing of Hiroshima are evoked through the face of a little girl hit by radioactivity. By Kiyoshi Awazu and Kohei Sugiura, 1960.

Left centre: Poster in favour of birth control. From the *Basta* series, a campaign of civil committment created by Giancarlo Iliprandi.
Below: A significant warning against atmospheric pollution, which has assumed dramatically disturbing proportions during the last few years. By Kenji Ito.

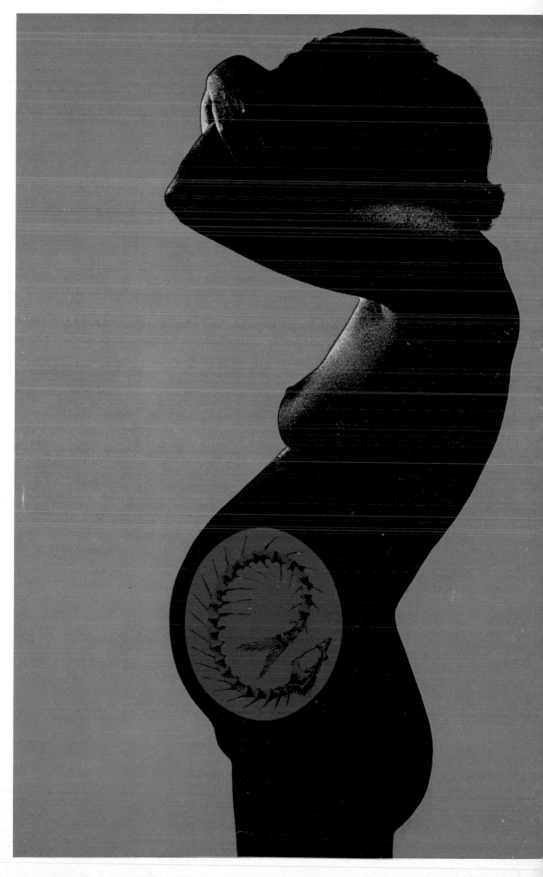

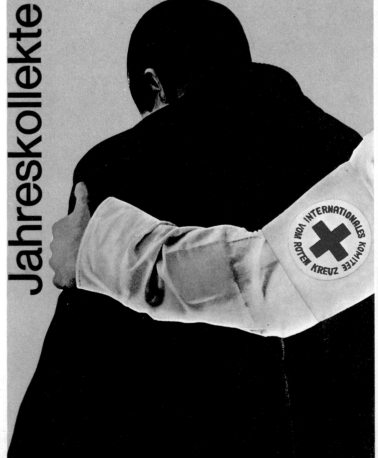

Above: Anti-accident propaganda formulated for the Polish workers. By Tadeusz Trepkowski, 1937.

Above right: Poster for the International Committee of the Red Cross. By Hans Neuberg, 1943. A new school of graphic artists formed in Switzerland in the 1940s, partly made up of the generation of pupils of the Bauhaus at Dessau. With their arrival, photography occupied a new place and was used to expressive new ends.

Right: A more recent poster to aid the International Red Cross. By André Masmejan, Switzerland, 1962.

WATER is LIFE

Below and bottom left: Two of the many posters devised by Josef Müller-Brockmann and circulated by the Helvetic Union from the early 1950s for the protection of individual citizens, and against the indiscriminate use of mechanical devices. The technique of photomontage, propagated by Heartfield, Moholy-Nagy, and El Lissitzky, is here explained in a quieter language and is characterized by contrasts in size.

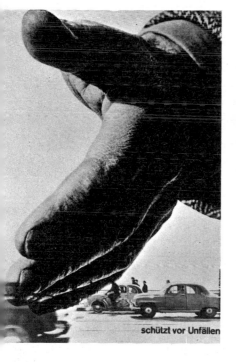

Organizations have sprung up throughout the world particularly since the mid-1960s, for the purpose of creating anti pollution movements denouncing all forms of oppression perpetrated by man on his environment. All this has been matched by an ample diffusion of graphic activity and visual communication; while this has spurred the creation of many valid posters, it has also served to show the weak side of such actions. In this instance, to articulate the problems unfortunately does not help to resolve them.

Near left, top and bottom: Two "water is life" posters, produced photographically, calling for ecological defence. The first by Hirokatsu Hijikata, the other by Stanislaw Podelko.

49

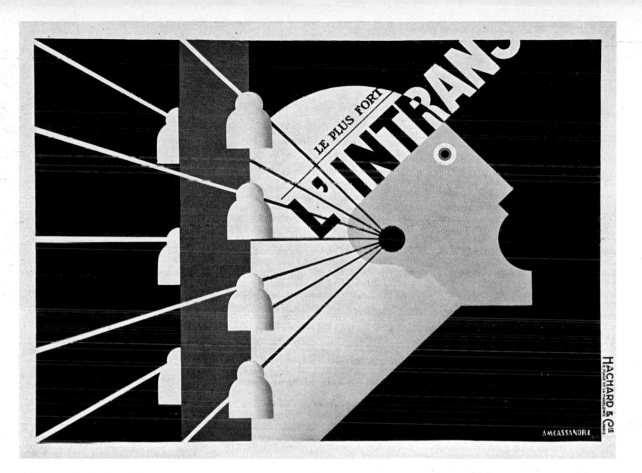

The News Interpreted

Opposite above: Publicity poster for the French satirical paper *L'Assiette au Beurre.* Even in advertising the popular vein of the publication is emphasized. By Eugène Cadel, late 1800s.
Opposite, below left: Poster for the German newspaper *Simplicissimus.* By Thomas T. Heine, who was for many years one of the paper's most worthy

contributors of political caricatures which had the virtue—besides being pungent and aggressive— of being executed with singular graphic elegance.
Opposite, below right: Dramatic illustration of an announcement in *Le Matin* publicizing the memoirs of the Abbé Faure. By Toulouse-Lautrec.
Above: Advertisement for the French

newspaper *l'Intransigeant.* By Adolphe Mouron Cassandre, 1925.
Below: This series of posters for the *National Zeitung* has a completely different concept from the previous ones: the maximum trust in a civil, essential, and—why not?—perhaps slightly iconoclastic communication. By Karl Gerstner.

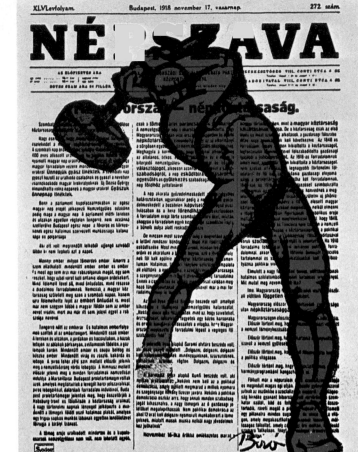

Above: Art nouveau version of an advertisement for the Chicago magazine *The Century.* By Maxfield Parrish, 1897.
Above right: Hungarian poster for the subscription to the Social Democrat party. By Mihaly Biro, 1918.
Below: The New York Times, advertised in cartoon style. By Tomi Ungerer.
Below right: A playbill devised according to the staunch canons of constructivism for *Il Politecnico,* a magazine of cultural and social commitment founded in 1945 by Elio Vittorini. By Albe Steiner.

The Birth of Illustrated News

Below, left and right: Cover and two-page spread of the American propagandist magazine *Front,* circulated by the Allied troops during World War II. Although illustrated magazines were being published throughout the world in 1936–37 (particularly the German *Signal*), it was the American publications that prevailed, with their innovative layouts, their strong, rich photography, and their illustrated-news format, which became a model for many countries after the war.

Even the choice of type size has an impact. On Tuesday, May 17, 1960, the front page of the British *Daily Mirror* carried just twenty-three words: "Mr K! (If you will pardon an olde English phrase) DON'T BE SO BLOODY RUDE! PS Who do you think you are? STALIN?" That was all. No pictures. No other text. Just the superlarge caps with their blank message: "Mr K! DON'T BE SO BLOODY RUDE!" It is an intriguing front page because it assumes that many of its readers already have some idea about what has happened and, presumably, that a large proportion would go along with this reaction. What had happened was that the Soviet premier Nikita Khrushchev, in Paris to attend a summit meeting, announced without warning that he would not take part in the meeting until the United States bound itself to make no more U2 flights over Soviet territory, and then withdrew an invitation to President Dwight D. Eisenhower to visit Russia.

Layout has a further effect in persuading readers that a publication is what it looks like. As readers, we are all aware of style and are conditioned by habit to accept certain forms as conveying a particular kind of reality. The sober layout of a newspaper such as the London *Times* or a magazine such as *Newsweek* acquires an aura that in turn lends authority to any material printed in that style. The form confirms reliability. That first issue of *The Berkeley Barb* in 1965 may have been an

Below: Poster emphasizing the virtues of *The Financial Times,* suggesting that it is a direct link with current economic events. By Abram Games.

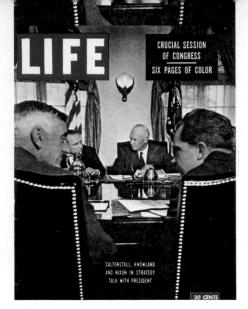

Above, left and right: Cover and a double spread from *Life* magazine, which laid down certain formulas in the field of illustrated news—such as detachable special features, for instance —which were then taken up all over the world. The magazine, which was a weekly, suspended publication for some years, finally reappearing in a new format as a monthly.
Below: Two covers and double spreads from *The Sunday Times Magazine*. They were considered for many years by graphic artists throughout the world to be important examples of layout and illustration. Art direction by David King.

MARINES WIN BLOODY BARREN SANDS OF IWO

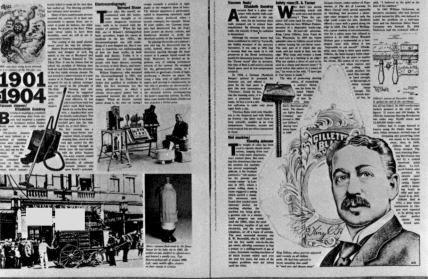

ugly thing, its stories packed into the page, its mast-head an immediate shock with its scrawled title set beside a drawing of Don Quixote on horseback that portrays rider and horse as skeletons. Yet it used news-paper conventions to make its point, and prospective readers thought they knew what they were getting. Editor Max Scherr was conscious of his aims: "What I was trying to do was to create credibility. The way I did it was by looking like a newspaper and printing mind-blowing facts down in straight columns." In the following years, the papers and magazines that assumed layouts where text and graphics merged into psychedelic swirls signalled in their very appearance that the readers they were after might well reject Estab-lishment views on drugs and other matters: "straight" columns provided its own double meaning.

Adopting the style of a particular kind of publication can be used both to present a point of view in a striking form and, perhaps, to bring it to the attention of readers who would not otherwise be made aware of it. The fantasy world of comic books, for instance, seems re-mote from political controversy, but their graphic techniques have been called to the aid of many causes. In the process, the stereotypes of popular imagery be-come the format of an analytical message. Comic books themselves sometimes make overtly clear their support for the forms of society and culture within which they flourish. Section A3 of the Code of the Comics Maga-zine Association of America advises: "Policemen, judges, government officials and respected institutions shall never be presented in such a way as to create disrespect for established authority." The Marvel Comics character Captain America, whose very costume incorporates the Stars and Stripes, corroborates that same support: "A man can be destroyed! A team or an army can be destroyed! But how do you destroy an ideal—a dream? How can you destroy a living symbol? How can the fearsome forces of evil ever hope to destroy the uncon-querable Captain America?"

In another example, Christopher Logue and Derek Boshier used comic strip conventions, heightened by the awareness of what Roy Lichtenstein had already done with them, to produce the poster-poem "Sex War Sex Cars Sex," which savaged the callous empti-

Above left: Cover of another influential weekly, *Paris Match,* which was also created along the lines of *Life.*
Above: Two-page spread from *The Sunday Times Magazine* featuring a photomontage on the end of the "Prague spring." Art direction by

David King.
Below: Amusing montage for the satirical monthly magazine *Esquire.* By George Lois.
Bottom. Cover of the Italian edition of *Esquire,* in the guise Giancarlo Iliprandi established for it. By Margaret Fodale.

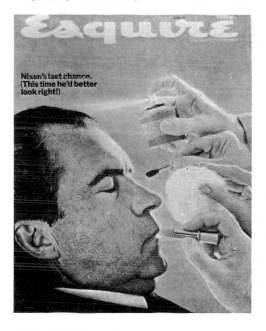

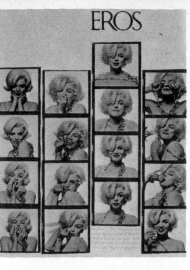

EROS

SHOW

Lollobrigida: One of Love's Many Faces

Toward an Haute Couture of Illustration

The development of technical possibilities in the field of photography, an ever-greater availability of means on the part of international editors, and the birth of art direction combined to bring about the publication, particularly in the 1960s, of "escapist" periodicals containing

elements of special distinction and new graphic ideas.
Above, left and centre: Double page and cover of *Eros* magazine. Art direction by Herb Lubalin; photography by Ralph M. Hattersley and Bert Stern.
Above right: Cover of arts magazine *Show*. Art direction by Henry Wolf.
Right: Cover of Japanese magazine *Now*. By Tamotsu Ejima and Shiro Tatsumi, 1970.
Below: Cover of *New York* magazine. Design by Milton Glaser; photography by Henry Wolf, 1972.

NOW

The Man Who Shot Rap Brown, by Robert Daley
Why the Power Vacuum Goes On and On at Time Inc.
Psyching Out McGovern's Mission, by Garry Wills

New York

OCTOBER 23, 1972

Special Section
THE WHOLE GRAPE CATALOGUE
Wine Buys and Wine Intelligence for The Passionate Sipper

Right: Anti-war poster, put together by *Avant-Garde* magazine. Design by Herb Lubalin, 1967.
Opposite top: Examples of two pages and a cover of the most prestigious of all European escapist magazines of the 1960s, *Twen*, edited by Willy Fleckhaus. For years it has produced an ever-new range of graphic ideas—in illustration, photography, printing, and layout. Photography, from left to right, by Otto Storch, Guido Mangold, and Peter Turner.
Opposite below: Two double pages from the French photography magazine *Zoom*, made up so as to require a way of reading opposed to the traditional way, according to a pattern also tried out for a long time by *Twen*. Photography by Franz Gruber.

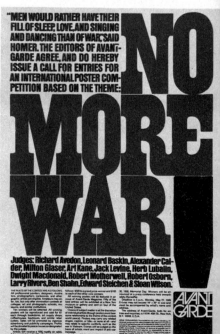

"MEN WOULD RATHER HAVE THEIR FILL OF SLEEP, LOVE, AND SINGING AND DANCING THAN OF WAR," SAID HOMER. THE EDITORS OF AVANT-GARDE AGREE, AND DO HEREBY ISSUE A CALL FOR ENTRIES FOR AN INTERNATIONAL POSTER COMPETITION BASED ON THE THEME:

NO MORE WAR!

Judges: Richard Avedon, Leonard Baskin, Alexander Calder, Milton Glaser, Art Kane, Jack Levine, Herb Lubalin, Dwight Macdonald, Robert Motherwell, Robert Osborn, Larry Rivers, Ben Shahn, Edward Steichen & Sloan Wilson.

AVANT GARDE

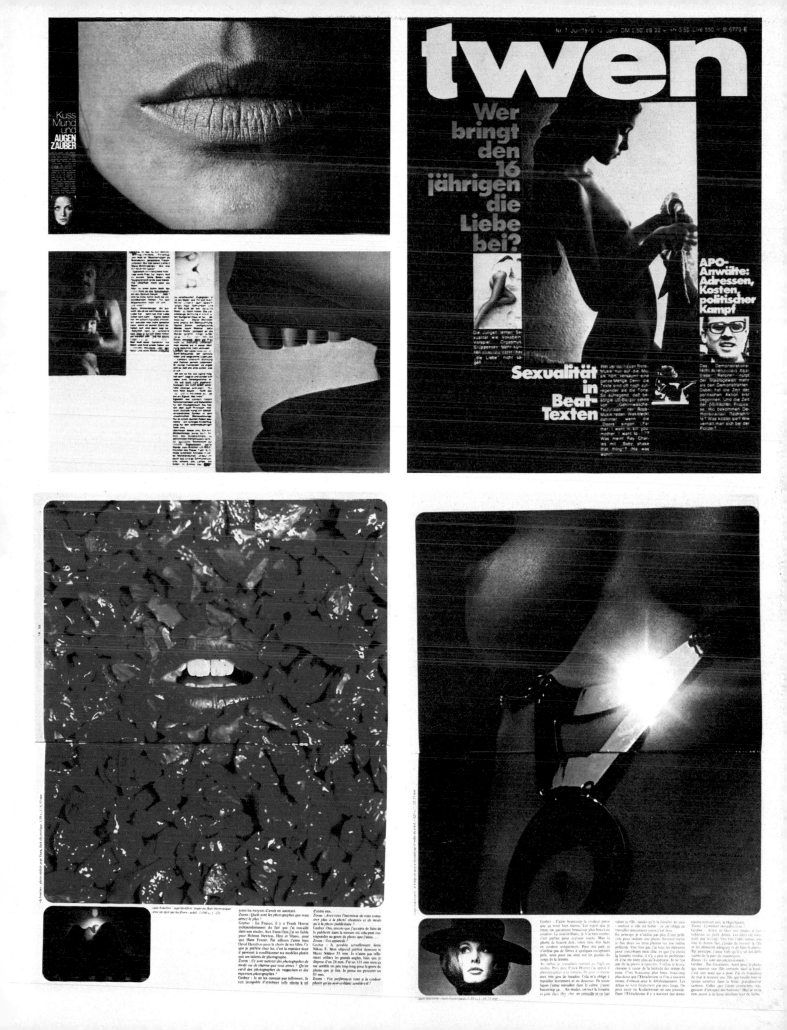

これが光なのだろうか, あふれでて私を抱こうとする, この大いなるもの。──HIRO

ness of some comic strip stories. "Please God!" a stylized heroine cries out in the last frame. "Let me die naked in a fast car crash with the radio turned on."

An example of comic books being used directly for political effect came from Chile during the years when Salvador Allende was president. One of the main magazine-publishing firms, Quimantú, began producing magazines, including several series of comic books, that supported the Allende government's policies. A particularly impressive series, in the fifty or so issues of *La Firme* that appeared between 1970 and 1973, featured strip after strip explaining the government's approach to Chile's basic problems.

Issue number 33 was devoted entirely to a confrontation with International Telephone and Telegraph (ITT), the multinational communications group, which has a massive presence in Latin America and had actually owned the Chilean telephone system. A typical page begins with the legend "The government decreed intervention." In the first frame two men dive into a murky heap from which they pluck an occasional telephone: "As government officers, we have to untangle this mess! To begin with, in the year 1971 the installation of 32,500 automatic lines was planned. . . ." The second frame continues: ". . . and not only were lines brought to regions which had never had any before but *socially equitable* tariffs were also introduced." A downtrodden member of the lower classes looks up

Photography has played a strong role in characterizing, idealizing, and mythicizing fashion figures, with all the ingredients that make up their microcosm.
Above left: Cosmetics advertisement. Photography by Hiro Wakabayashi; art direction by Hiroshi Kojitani.
Above and top: Male and female fashion advertisements. Art direction and design by Osamu Hoshi; photography by Richard Avedon.

Left: Japanese cosmetics poster. Design by Makoto Matsunaga; photography by Noriaki Yokosuka.
Below and bottom: Pages from *Harper's Bazaar,* where the photography assumes a symbolic value, and is stretched to exalt the predetermined element to the full. Photography by Hiro Wakabayashi (below) and Silano (bottom, left and right).

⊛ 資生堂化粧品

次々に生まれる流行をいち早くとり入れる資生堂化粧品はいつもフレッシュな感覚にみちています

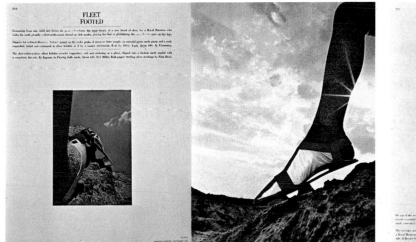

The very least, far left: bare bikini panties and top, bare beige chiffon. Jon Haggins. Two and total, far left below: bikini top with built-in bra, wide-legged pants with built-in pantie-girdle—now you have the whole inside-outside story in a double play of polka dots. By Warner's. Top-to-toe body stocking, centre, doing your thing for you at a single ribby black stretch. By Hudson. Lasting attachment, left: sheer black tights and bikini panties hit it off together—for good. Rudi Gernreich for the McCallum Boutique. The most, above: if you need a bit of help, you've got it—a holding operation that makes one trim line of stockings, panties, you. Hanes. Out from under, right, comes the jump suit—bitter-brown ribbed wool by Ungaro wrapped by an unbleached denim Phelps mini-jupe. This one's really got pull, far right, snugging up to a perfect fit whether you're 5'10" or just 5'1". In brown. By Berkshire.

Far left: Silk bikini, about $60. Bonwit Teller S'fari Room, Joske's Houston. Far left, below: Navy and white dots in Arnel and Lycra. Top, $6; pants, $15. February 1, at Bonwit Teller. Centre left, below: Body stocking, $8 Bergdorf Goodman. Near left: Agilon bikini tights, $6, Henri Bendel. Near left above: Pantie stockings, of Cantrece nylon and spandex, $5, Alter'ars. Right: Jump s. t, $100. Bonwit Teller S'fari Room. Skirt of Dacron and cotton (Avondale fabric). $23. Lord & Taylor. Berkshire knee socks. Capezio shoes, Lord & Taylor. Far right: Act on wear tights of Monsanto Blue C nylon. $3. Arnold Constable. Trifari chain. Accessocraft pendant. All coiffures: Mr. Chin of Charles of the Ritz.

FORECAST
1969
doing your
under thing—
the least
you can do

WALDECK

Above and right: Double page and cover of *Vogue,* the American fashion magazine that boasts a long tradition of being a trend-setter in the field. Many major illustrators and photographers have worked for the magazine in their time; its character is at once modern and classical, and its pages are often set in eighteenth-century type.
Left and below: Some pages from *Harper's Bazaar,* which vies with *Vogue* for leadership in the fashion-magazine field, sharing its aesthetic philosophy. Photography by James Moore and Hiro Wakabayashi.

75c. NOV. 15
VOGUE
LOOK
MARVELLOUS
RIGHT NOW
AT NIGHT...IN THE SUN...
75 SMASHING
ACCESSORIES...
PLUS 102 GIFT IDEAS

WHAT YOU MUST
KNOW ABOUT YOUR
SLEEP
AND DREAMS:
THE LATEST
MEDICAL
DISCOVERIES

THE HUFF
AND PUFF
THEORY OF
EXERCISE

MEN IN
VOGUE

ARTICLES
BY:
ANDRÉ
MALRAUX,
ROBERT
GRAVES,
DAVID
SMITH

PARIS

BALMAIN
GRÈS

FORECAST 1969

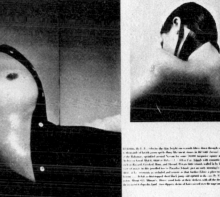

Above: Two double pages from *Vogue*. Photography by Richard Avedon; art direction by Priscilla Peck.
Below: A double page from *McCall's*, which established an editorial policy of dealing with a number of widely varied topics in a spirit of maximum practicality. It is thus markedly different in attitude from *Vogue* and *Harper's Bazaar* although in all three the picture and the colour prevail to the full. The spread here presents a picture which was destined to be used in another vehicle of communication, such as this advertising board in a landscape. Roland Barthes, writing on fashion, stated: "In order to obscure the financial awareness of the buyer, it is necessary to stretch before the object a veil of images, reasons, senses, to elaborate around it an intermediary substance, in short to create an effigy of the real object, substituting the sad time of wear and tear with paramount time."

A SUMMER BEAUTY PLAN TO DISPLAY YOU AT YOUR BEST

BINZEN and PRIGENT

Specialized Magazines

Above: Cover of a promotional publication, in which the design takes into consideration the casual intervention of the postal service, the means through which the publication is dispensed. Design by Ryuichi Yamashiro; art direction by Ikko Tanaka.
Above right: Cover of the international architecture, art, and design magazine *Form,* published in Switzerland. Design by Karl Oscar Blase.

Right and below: Cover and some pull-out supplements from the Italian architecture, art, and design magazine *Domus,* founded by Gio Ponti in 1928, and still edited by him. While retaining an ideal level of continuity, this magazine has always known how to keep up to date, even in its graphic aspect, and how to be well ahead in the field of information-giving through each period of history.

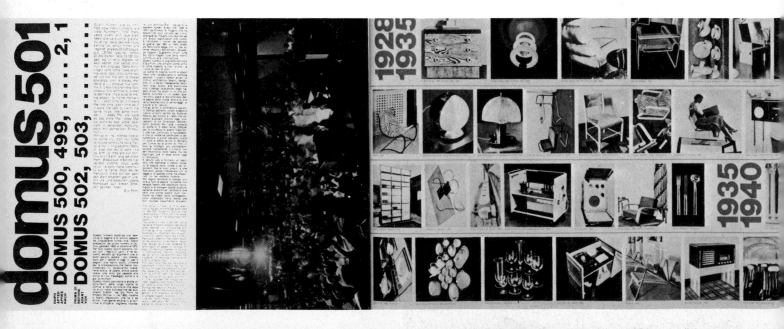

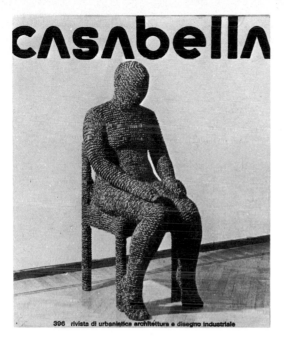

Casabella

ABITARE
vivere nella casa, nella città, nel territorio / living at home, in town and in the country

Nell'anno della crisi tutto per abitare meglio: ma a che prezzo? All you need for better living in this year of crisis: but at what cost?

Above and below: Cover and double page from *Casabella* in the early 1970s. It, like its sister publication *Domus*, was founded in 1928, and has weathered not insignificant difficulties through the years; it has nonetheless always found extremely valid directions, notably during a glorious phase under the leadership of Pagano and Persico. The pages here represent its "radical design" period. Graphics by Luciano Boschini; art direction by Alessandro Mendini.

Above and top: Double page and cover from *Abitare*, another Italian design magazine, more sensitive to the phenomenological and social problems of living than to the purely formal aspects. Illustration (above) by Paolo Guidotti; art direction by Italo Lupi.

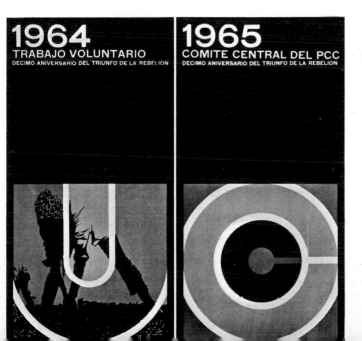

Left: Pamphlets produced to commemorate the tenth anniversary of the Cuban Revolution.

Visualizing the Contents of a Book

Above left: Cover from Penguin Books. Their books have been updated in their presentation under the art direction of Germano Facetti. Illustration by Romek Marber.

Above centre: The Oscar Mondadori series, which, after initially adopting a fixed pattern, was liberated from any artistic shackles in order to give each cover an appropriately thought-out, individual presentation. Design by Paolo Guidotti; art direction by Bruno Binosi.
Above right: Recent cover from the German publishing house Klett-Cotta, with a journalistic layout.

Below, left and centre: Two covers in which the artist intervenes with fantastic ideas that enhance his strong illustration. By Heinz Edelmann.
Right: Cover by John Alcorn, who for some years has brilliantly sustained the entire book output of the Rizzoli publishing house in Italy. Art direction by Mario Spagnol.

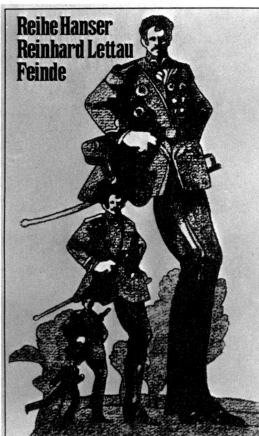

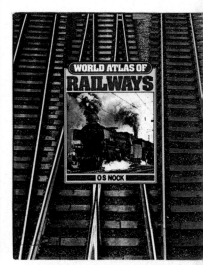

Top left: Jacket created for a Colette series published by Penguin Books. By Alan Fletcher.
Top right: Cover for a series of prose works put out by Penguin Books. By Bentley, Farrell, and Burnett.
Centre left: Graphic creation for a story published by the British publishing house Corgi. By John Munday and Chris Moore.
Centre right: Jacket for a Signet Classics Shakespeare series. By Milton Glaser.
Left: Jacket for the Fischer publishing house. By Jan Buchholz and Reni Hinsch.
Opposite, near right: The illustrated book usually requires visualization distinguishable from that used in fiction. Shown is a jacket for a book published by Mitchell Beazley. Design and illustration by the QED group; art direction by Roger Pring.

at a plutocrat lounging in a cushion-stuffed chair (both characters have telephones in their hands) and remarks: "That seems only fair, I can't pay the same as that fat cat." In the third frame a woman picks up a telephone to hear the message: "And in addition, NATIONALIZATION is definitely being planned—in most of the world the telephones are state-owned."

In a last step, communication shifts from espousing a point of view to persuading people to support this or that action, getting them to behave in a particular way. In a commercial culture the most obvious example of persuasion is advertising. Although its primary intention is to coax the consumer to spend money, advertising can have other functions. Sidney Webb, the British socialist thinker, pointed out that "even when all our various manufactories have become public services, we can easily imagine the various public health departments advertising their baths and the educational authorities importuning every young man and maiden to try their attractive lecture courses and organized games."

One area in which advertising plays a part is in the struggles that develop between businesses or other corporate institutions and political activists and consumer groups. In general, these groups bring pressure to bear by organizing boycotts, rallies, and demonstrations, lobbying individual politicians, and planning stunts or holding conferences that will attract media attention. In order to combat this kind of public pressure, corporate interests have developed concepts such as advocacy advertising. One of the first people to use the term was John O'Toole, president of the New York advertising agency Foote, Cone & Belding, who wrote, "Advertising is the only means available to provide the balance—an advocate for the system and for individual corporations within that system. It is a different kind of advertising than most of us are used to, but it is a legitimate and, for the times, a highly appropriate mutation."

An example of this style of advertising was a campaign by the American Electric Power Company attacking demands by environmental groups and government agencies for more stringent controls on pollution from coal-mining operations and electricity-generating plants. An even wider-ranging campaign, launched by the Warner & Swasey Company, an Ohio-based manufacturer of construction machinery, has endorsed a tough-minded approach to the problems of the American economy. A sample advertisement begins with the copy line "No wonder we're broke! When we're giving away money we don't have, and getting hatred and antagonism in return." It continues with a list of American loans and aid to other countries.

Advocacy advertising such as this shades off into campaigns by more purely political pressure groups and appeals by political parties themselves. In the run-up to an election perhaps the most important message

IELA AND ENZO MARI

THE APPLE
AND THE BUTTERFLY

ADAM & CHARLES BLACK

THIS EDITION FIRST PUBLISHED 1970
REPRINTED 1972
A. AND C. BLACK LIMITED
4, 5 AND 6 SOHO SQUARE LONDON W1V 6AD
© 1969 IELA AND ENZO MARI
PRINTED IN ITALY
BY FANTONIGRAFICA - VENICE
ISBN 0 7136 1192 9

Left: A book for very young children; the criterion of learning, which combines the principles of pedagogy and the theory of Gestalt psychology—to which graphic design frequently resorts—is fulfilled here through the use of simple shapes and primary colours. Created by Iela and Enzo Mari.

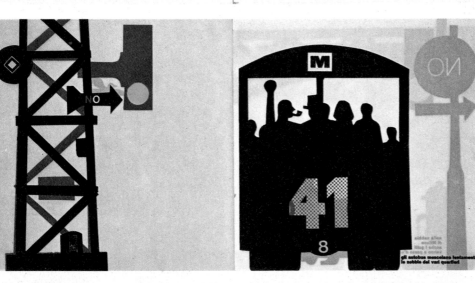

An amusing little book devised by Bruno Munari, who for many years has devoted part of his energies to the problems of communication and visualization, always putting himself in the child's position. His *Nella Nebbia di Milano (Through Milan's Fog)* was created by printing the various drawings on transparent vegetable paper in such a way as to cause all the components to be superimposed and slowly become evanescent, as if they were lost in the fog. The effect is achieved through the impure transparency of the paper.

I know a cat goes meow

I know how things are made.
A house has glass
and bricks
and lots of sticks.
A square box has
a top as wide
as its side.

conveyed by a party's advertising is that it exists and is able to advertise itself. The graphics may be striking: the aim is to grab attention rather than present policies, to invite support by appealing to the emotions as much as to the intellect. For example, the British Labour Party once produced an ethereally beautiful poster portraying the standing figure of a cloaked woman holding a baby In order to make the plea "Mothers vote Labour." In another example, Saatchi & Saatchi, the agency that handled advertising for the British Conservative Party in the 1979 election, noted: "The truth is that people succumb to simple arguments," and went on to produce a poster showing an endless unemployment queue with the copy line "Labour still isn't working."

Political struggle, the last extreme of which is war, has always required the exhortation of supporters and potential supporters, often stimulating the creation of graphic images that become particularly memorable. War itself, with its obvious division between allies and enemy, invites reduction to the symbol: even a waving flag becomes deeply significant. The basic message is simple, yet it can be powerful in the emotions it stirs: "You can help us to beat them." It crops up again and again.

Consider the posters built around the theme "Your country needs you." Alfred Leete's British version from World War I pictures Lord Kitchener gazing out directly at the viewer while his foreshortened index finger pins down the viewer's soul. James Montgomery Flagg's American version has Uncle Sam fixing his eye and finger on the audience. There is a Russian poster with a similar motif, painted in 1920 by Dmitry Moor (D. S. Orlov) when the Red Army was fighting against the White. "Have you volunteered?" it asks.

Dmitry Moor described the effect his poster produced. "In this poster, the Red Army soldier, pointing with his finger, fastened his eyes directly on the viewer and turned in his direction. I had many conversations about the poster. Some even told me they were made ashamed by it, that it inspired shame if one did not volunteer."

Political struggle calls forth a ferment of activity. In the year that Dmitry Moor painted his poster, the revolutionary movement in Russia produced over fifteen hundred posters, circulating them in print runs of fifty thousand or more. An interesting development in this type of propagandistic art was reflected in the window posters rushed out by ROSTA, the Soviet telegraph agency. These collections of drawings, cartoons, slogans, and text were stuck in shop and house windows and changed rapidly in response to reanalysis of the revolutionary stance or to new information about the struggle against counterrevolution.

In such circumstances the process of producing posters may affect the decisions reached, as well as communicate those decisions and urge others to act on them. This has been especially noticeable with the Chinese wall-posters that have come to play a prominent part in conflicts between governing factions. The Cultural Revolution of 1966, for example, in which the Red Guards set out to destroy the "four olds"—old ideas, old culture, old customs, and old habits— virtually launched itself with a wall-poster that appeared at Peking University attacking the university president. Some of the wall-posters of the subsequent struggle were purely products of an ethos of incivility: "Any rat that dares to try to shift the revolutionary pacemakers half a hair's breadth off course will be smashed to a pulp." Some presented cogent arguments

With the arrival of László Moholy-Nagy at the Bauhaus, formal and spatial strictness were emphasized even in graphic and printing compositions, with a marked tendency toward dynamism. The cultural climate of the artistic avant-garde, particularly in the magazines *De Stijl, Ma, Broom,* and *Merz,* where Theo van Doesburg, El Lissitzky, Alexander Rodchenko, and Moholy-Nagy worked, was also reflected in the Bauhaus environment.
Opposite: Poster for a Russian exhibition in Zurich, exalting the revolutionary power of the Soviet people and realized according to the patterns of construc-tivism. By El Lissitzky, 1929.
Below left: Poster for two ballets put on in Weimar in 1922; the illustrative style was created by the artist while at the Bauhaus. By Oskar Schlemmer.
Below right: Poster for an exhibition held at Weimar in 1923. By Joost Schmidt.

that were picked up and republished or answered in other wall-posters.

In the same way, the action committees of the militant student movements in France in May 1968 poured out posters and leaflets that displayed all the immediate liveliness of hastily prepared broadsheets. They were both a source of information and a call to action. The discussions that produced these texts and visual images were themselves significant in clarifying the aims of the various sections of the movements. One group produced a list of slogans to be circulated by any means: "Occupy the factories!" "Power to the workers councils!" "Abolish class society!" "An end to the university!" and so on. Another faction commented on the nature of the contribution made by such posters: "Experience has taught us the danger of ambiguity and the necessity of incorporating slogans as an integral part of the design. Sincerity, fantasy, are only effective when they interpret and reinforce the attack made by the slogan."

Here is some sort of key to the function of both words and pictures in influencing social and political movements. Both need a context, an exploration of their significance, although in a specific situation and when aimed at a specific audience much of that context may already be understood. A picture by itself may always contain some ambiguity: spelling out the context ensures that when interpretations differ it has something to do with real differences in point of view rather than sheer vagueness of response. Take, for example, Joe Rosenthal's famous photograph of the flag raising on Iwo Jima during World War II. Given some knowledge of the war in the Pacific and support for that kind of military endeavour, it raises the spirits; given the same knowledge and a distaste for militarism, it depresses. Without the knowledge of when and why it was taken, and of what it actually shows, it may still produce these reactions but without the resonances that give them depth.

The Cultural Poster in Show Business

Left: A singular cinema poster created by means of the photomontage technique and the use of certain typographical elements. By Roman Cieslewicz.
Above left: This poster was created along the lines of Dutch neoplasticism and Russian constructivism, which were the major influences on the artist. By Max Bill, 1945.

Above right: Poster for a private exhibition of the artist's work. By Shigeo Fukuda.
Below left: Poster in which references to Utamaro's art can be found in the stylization of the traditional Japanese landscape. By Ryuichi Yamashiro, 1960.
Below right: A richly graphic poster, full of little calligraphic inventions, created for a series of musical performances held at the Fondation Maeght. By Saul Steinberg.

Left: Cinema poster that shows some film sequences according to the scansion of the roll of film. By Wojciech Zamer-cznick, 1959.
Below: Two posters for the International Exhibition of Prints, held every two years in Tokyo. Each reflects a very different conception: one is made up of a fantastic illustration, while the other is a dense composition of textual matter and fragments of illustration. By Tadanori Yokoo (left) and Kohei Sugiura (right).

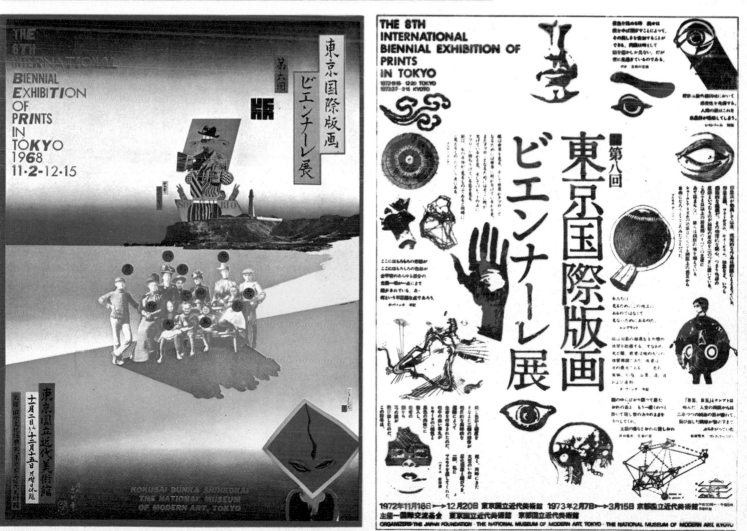

The Theatrical Poster and the Polish Tradition

Polish posters have been a veritable "footlights school" for the past few decades. Although they convey their messages by means of expressionistic signs, they are striking because of their modernity and their dramatic quality.

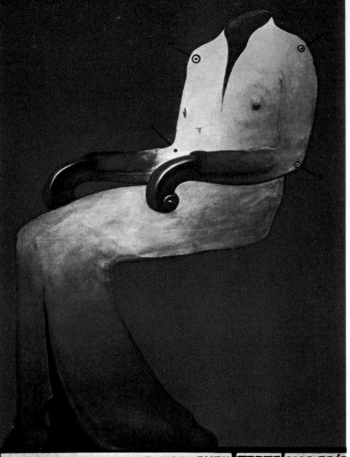

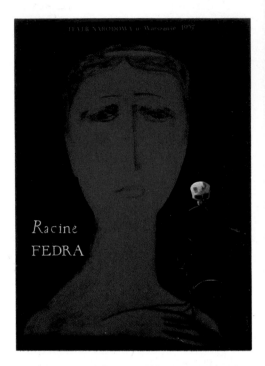

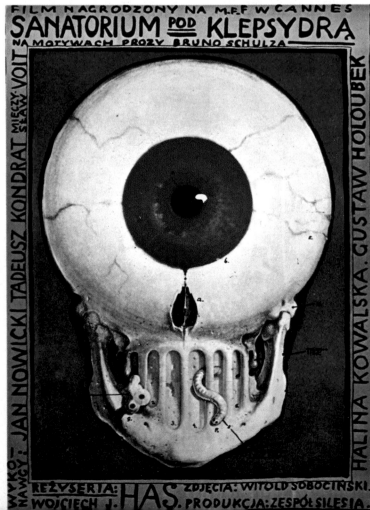

Top left: An interpretation of Racine's *Phèdre*. By Jan Lenica.
Top right: Graphic visualization for a Pinter play. By Franciszek Starowieyski.
Above: A highly personal poster for Verdi's *Otello*. By Jan Lenica.
Right: A grotesque mask created for a film. By Franciszek Starowieyski.

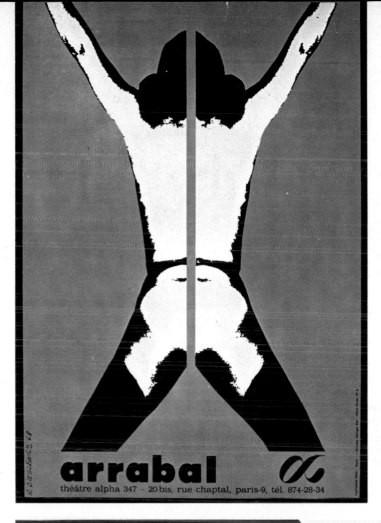

arrabal

théâtre alpha 347 - 20 bis, rue chaptal, paris-9, tél. 874-28-34

Left: Theatrical poster. By Roman Cieslewicz, who was the first among the artists of the Polish school to abandon traditional techniques of expression in favour of a more sharply graphic presentation.

Below: Poster for a personal exhibition of the artist's work. By Jan Sawka, 1974. *Bottom:* Photomontage for a playbill. By Gan Hosoya.

Ambler Music Festival / Institute of Temple University

Left: Calligraphic poster for a concert.
By Kohei Sugiura, 1959.
Above: Poster for Amber Music Festival.
By Milton Glaser.
Below, left and centre: Two theatrical
posters by Tadanori Yokoo.
Below right: Poster for a Dionne Warwick
concert. By Milton Glaser.

To a Musical Rhythm

Below left: Poster for a music festival in Hong Kong. By Henry Steiner.
Below centre: Poster for the film of the musical *Hair*. It is partly photographed, partly drawn, attaining a perfect connection between all the parts, in a magical

light that evokes the mood of rock. By Eiko Ishioka.
Below right: Programme for a jazz concert, with a tone-colour symbol that heightens its portrayal. By Seymour Chwast.

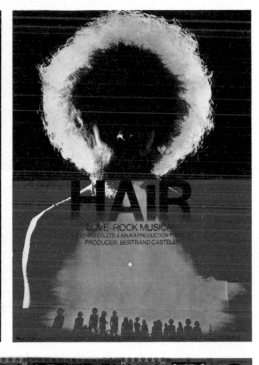

Left: A complex composition within a thick geometric decoration, which answers a typically Japanese concept of graphic art. By Kiyoshi Awazu, 1973.

The Language of Symbols

Above left: A free interpretation for a musical poster for the Poppy Record Company. By Milton Glaser.

Above right: Real images mingle with fantastic ones in this poster for National Book Week in America. By Peter Max, 1969.

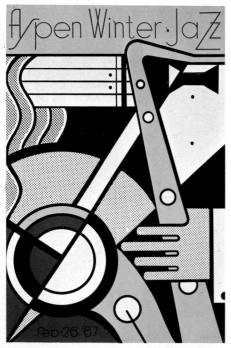

Left: Poster for a jazz concert which uses a mixture of art deco and cartoon-strip techniques. By Roy Lichtenstein, 1967.
Opposite: Another surrealist fantasy by Milton Glaser.

Pictures affect the public consciousness in many different ways. Photographs, in the main, are seen as standing in a direct relationship with the real world. As a result they have a powerful effect in making people aware of that world and their identity within it. A photograph of a political demonstration, with the banners and slogans showing, is proof that that demonstration occurred. The photograph is evidence, it provides a record. It also conveys some of the atmosphere of that demonstration, of the political energy involved. More generally, a photograph allows identification with a human experience: a photograph of the twisted limbs of a victim of mercury poisoning from industrial waste stirs compassion and may lead to an urge for action. By pinning down and isolating an incident with an image in time, a photograph forces some reaction from the viewer. Yet photographic "reality" may be heavily slanted in order to emphasize a point of view. *Picture Post* chose to print a photograph of Adolf Hitler showing him as a dowdy middle-aged militarist; the Nazi Party paper *Völkischer Beobachter*, on the other hand, picked shots that presented a confidently sublime, almost godlike human being.

Pictures of all kinds have the power to present abstract concepts in concrete images to devastating effect. In one example, John Heartfield in 1932 summed

MILTON GLASER

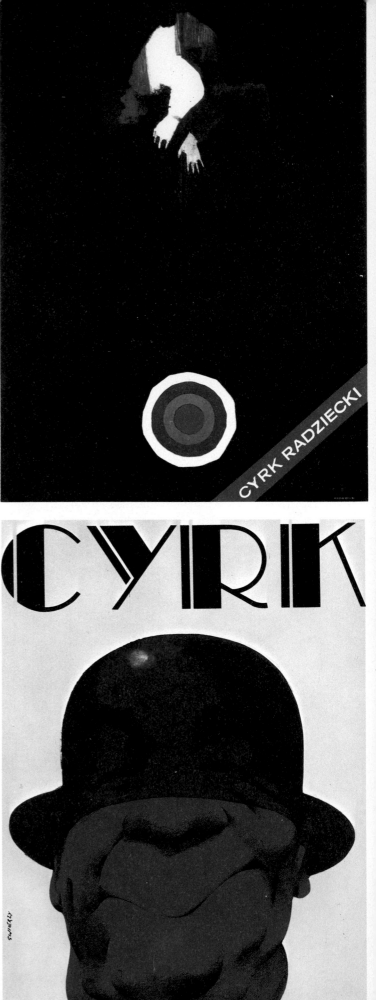

up the relationship between the Nazi Party and business interests in a photomontage entitled "Millions stand behind me": Adolf Hitler lifts his right arm in a salute that becomes supplication, while a giant figure standing behind him slips bank notes into his upraised hand. A picture can encapsulate and refine an argument or an appeal to the point where it focuses myriad strands of analyses and potential reactions into a single frame. The image, with its own complexities and in tension with the context, becomes a social force.

The Fascination
of the Circus

The pictorial tradition of Warsaw artists
is expressed with skill and subtle irony
in these posters for circus performances.
Opposite, far left and left : The graphic
representation of the acrobat's balancing
act is itself balanced between the pic
torial quality of the figure and the
decorative symbolism of the circle
design. By Maciej Urbaniec.
Opposite below: A particularly striking
drawing between realism and colour
abstraction. By Waldmar Swierzy, 1970.

Right: The chance to present a Polish
circus enabled Maciej Urbaniec to parody
Leonardo's Mona Lisa with a graceful
composition that is vividy colourful.

INTERNATIONAL CANVAS FURNITURE DESIGN COMPETITION

Above: Poster for a cultural exhibition.
By Jean Picart le Doux, 1947.
Right: A symbolic form, covered in
cloth, for a clothing-fabric fair. By Eiko
Ishioka.

Above: Cover of an internal publication
for the staff of RAI (the Italian broadcasting network); the characters evolve
simultaneously, seeming to acquire
movement through the repetition of the
picture. By Giancarlo Iliprandi.
Right: A horse, rampant between the
return to classicism and metaphysics,
designed for the Milan Trade Fair. By
Marcello Nizzoli, 1931.

Above left: Poster for the 1960 Rome Olympics, inspired by the symbolic values of the eternal city. By Armando Testa.
Above centre: An English pop artist has visualized the Olympic Games as a synthesis of strengths and balances. By Allen Jones.

Below: Continuous poster in which the photographic images of sports alternate with the symbol of the Olympic Games, associated with the Japanese flag for the 1964 Tokyo Olympics. By Yusaku Kamekura and Jo Murakoshi.

Above and below: Two posters from a series created by Otl Aicher for the 1972 Munich Olympics. Reproduction methods lend themselves to various technical possibilities which are skillfully exploited in the poster above.

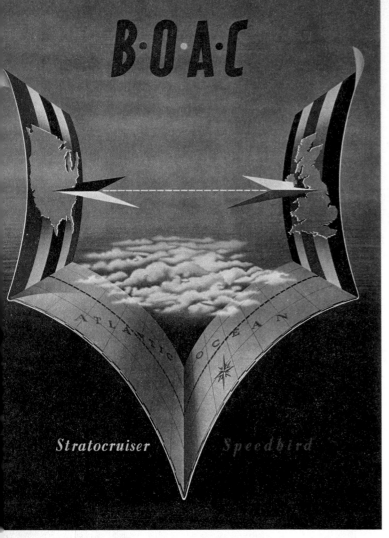

FLY TO THE U·S·A BY

B·O·A·C

ATLANTIC OCEAN

Stratocruiser *Speedbird*

To Dream of Great Travels

verkort uw reisduur

AMERICAN OVERSEAS AIRLINES

Left: Poster for British Overseas Air Corporation (now British Airways). The pages of an atlas, projected into space, indicate the trajectory of intercontinental flights between Britain and America. By Abram Games, 1949.
Above: Another free interpretation of journeys around the world. By Jan Le Witt and George Him, 1948.
Below left: A poster for Britain's trans-continental postal route that conveys its message subtly, the lines of the hand implying that the places are all within hand's reach. By E. McKnight Kauffer.

Below right: Tourist poster for the French Line. By Paul Colin, 1930s.
Opposite: Poster for British Rail. By Abram Games, 1952.

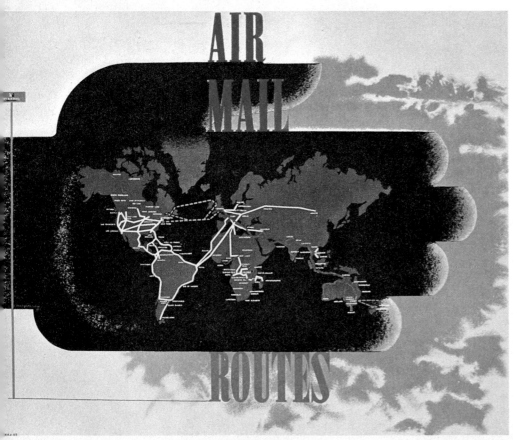

AIR MAIL ROUTES

Cⁱᵉ G.ˡᵉ TRANSATLANTIQUE
French Line

ATLANTIQUE · PACIFIQUE · MÉDITERRAN

Above left: A spectacular poster for
Swissair, created with a photograph
by Emil Schulthess; graphics by
Manfred Bingler.
Above: Tourist poster for Pan Am that
seems to offer a dream vision. By Peter
Max.
Left: Another poster for Swissair,
advertising the beauty of Swiss tourist
resorts. Photography by Georg Gerster;
design by Emil Schulthess and
Hans Frei.

Right: Scandinavian advertisement crystallizing a magic moment in the Nordic landscape. Photography by Mike Cuesta; graphics by Amil Gargano.
Below: A flag across the pages of a magazine welcomes overseas tourists. Photography by Elliot Erwitt; art direction by William Taubin.

"'Tis now the very witching time of night,
when churchyards yawn,
and hell itself breathes out contagion to this world..."

Visit Hamlet's castle at Elsinore, Denmark at night, and you can almost see him moodily ranging the battlements, talking of ghosts and murder.
If the castle of the melancholy Dane is a little too eerie for your tastes, remember Elsinore is less than an hour from Copenhagen. Copenhagen is as modern and gay as Elsinore is ancient and brooding. As you get to know the people of Copenhagen, you'll swear that Hamlet must have been the only Dane who was ever melancholy.

SAS flies to Copenhagen (and Stockholm, Oslo, Helsinki and Bergen) from New York, Chicago, Los Angeles, Anchorage and Montreal. A total of 18 jet flights a week now through spring . . . 34 a week beginning June 1. And, in case you want to travel on (although hardly anyone ever leaves Copenhagen willingly), SAS serves more cities within Europe than any other transatlantic airline.
For more information contact your travel agent or write: Scandinavian Airlines System, Dept. SX, 138-02 Queens Boulevard, Jamaica, New York 11435. **SAS** *Scandinavian Airlines System*

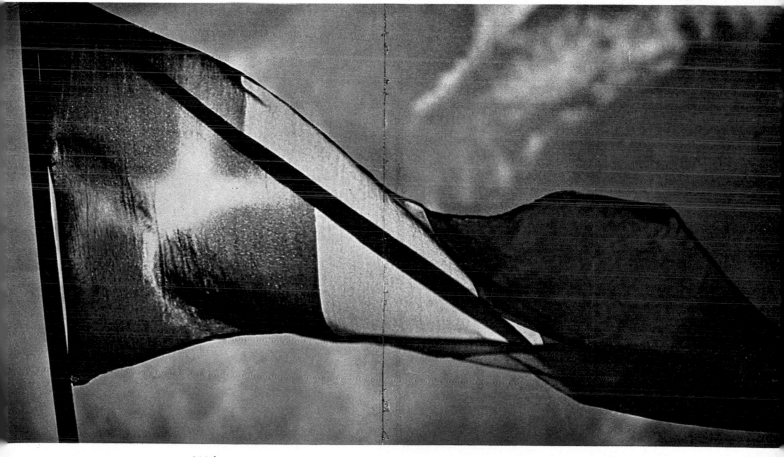

Welcome.

The Place de la Concorde is scrubbed and gleaming. The sommelier of a 4 star restaurant says it will be a great wine year. And the provinces report the geese look extra fat. For the first time since Louis left, Versailles is dazzling in candlelight. And the Louvre has 26 new halls filled with dramatic antiques. We've turned a lot of picturesque castles into charming inns for you and opened a lot of new hotels. We've even planted flowers all the way from Paris to Nice so we'll be coming up roses. In other words, we hope you'll have a wonderful time. If there's anything we can do, any literature you need, just write Dept. NY-A, Box #221, New York 10. Or see your French Government Tourist Office in New York, Chicago, Beverly Hills, San Francisco, Miami, Montreal. Or see your own travel agent. We'll all help you in every way.

See.
All lipsticks are not alike. This one is Stained Glass by Fabergé.

3. THE STRATEGY OF COMMUNICATION

Vocal to the wise,
but for the crowd they need interpreters.
PINDAR

Art in advertising has many roles to fulfill. It may be required to communicate an idea, a thought, or a message. On another level, it may have to act as one of several elements designed to achieve a degree of persuasion. Or it may simply be required to be remembered, to be memorable on its own. But above all else, its principal function is one of interpretation.

In the logical order of all advertising and selling activities, it is, in the first place, the responsibility of industrial management to produce the goods or organize the services offered by the company. Historically, many of the products now taken for granted were developed as a result of man's basic needs for clothing, housing, food, and recreation. They needed no advertising because their worth was evident in their usefulness. A crusading knight needed no persuasion about the value of armour. A country squire needed no introduction, other than word of mouth, to the idea of roofing tiles for his house—their value was self-evident. And those with time on their hands needed no indoctrination into the gentler arts of music and drama. Such diversions developed because man recognized his basic needs for entertainment and instruction.

But, in the years since the industrialization of society and its production methods, since the massive growth of the world's population and its increasing mobility and international communication, there has developed a fundamental need for industry to engage interpreters whose job it is to act for them in the next step of their production cycle: the creation of effective messages that will appeal to the potential consumers of their products or services.

With the help of these interpreters, the simple cycle becomes complete, despite the complexities of society today. Industry produces goods or services. Advertising agencies interpret their value. The consumer buys the goods.

Yet this simple pattern is surrounded by geographical, sociological, and ethnic complexities which can be re-solved only by strategic application of strict disciplines. The creative discipline is one of the most crucial.

To understand the fundamental importance of creativity, whether verbal or visual, it is necessary to understand the ultimate link in the selling cycle—the consumer. In markets flooded with as many useless products as useful ones, the consumer has many choices open to him. In some sectors of the market he may have as many as fifty to a hundred brands to choose from, each varying only slightly from the rest. Even before he makes any kind of considered choice about one brand in preference to another, he will make a number of fundamental decisions, some subconscious, others conscious. He may begin by asking himself whether a particular product or service is necessary to his existence, whether it will enrich his life. Next he may consider whether the product is something he genuinely wants, even though he knows it has no value to him as a necessity. Finally he may decide that the product is valuable to him because, as a result of innumerable received opinions and messages, he has become convinced that, for good or ill, the product is desirable or should be desired.

Recognizing that these patterns of choice exist, industry is geared to the production of goods or services which are either necessary, or desirable, or marketable. They satisfy the areas of choice.

In the selling process, it is the advertising agency's job either to inform the consumer that the company's products are on the market (if those products can be considered necessities), or to display the products in a way that will increase their inherent desirability (even though the products may be considered purely ephemeral), or to capitalize on the perceived knowledge that the consumer has grown used to the idea that the products contain a degree of desirability, albeit a desirability that has been created and communicated through a process of indoctrination.

Modern life offers many examples of these classifiable products. For instance, milk is generally held to be a staple of the human diet. In many parts of the world its sales are virtually guaranteed without the help of advertising. Elsewhere, milk is actively advertised as a food which, with a little imagination, can be turned into an appetizing health-giving drink. But a food, and an important food, it remains. On the other hand, many people can and do live quite satisfactory lives without

A lipstick advertisement in which one is invited to admire the product as well as use it; to make the object more precious, the name Fabergé is wielded. Art direction by George Lois.

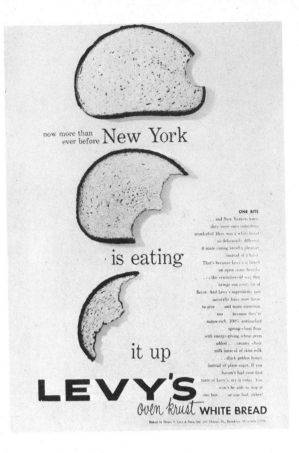

now more than
ever before **New York**

ONE BITE

...and New Yorkers knew
they were onto something
wonderful! Here was a white bread
so deliciously different
it made eating bread a pleasure,
instead of a habit.
That's because Levy's is baked
on open stone hearths
...the centuries-old way that
brings out every bit of
flavor. And Levy's ingredients just
naturally have more flavor
to give ... and more nutrition
too ... because they're
nature-rich. 100% unbleached
spring wheat flour
with energy-giving wheat germ
added ... creamy whole
milk instead of skim milk
... thick golden honey
instead of plain sugar. If you
haven't had your first
taste of Levy's, try it today. You
won't be able to stop at
one bite ... or one loaf, either!

is eating

it up

LEVY'S
oven krust **WHITE BREAD**

Baked by Henry S. Levy & Sons, Inc. 165 Thames St., Brooklyn 37, N.Y.

FRESH KEWPIE
キユーピーマヨネーズ

自然主義

キユーピーマヨネーズの黄色は純粋に卵の黄身の黄色です

Ecco la prova del fuoco
per gli Ziti

Quando la ricetta
vuole anche la cottura in forno
civogliono Ziti Barilla

Ziti Barilla alla ciociara

Barilla

Above left: Advertisement for a type of
bread. By Robert Gage.
Left: A Japanese advertisement that links
the freshness of the product with its
natural habitat. Photography by Tadao
Yoshida; art direction by Katsumi Asaba.
Top centre: Created by the same people
for the same agency, this advertisement
presents the integrity of an egg yolk,
substituting the shape of the eggshell
with the analogous shape of the spoon.
Above: In offering a slightly unusual
brand of pasta, some recipe suggestions
are added, making the advertisement
more attractive and offering the consumer
a useful service. Photography by Tony
Copeland; art direction by Raymond
Gfeller.
Right: Television is undoubtedly one of
the most effective means of advertising;
besides supplying images, it contributes
to the power of suggestion with the spoken word. Shown is a short segment of
film. Art direction by Ron Collins;
production direction by Terence Donovan
& Partners.

FRESH KEWPIE
キユーピーマヨネーズ ®

私たちは食卓の上の自然を守ります。

キユーピーマヨネーズは新鮮な卵の黄味が原料。着色料、乳化剤、防腐剤などの添加物は使っていません。さわやかなオイシサの自然食品です。

Le dessert 2 secondes

(ou le hors-d'œuvre 2 secondes)

PAMPLEMOUSSES
Jaffa

Make Hovis your daily bread.

Above: Photography can reach levels of high quality in the advertising "still life." This grapefruit advertisement won an international prize in the field. By the French agency Intermarco-Elvinger.
Right: A picture created by means of the cinematographic technique of environ-mental reconstruction, and with the help of a character actor, to advertise a type of wrapped bread. By Richard Dearing; photography by Peter Webb.
Below: Three newspaper advertisements for tinned vegetables. By Tadashi Ohashi.

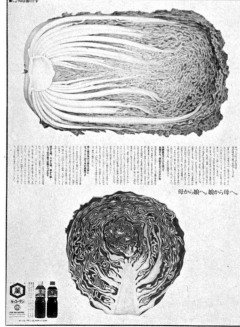

Right: An advertisement presented as simple visual information, without the aid of any other supporting elements. By the Swiss agency Victor Rutz, 1948.
Below: Swedish advertisement aimed at breeders, suggesting how to get twenty piglets of prime quality each year from each piglet. Art direction by Christer Eriksson.
Bottom left: Fruit juice visualized in a poster drawing. By Willy Trapp, 1941.

Frutta da spalmare

O scegliete Arrigoni
o rinunciate al meglio.

Med Suggex får ni 20 prima smågrisar på varje sugga år efter år.

Above: An essential composition, a powerful picture, and a text that is immediately understandable are the main ingredients for this advertisement. By Luigi Montaini Anelli.
Below: A graphic advertisement for a Japanese tomato sauce. By Shigeo Fukuda.

ひかりの味。
ひろがる人間
カゴメケチャ

According to a concept of advertising that evolved after World War II, commercial design frequently resorted to the pictorial find by means of a design that was gently ironic.

Below: Raymond Savignac was undoubtedly one of the major exponents of this type of advertising, with a prolific output over many years.
Bottom: Meat products. By Herbert Leupin.

so much as thinking about a need for hi-fi equipment, records, or sailing yachts. Yet effective advertising is widely used to stimulate a person's latent desire for something he may grow to genuinely want, could probably live without, but will eventually buy. Finally, in an increasingly energy-conscious era, man's dependence on the automobile serves as an historic example of the way in which implanted desires can produce massive sales, and provides us with a warning. Once cars had become readily available, once the production methods had been perfected and thousands of men had become dependent on the automobile industry for their livelihood, the mass of the world's population was introduced to the joys of motoring, persuaded that their lives would be transformed simply by car ownership. In the early days of the automobile, this proposition held a great deal of truth. Today, however, the results speak for themselves as motorists find themselves having to contend with the world's choked and overcrowded cities and the highways that link those cities. And, paradoxically, governments now have to spend large sums of money on advertising campaigns designed not only to warn the motorist of the inherent dangers of driving but also to draw their attention to the fact that the automobile presents a genuine threat to the world's major energy source, oil.

The clock cannot be put back. These are the circumstances in which the creative person has to ply his trade. These are the conditions under which he has to act as interpreter for those whose job it is to ensure that industry produces the various goods and services that consumers either need, or want, or can be persuaded to want.

Since man first made a mark on a wall, using berry-juice ink, creative people have had an important role to play in society. For the painter, poet, author, essayist, musician, actor, or dramatist the role remains the same: to show us what we are really like, or to stimulate us into seeing ourselves in a new, perhaps unusual, light.

In advertising, the creative person's point of view, his imaginative interpretation of his brief, and his contribution to the selling process should all reflect this fundamental principle. The difference is that, in his case, he is working with the substance of a product or service, whereas the fine artist is working with the substance of life. Yet there is an overlapping of both substance and technique. For the creative person working in advertising must produce work that is not only relevant to the product or service the client has for sale but relevant, too, to the society and the market into which the product or service will be sold. Th where the interpretive element of his work becomes crucial. It must form a link between the inanimate product and the animate life it serves.

Working toward this end, the creative person's role will inevitably interplay with the crafts and disciplines

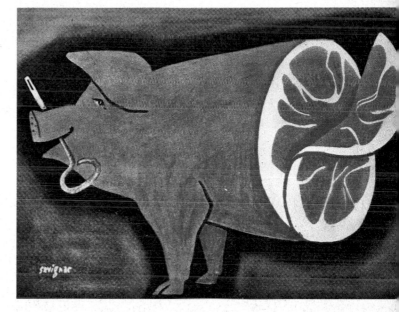

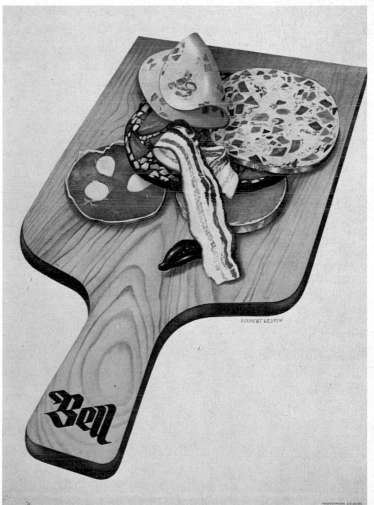

Drinks—Hard and Light

Left: An historical reconstruction that evokes a turn-of-the-century atmosphere to advertise beer. Photography by Howard Zieff; art direction by Robert Gage.

Opposite: The photomontage technique is used to project a brand of whisky onto the skyline of the large metropolis of Tokyo. By George Lois.

One has only to read Molly Bloom's soliloquy at the end of *Ulysses* to appreciate how accurately Joyce captures the essence of undisciplined thought, the ceaseless stream of confusion that exists in the minds of all before the rigid disciplines of creativity are applied to the articulation of thoughts.

Like Joyce, McLuhan, in *Understanding Media*, uses aural as well as visible puns to build meaning upon meaning, employing words that sound alike to create equations and reveal unexpected, yet at once obvious truths.

In *War and Peace in the Global Village* McLuhan explains this aspect of communication in greater depth. He states that all forms of popular culture are always at the height of their powers and effectiveness when they are at work shaping, or reflecting, the immediate present of the society that spawned them. Yet, at the time, such techniques are often considered to be rubbishy in content, irrelevant in meaning. For example, early comic books were deemed junk when they first appeared. But now they have become a collector's item, valuable as a vital link in understanding our immediate past and the society from which our present-day world has grown. Similarly, until television took them up as programme material, old movies were thought to be fit only for the rubbish bin. Today they are considered an art form in themselves and are, fittingly, the genesis of an entire, cinema-based culture. It is obvious that television, too, fits into this pattern of contemporary disdain and nostalgic acclaim. In time, with the increasing use of satellite-communications technology and space exploration, television itself, and its present content, will become a cultural art form in its own right.

In the day-to-day business of advertising, the creative person has little time to reflect on the global implications of society's shifting points of view and its developing technology. He must concentrate on keeping in touch with the immediate present, on continually developing his craft so that he is able to make his own contribution to the strategy of advertising communication.

In terms of television alone, the creative person has his work cut out for him. As McLuhan has pointed out, advertising, as a mode of communication with and education of the public at large, has changed radically since the industry first was able to use the commercial channels. Now, as then, to maintain its effectiveness, the television commercial must always be immediate. Indeed, so immediate is the rapport between advertiser and audience, and so intense the mass response, that lack of a contemporary stance within the media can mean overnight defeat for the advertiser's product. Thus, the creative person must be in constant touch with the shifting attitudes and aspirations of the society

of others working in his advertising agency or group. The most important interaction of this kind takes place between the application of creativity and the selection of media. Until the early 1960s, this interaction had largely been ignored. Then it was enough for advertising agencies to employ writers and artists whose job it was to create interpretive messages for a limited variety of media. Newspapers, magazines, and posters were the main channels of communication. Leaflets and brochures were also in use. But advertising relied mainly on tried-and-tested, comparatively predictable methods. With the advent of television and the increase in the use of commercial radio stations and cinema advertising, change was inevitable.

Perhaps the single most powerful influence for change was Marshall McLuhan's book *Understanding Media* (1964), in which he first propounded his controversial thesis that "the medium is the message." Widely misquoted today, even still misunderstood by some, McLuhan's treatise, and the subsequent volumes he produced, have had nonetheless a profound influence on man's thinking about his communications techniques.

McLuhan maintained that James Joyce understood more about the media, and the various effects on society at large, than any other man in history. *Finnegan's Wake* may be seen as a guide to the media, but a guide presented in language entirely different from that used and understood in books published at the time. Joyce's great gift was his ability to employ language as much for the ear to understand as for the eye to assimilate.

Inver's in in Tokyo

Colorful, bustling, exotic Tokyo is as friendly
as it is fascinating. And nowadays it's
even friendlier. Its people have found
the Scotch that's Soft as a Kiss.
(Because Tokyo's now drinking what
Rome, New York, Paris, Chicago and
San Francisco are drinking.) Inver House,
the international Scotch, shall be
America's next No. 1 Scotch.

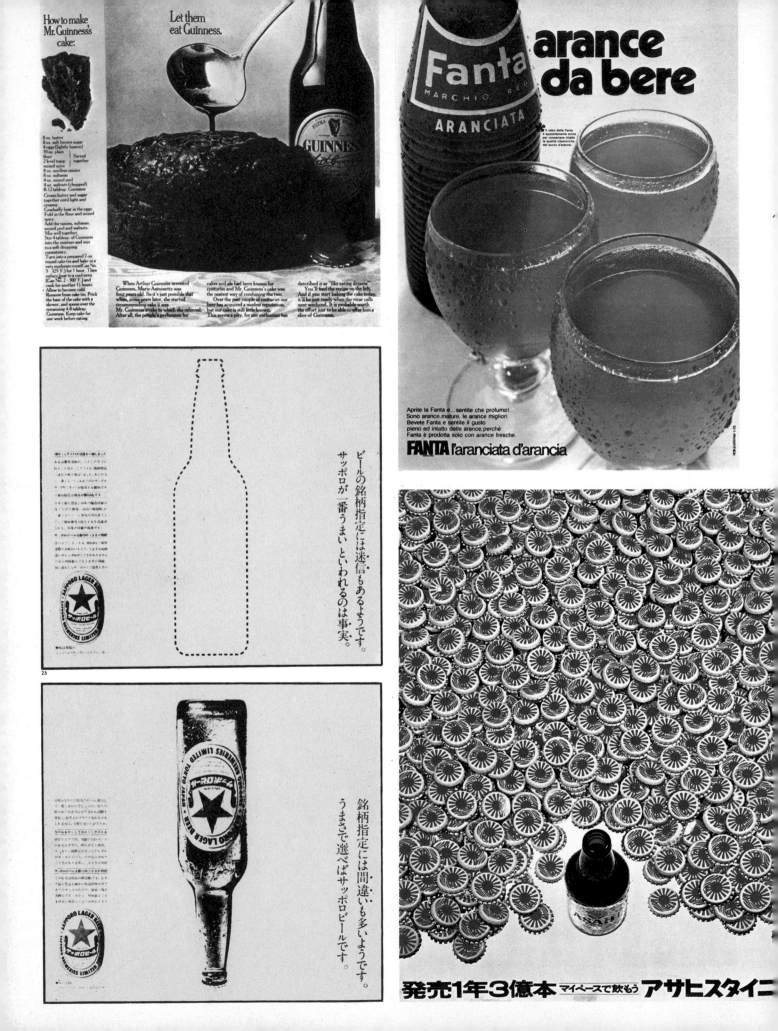

Opposite, above left: "Let them eat Guinness," an appetizing recipe suggestion. Art direction by Anne Leworthy; photography by Peter Mercier.
Opposite left, center and below: Advertisements for a Japanese beer. By Gan Hosoya.
Opposite, above right: Advertisement that relies on the effectiveness of the photographic image, and on a powerful headline. Design by Ennio Sozzi; photography by Serge Libiszewsky.
Opposite, below right: Advertisement for a Japanese drink, achieved by the repetition of the graphic trademark on the bottle top. Art direction by Kazumasa Nagai.

Left: A sober advertisement created by means of a treated photograph. By Karl Gerstner, 1963.

Below left: A poetic poster for Coca-Cola. By Herbert Leupin, 1953.
Below right: Poster advertising a fruit juice, using a sign that takes into account the beholder's experience of pop art and cartoon strips. By Ruedi Külling, 1972.

美味 滋養 葡萄酒
赤玉ポートワイン

A series of advertising messages through different periods of time, all promoting alcoholic beverages, emphasizing the various graphic artists' differing approaches and techniques of visualization.

Above left: Advertisement for a French champagne. By Pierre Bonnard, 1898.

Above centre: Japanese photographic poster that adopts the technique of contemporary Western postcards. 1922.

Above right: Advertisement for Campari soda. By Celestino Piatti, 1960s.

Right: A caricatured portrayal. By Herbert Leupin, 1950.

Far right: Photographic composition. By Josef Müller-Brockmann, 1952.

Below: An amusing picture that exalts the power of the beverage to "fill one up." By Adolphe Mouron Cassandre, 1932.

Opposite, above right: Magazine advertisement. Art direction by Hershel Bramson. With strategies of communication becoming more subtle, refined by the work of international advertising agencies, even publicity is becoming more sophisticated in its message, and ever more rich in connotations.

Opposite, above left: A page in which a story is set up within moments in order to promote a type of vodka. By George Lois; art direction by Carl Fischer.

Opposite, below left: A magazine advertisement that humorously emphasizes the delicate characteristics of a bitter digestive drink, normally considered to be too bitter. By Paul Leeves; photography by Bruce Fleming.

Opposite, below right: Men have always been the favourite subject of alcohol advertisements, but in this instance, as a tribute to sexual equality, "Aunt Agatha" is called upon to promote a kind of rum. By George Lois.

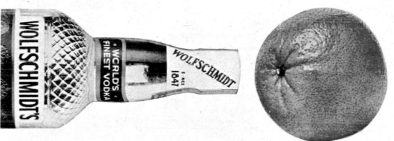

Keeping Pace with Fashion

Opposite left: The reading characteristics
of Japanese texts make it possible to
create layouts that are inaccessible to
Western graphics. Design by Ikuhiro
Kotani; illustration by Akira Moori.

Opposite right: One of the many ways to
promote a T-shirt, inspired by the world
of horse racing. By George Lois.
Opposite below: No less than the Flood is
evoked in an advertisement for British
raincoats. Art direction by Gennaro
Andreozzi.

in which he lives, particularly those of his immediate
surroundings, bearing in mind the international
influences that all countries are subject to.

Ours was once a society in which business was our
culture, capitalism and the amassing of capital the
principal work ethic. This was a period of private jobs,
distant goals, and high ambitions of the self-made man
(and the man-made self) climbing the ladder of success
in a material sense. In the past fifty years, and, in
particular, in the past fifteen, Western culture has
reached a totally new plateau in its evolutionary progress. In a sense, and in many areas of activity, a
complete reversal of the old ethics has taken place.
We now live in a society in which culture is our
business; our goals are more immediate, our aspirations
less concerned with material growth, more concerned
with realizing harmony within the planet.

In terms of advertising, and particularly in relation
to the strategy of communication, this change has had
far-reaching consequences.

In a sense, the change was predicted by McLuhan.
The widespread use of television would, in his view,
bring about a global village—a vast urban area covering
the whole world in which, through television, it would
be quite possible for a housewife in Rome, Sheffield,
or St. Louis to have a first-hand impression of life as
a housewife in Calcutta, Hong Kong, or Sydney. Or
to be aware of the effects of war in Vietnam, an earth-
quake in Yugoslavia, or a tornado in Florida. And, of
course, the world's population would be aware of the
external images of each other's lifestyle. Through television we would come to know each other so well that
even our clothes would take on a universal appearance.
McLuhan's prediction has, largely, been borne out by
the "denim revolution." Where denim was once worn
only by working people and then by the young who
wished to identify with the work ethic, it is now worn
by anyone and everyone from a wide and disparate
variety of professional and sociological groups, from
presidents to parsons.

Thus, out the window go the time-honoured concepts
created by advertising media buyers and researchers.
The old social categories are of diminishing relevancy,
the class and age barriers are breaking down. Today,
where once the son was given example by the father,
the father takes his example from the son, buying similar
clothes and cars, taking up similar interests and beliefs.
Grandmothers buy the same skirts and trousers worn by
their granddaughters. In contemporary circles, the new
"swinger" is the man of forty-eight, and the break with
tradition is complete.

In selling activities, this change shows in the way
in which the buying power of the younger generation
influences the marketing of many products that have no
specific generational appeal. What happens now is that

Above: Advertising often tends toward
a paradox in order to attain its aim, which
is always to draw attention back to the
product being presented, sometimes by
creating scripts that are altogether
extraneous to the actual content of the
message. In the case of these stockings,
the advertisement does not point to the
stereotyped image of the perfect pair of
legs, but stresses instead how economical
the product is: twenty-five cents per leg,
says the pack, a concept which is backed
up as a recommendation by the bride's
mother. By George Lois.

no spettro si aggira per l'europa:

king's jeans

Chi mi ama mi segua.

jesus jeans
original american fabric

Non avrai altro jeans all'infuori di me.

jesus
jeans-original american fabric

If there is a consumer product that has in the past years more than any other been promoted with a mixture of strong doses of sex and ideology, in the portrayal of which women, more than with other products, have shown the signs of a modern eros, it is undoubtedly jeans.
Above: A poster in which Marx is directly connected with the maxim, ''A spectre is moving across Europe.'' The poster appeared in Italy after 1968 but was almost immediately withdrawn from circulation.

Right: Two posters for an Italian jeans firm, which chose its logos in the wake of the musical *Jesus Christ Superstar*; their appearance caused much scandal and complaints (the one below was seized, with legal consequences). Art direction by Michele Goettsche; copywriting by Emanuele Pirella; photography by Oliviero Toscani.
Opposite: A famous model, the Stars and Stripes, and a name worthy of the seventies are used to represent these jeans. By the creative group of Adas; photography by Oliviero Toscani.

Ufo... **all way identifiable**

A Touch of Class

An item that has fallen slightly into disuse nowadays—the hat—was in the past considered an irreplaceable part of both men's and women's wardrobes, adopted not only by the upper classes but also by people of modest means.

Below: Turn-of-the-century poster for the opening of a hat shop. By Albert Guillaume.
Bottom left: The hat used as a signal to denote the shop it is sold in. By Otto Baumberger, Zurich, 1919.

Bottom right: Poster for a clothing shop. By Otto Baumberger, 1923.
Opposite: Poster created after World War II. By the Studio Boggeri, which, using the mixed techniques of photography and design, has helped to innovate the process of advertising communication in Italy.

GOT THE TIME?

New faces for $50 and under

The watch you now own no doubt serves you well as a timekeeper but may be a little too dressy for weekends in the country or too sporty for dinner at the Top of the Tower. Good-looking yet inexpensive watches are now on hand for just such occasions. For that extra time on your hands, why not build a watch wardrobe? Opposite page, from top: automatic calendar watch by Wakman in silvertone has a blue face; $50. Vantage stainless steel by Hamilton has markers in red, sweep second hand, flexible metal band; $35. Skin diver's watch, Caravelle by Bulova, in stainless steel, has a rotating bezel for gauging time under water; $30. Automatic waterproof calendar watch by Enicar is completely stainless steel; $49. Blue-faced, stainless steel waterproof watch by Wyler; $40. Goldentone digital watch by Schiaparelli shows date, hour and minutes in three windows; silvered face, steel back; $33. Round tortoise-faced watch in golden oval frame is by Rodenia; $35. This page, from top: golden nautical watch by John Weitz for Destino has unusual rope looped band and sweep second hand; $40. Polished stainless steel calendar watch has perforated strap; Commodore A by Wittnauer; $50. Electronic watch by Sheffield has large script numerals and a sweep second hand; $40. Goldentone square-faced watch with Roman numerals is by Old England; $30. At jewelry and department stores throughout the country. Write for stores nearest you selling specific watches.

BRÜHL

The Object Symbol

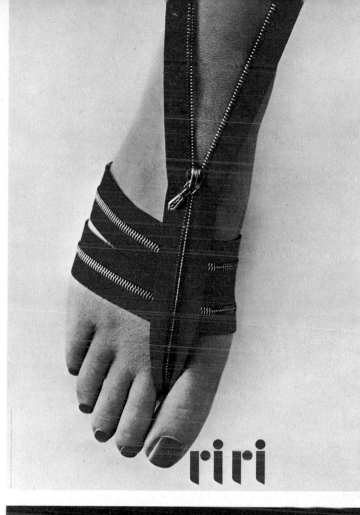

older people follow trends in advertising that are dictated
by the aims and aspirations of the young.

This is due partly to the extraordinary influence of
television itself, an influence seen by McLuhan as
causing the young to "grow up absurd." In his view
they are "grey" at three years old. They have been
exposed, through television, to more information
concerning the world's affairs—while they are still in
their playpens—than their grandparents might have
assimilated in an entire lifetime. By their early teens
they are as mentally tired of life as their grandparents
might have been at ninety.

Yet, against this background of dramatic change—
of continuing and developing changes—the creative
person works at interpreting his client's brief in such a
way that, when presented to the customer, the product
or service in question will be seen as fresh and contemporary as it was the day it was invented. For despite
mass education and despite television's profound
influence, the public still craves a new experience, a
challenging way of seeing things.

Let us now consider the practical aspects of the
function of the designer or art director in the overall
strategy of communication.

In every case, his work with the other members of his
advertising group will begin with an assessment of the
product, its market, and the media most likely to achieve
the required objective, be it pure sales, public education,
or the straightforward communication of factual information. In some cases a combination of media will be
required. In others, a single medium will be the obvious
choice for the message. For example, some products—
and some types of selling—do not lend themselves
to television. In recent years there has been an increase
in direct-response advertising, where the product is
bought by the consumer who reads of its existence in
the press, completes a coupon, and pays the selling
organization direct. Obviously, this kind of selling
cannot be carried out on television. In the field of
impulse buying of low-priced items such as foods and
cosmetics, it will probably be necessary to choose a
combination of media: press, television, radio, and
outdoor advertising. Press advertising may concentrate
on an educational function, relying on the static medium
to furnish advice and ideas on cooking methods, recipes,
and the presentation of food. Television, on the other
hand, will set the product in a chosen environment,
carefully conceived to achieve a positive rapport with,
and response from, the consumer.

These decisions about the choice of media will be
made not only in the light of experience and research,
but, increasingly, within the constraints of governmental
restrictions as well. Cigarette advertising, for example,
is banned from television advertising in the United
States and the United Kingdom. Alcoholic beverages

Questions of Beauty

Below: An oriental cream presented in an exotic environment. By PAL (Paléologue).
Right: Poster for a unique nail varnish. By Makoto Nakamura and Reikichi Nakayama; photography by Takayuki Ogawa.
Below, left centre: Decorative poster, not created for advertising means. Photography by Sam Haskins. During the 1970s, the poster, aimed particularly at young people, became widespread as a substitute for other, more traditional decorative elements.
Below, right center: A delicate design that sums up the effects of a vitamin cure for the hair. By Herbert Leupin, 1945.
Bottom: Advertisement for a department store. By Seiji Suzuki; illustration by Harumi Yamaguchi.

指先と目元の新感覚。⑧ 資生堂ネイルアート・資生堂フラッシュアイズ

Crème Orientale
Poudre & Savon

POUR
LA BEAUTÉ
ET LA
SANTÉ DE LA PEAU

PARFUMERIE ORIENTALE
17-19, RUE DE MAUBEUGE. PARIS
EN VENTE PARTOUT

IMP. PAUL DUPONT.

Panteen
DAS ERSTE VITAMIN HAARWASSER

おしゃれの嫉妬は美しい。

有名ブティックバザール

見つけてください。赤坂 青山 六本木の安さと傾向を。
●山本寛斎/すごろく/グラス/弐番手/ドウファミリー/BIGI
ムッシュスク/メルローズ/RIGORO/自由ヶ丘ろまんシューズ

渋谷 PARCC
●5F・特設会場 3⁄8 (金)

Right: The effect of a lipstick, seen in relation to nature. Art direction by Martin Stevens; photography by James Moore.

SHISEIDO

COSMETICS PRIOR
PRIOR CLEANSING CREAM
PRIOR COLD CREAM
PRIOR MAKE-UP FOUNDATION
PRIOR SKIN MILK
PRIOR SKIN LOTION
PRIOR SKIN TONIC
PRIOR BRUSH PACT
PRIOR FACE POWDER
PRIOR HAIR TREATMENT
PRIOR PERFUME
PRIOR EAU DE COLOGNE
PRIOR NIGHT CREAM LIQUID
PRIOR FANCY POWDER
PRIOR NOURISHING CREAM

COSMETICS SPECIAL
SPECIAL CLEANSING CREAM
SPECIAL COLD CREAM
SPECIAL NIGHT CREAM
SPECIAL SKIN LOTION
SPECIAL MILKY LOTION
SPECIAL HONEY & LEMON
SPECIAL CLEANSING LOTION
SPECIAL SKIN LOTION
SPECIAL SKIN TONIC
SPECIAL MAKE-UP CREAM
SPECIAL CREAM FOUNDATION
SPECIAL PRESSED POWDER
SPECIAL LIPSTICK
SPECIAL BEAUTY CAKE
SPECIAL EYEBROW PACT
SPECIAL BRUSH PACT

COSMETICS DE LUXE
DE LUXE CLEANSING CREAM
DE LUXE COLD CREAM
DE LUXE COLD CREAM
DE LUXE MOISTENING CREAM
DE LUXE ACNE LOTION
DE LUXE MAKE-UP CREAM
DE LUXE ACNE CREAM
DE LUXE FRESHENING CREAM
DE LUXE COLD CREAM
DE LUXE EAU DE LUXE
DE LUXE EAU DE CARMIN
DE LUXE CLEANSING LOTION
DE LUXE EAU DE VERT
DE LUXE PAPER POWDER
DE LUXE FACE POWDER
DE LUXE FOND DE TEINT
DE LUXE EAU DE BLAC
DE LUXE LIPSTICK
DE LUXE ROUGE PACT
DE LUXE CREAM PACT
DE LUXE EYESHADOW
DE LUXE HAIR TREATMENT
DE LUXE HAIR CREAM OIL
DE LUXE HAIR OIL
DE LUXE HAIR SPRAY
DE LUXE PERFUME
DE LUXE EAU DE COLOGNE
DE LUXE NOURISHING CREAM
DE LUXE AFTER SHAVE

FATE BLEAH AI VECCHI TRUCCHI

danuselle ha pronto il tennis-look

Left: Woman is nearly always present in messages that are aimed at her, especially in the case of cosmetics advertising in which the virtues of her beauty are stressed and often exalted. By Makoto Nakamura and Reikichi Nakayama.

Above: An unusual and humorous way of presenting a cosmetic product to the modern woman, to whom one wants to suggest an attitude. This is part of a campaign created by Titti Fabiani; photography by Lou Zan.

Pharmaceutical Products

Above left: Jules Chéret's characteristic jollity is present even in this poster advertising a coughdrop.
Above right: "Accidents happen easily, use Salvekvick," says this amusing

Swedish poster, which leans toward a modern concept in advertising. Art direction by Wilhelm Giesecke.
Below left: Poster for toothpaste. By Fritz Bühler, 1947.

Below centre: This poster for a pain-killer appeared in 1947 also, and is realized with similar techniques. By Donald Brun.
Below right: The agency in charge of the

Alka-Seltzer campaigns in the press and on television created cartoon characters, producing cartoon-type stories. Illustration by R. O. Blechman; art direction by Joe Panza.

Alka-Seltzer.
When you and your stomach don't agree.

Picture, if you will, a salami-pepper-and-onion sandwich entering your stomach.

It arrives, un-announced, and upsets your stomach. Blindly striking back, your stomach upsets you and you get heartburn.

That's his way of saying "Watch it, Mac."

It's a pity you can't get together with your stomach, and decide what foods you can both agree on.

There is a communica-tions problem.

Therefore, you must speak to your stomach in a language he understands, like Alka-Seltzer.

Alka-Seltzer is your way of saying "Forgive me."

It has alkalizers which will soothe your upset stomach and reduce excess acidity.

You take care of your stomach.

Your stomach won't bother you.

may be advertised in the United Kingdom during certain periods of the day, and then in a controlled way.

All these considerations will affect the art director's thinking when he is planning the visual presentation of his client's product or service. His job, as interpreter, is to divine the thinking of the market at the time of advertising, and to assess the environment in which the advertising will appear. In simple terms, the disciplines of television art direction are not like those of outdoor or press advertising. And they differ from other forms of art direction when mass communication is the objective.

Frequently, of course, this early thinking about the nature of the message will be carried out within the framework of a group discussion. The art director is aided by his copywriter while both of them, in turn, are helped by others whose work covers media selection and buying, printing, production—for either television, or film, or print—the functions of research, and the interests of the client.

Once the medium has been decided on and the nature of the message and its required effect arrived at, the art director and copywriter begin their work, their crucial contribution to the strategy of communication having been agreed upon and accepted as a group decision. It is now their job to interpret that group decision, to make it viable within the framework of the media.

The tools at their disposal are words and pictures, sounds and images, the common language of communication. Music may be used as well. The effect they achieve must reflect both the group decision and the client's position in the marketplace. They must decide how the client will best be seen as a responsible member of an industrial society. This consideration may have been less important in the past than it is today. There was a time when manufacturers just sold and consumers just bought. But the example of the automobile, cited earlier, illustrates the ways in which this approach can, quite literally, backfire on the producer.

Let us look at this element of responsibility as it affects products and services that are necessities, genuine desires, or indoctrinated desires.

The necessities of life need not, some may say, be advertised at all. Yet many of these necessities vie with each other for shares in very large markets.

Bread is a good example. The "staff of life" comes in many forms. It is produced in many ways, some traditional, some technologically advanced. In the strategy of communication, a decision must be made as to the way a particular bread is to be presented, taking into account not only its production method but also its likely market. Mass-produced sliced white bread garners by far the largest piece of the market. Yet it is viewed with some suspicion by housewives and their families.

It is seen as chemical, or artificial. But it is still bread, baked in a traditional way, albeit in huge quantities.

How can the art director and copywriter persuade the public of its natural goodness?

As a necessity, even mass-produced bread needs no introduction. Suspect though it may be, it is still considered necessary to life, still vital as a food source. People need, perhaps, to be reassured of this fact. They don't so much need to be sold the idea of eating bread; rather, they need to be reassured that bread-eating is a natural habit, one which man has developed since pre-Christian times, one which may even have post-Christian overtones, as well as overtones of traditional certainty in a world in which modern food-production methods have introduced us to frozen, precooked foods and foods produced from substances most people would previously have shunned.

Thus, in Britain, advertising concepts have been developed that present various brands in differing ways, each concept designed to achieve the same level of reassurance, or acceptability, according to the way in which each bread is produced.

The makers of Wonderloaf, discovering that housewives would always prefer to buy their bread from "the little man round the corner," capitalized on the fact that they had more mass-production bakeries in operation than any other similar baking chain. This geographical advantage allowed them to describe their product as "your local loaf." Basing their ideas on this central theme, the art director and copywriter worked together to produce a series of television commercials that emphasized the human friendliness of the people who worked in the bakeries, thus augmenting the idea that, despite their size, those bakeries were run by men and women who were part of the local community. The effect was both responsible—in the sense that it echoed a fact of distribution—and successful—in that it created a greater degree of human rapport between the manufacturer and his market.

Another bakery chain, producing a similar loaf, focused on its brand name, Mother's Pride. Television advertising featured a middle-aged mother, the symbolic representation of the company, who took evident pride in the loaves available on supermarket shelves. Handled with the right degree of wit and charm, these commercials were designed to reassure housewives that, at least so far as bread-buying was concerned, the old adage of "Mother knows best" had more than a ring of authenticity.

Hovis is another British bread brand. Smaller, brown, and sold as both a sliced and an unsliced loaf, it has been part of the British way of life for several generations. It has connotations of prewar simplicity, of a time when life was less pressured, more tranquil than it is

Household Accessories

Below: An advertisement for specialized magazines in which the picture of the desired kitchen reflects the delight of those who may benefit from it. By Giulio Confalonieri.

Bottom left: An extraneous, outrageously dressed character draws attention to the sofa, replacing the more conventional image of the distinguished woman associated with consumer products. By Gianni Sassi of the creative group of Alsa.
Bottom right: "If your Harvey Probber chair wobbles, straighten your floor."

An example of integration between picture and text; it is obvious that art director and copywriter (George Lois and Julian Koenig, respectively) have worked closely together. The advertisement is devoted solely to a detail, albeit one which is by no means secondary.

Boffi arredamento cucina
Cesano Maderno / via Padre Boga 31
telefono 51.412

eccola! è questa! la inconfondibile, originale, unica, vera cucina Boffi!

che c'è da guardare?
non avete mai visto la pubblicità di un divano?

hidalgo
un progetto di Arrigoni & Giannobi
per star seduti (da adesso in avanti)

GRUPPO INDUSTRIALE BUSNELLI Meda/Italy
Divisione poltrone e divani

If your Harvey Probber chair wobbles, straighten your floor.

Every piece of furniture that Harvey Probber makes at Fall River, Mass. is placed on a test platform to make sure it's on the level. If you get it, it is. Mr. Probber loses a lot of furniture this way.

This luminous finish takes a long time to achieve, but it lasts a long time. The lovely chair above could be made with 14 less dowels, 2 yards less webbing, thinner woods and so forth. You wouldn't know the difference,

Skin Problems

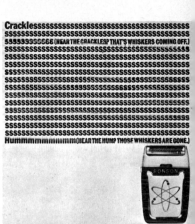

today. Perceiving this attitude toward the brand, the agency acting for the manufacturer developed a suitably tranquil series of commercials for television, each one cleverly shot in a part of the country where the so-called old-fashioned values are still held to exist. In this case, the writer and art director devised a strategy of communication that would reflect known attitudes toward a brand of bread which, by its very substance and texture, size and flavour, evoked images of a lifestyle few of the present generation can remember, let alone have experienced.

Yet the loaf itself and the vogue for nostalgia were brought together through the medium of television to create a strong feeling of security, a form of reassurance—the message being that, as long as Hovis was available, life could hardly be as difficult and as violent as it may indeed seem in reality. The function of the advertising was to convey the sense that one brand of the ''staff of life'' was as good as it has always been. In fact, this generational aspect of the loaf's image was projected through the commercial by the introduction of two generations of one family, a family whose life's work had been concerned with baking.

In these three cases, the strategy of communication was arrived at as a result of a responsible group decision which was then interpreted by the art director and his writer so that, through a combination of careful scripting, equally careful casting, and the perfect location, a selling message was produced that not only informed the audience of the value of bread as a food and a necessity, but also reassured them that the bread they buy today is as good—indeed, may even be better—than the bread sold in the days before technological advances made it possible for loaves to be mass-produced.

But how does the strategy of communication work when the product or service is not a necessity, when it has not become an indoctrinated desire, but when it is, for whatever reason, something that the consumer genuinely desires but feels confused by? Hi-fi equipment is one such example. Others include cookers, refrigerators, television sets, and cosmetics.

Let us consider hi-fi equipment as the example to work on. Here the genuine desire is for entertainment. "If music be the food of love . . ." wrote Shakespeare in *Twelfth Night*. He might not have taken the same stance in the twentieth century, but music has an undeniably universal appeal, whether it be baroque or rock, romance or the rhumba. It is, for hundreds of thousands, one of the most accessible—and most rewarding—forms of relaxation. Moreover, since the invention of the gramophone record and, later, the magnetic tape, music has become a major industry, one in which record companies and equipment manufacturers measure their turnover in millions of dollars each

Pee Wee Tee Vee

Climb upon my knee, Sony boy. The 4″ Sony pee wee tee vee, otherwise known as pee wee knee tee vee. (It only weighs six pounds so you'll never get water on the knee no matter how long you watch it.) For knee TV the pee wee Sony operates on a built-in rechargeable battery pack. Thanks to its flat-faced, non-distorting picture tube and directional master antenna, the picture will stay steady even if you're in a rocking chair. For sitting-watching, it has an AC plug that fits in your wall outlet. And the nice thing about it is, when the Late, Late Show finally brings you to your knees, you can always take the Sony off your lap and put it to bed in your nighttable.

The 4 inch SONY television

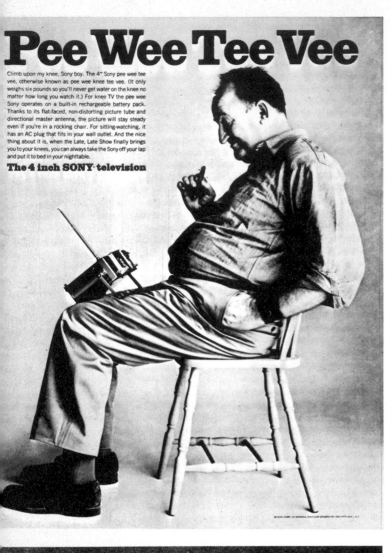

The Sony for Sun-Lover

If you're a person who hates to stay indoors watching television on a bright sunny day, we've got the perfect set for you. Because with the all-transistor Sony Sun Set, you can go outdoors and watch television on a bright sunny day.

The secret is the screen. Instead of a conventional white screen, the Sun Set has a special black screen that cuts down the glare. Which means that the picture won't fade out unless it's supposed to. And since it plays off AC current as as rechargeable batteries, there's nothing to stop you from going indoors and watching the Sun Set after the sun goes down.

The Sun Set

Telecommunications

Above left: An appliance suited to individual pleasure. Advertisement for the American branch of Sony. By Leonard Sirowitz; photography by Howard Zieff.
Above: A television set for communal living. Photography by Carl Fischer; art direction by Frank Camardella.

Left: Photomontage with a surrealist bent, created for an Ogden advertisement. By Henry Wolf.
Below: "No one ever ignored a telegram." Two magazine pages advertising the telegraphic services of Western Union. By Dan Cromer; copywriting by Jay Folb.

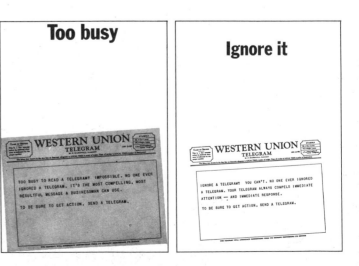

First of a
seven-part series

"Black History;
Lost, Stolen or Strayed."

Tonight, in the first of a seven-part series broadcast on Tuesdays in the coming weeks, CBS News tries to set the record straight to help close some of the gaps of understanding that separate black and white America.

In tonight's broadcast, Bill Cosby, actor and comedian, guides us through a history of the attitudes that have distorted the image of the Negro in America. He shows how those attitudes were formed and what they have done to us. He shows the black man's need to know who he is and what happens to him when he cannot find the answer.

On succeeding Tuesdays, Of Black America will present a study of the Negro soldier, a conference of black American and African leaders, a public opinion survey of black and white attitudes, a look at what the black American has contributed to sports and music, a history of slavery, and an examination of African life and

civilization through the eyes of three young black Americans.

Sponsored by Xerox Corporation, with Perry Wolff as Executive Producer, Of Black America presents the Negro in a new light, with balance and perspective. If it helps both black and white Americans to understand each other a little better, if it helps to change some of their attitudes toward each other, it will prove to be one of the most rewarding series ever presented on television.

America has camouflaged the black man. For three hundred years the attitudes of white Americans to black and black Americans to white have been subjected to misunderstandings, erasures and distortions damaging to both. The black American's achievements have been replaced, his contributions obscured. He has been told so often who he is not that he no longer knows who he is. And the frustrations of his search for identity and recognition underlie much of today's crisis of alienation in American society.

OF BLACK AMERICA

10 TONIGHT CBS NEWS ⓞ2

THE ROCKET'S RED GLARE...

HOW TO FLY A CAPSULE

REPORT ON RECOVERY

FAMILY REACTIONS

CBS ⓞ2

Above: Two advertisements for television programmes. By Louis Dorfsman; photography by Ronald Borowski and the photographic department of CBS.
Left: Movie-programme advertisement.

By Saul Bass.
Below: Poster extolling the virtues of the old gramophone, considered the first real mass medium in the field of audio-communication. 1905.

In all the years no picture has said *this!*

ETTE DAVIS IN STORM CENTER

EL GRAMOPHONE

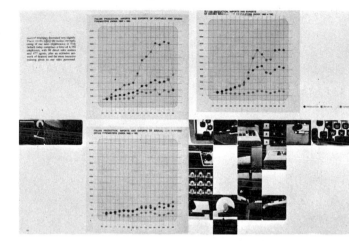

Opposite: Poster for Olivetti, intended purely as a divertissement. It is inspired by the inlaying of Federico di Monteteltro's small study at the ducal palace of Urbino; the artist has grafted the image of the modern streamlined Valentine typewriter onto a typical Renaissance iconography. By Milton Glaser.
Above and right: Pages from an institutional periodical. By Franco Bassi; photography by Gianni Berengo Gardin
Below: Advertisement for the diffusion of Olivetti products into the international market. By Franco Bassi.

Information is the impulse which processes and produces further information. It is logic, and calculating power. It is the means with which to forecast production and sales; or the average height of the population in Vienna in 1999; or to determine the structural design of a viaduct; or the streamlining of a record-breaking car. Information is a magnetic impulse which controls a computer from a simple card. Information is an electronic impulse which flashes through the circuits of a computer — the microcomputer which was first put on your own desk by Olivetti.

Information travels through Olivetti

Programma-101 the World's first desk-top computer with programs recorded on magnetic cards — P. 203 the office computer, for business analysis and estimates

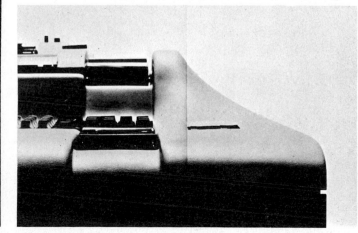

Don't just stand there: do something!

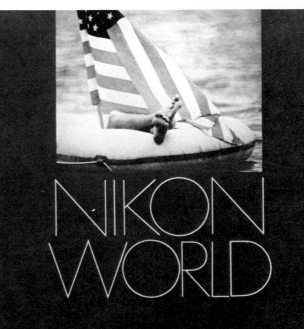

year and their successes by the placing of their latest releases in the current listings of popular hits.

With invention, however, comes confusion. The consumer—confronted by a bewildering array of machinery, each piece seemingly more complicated than the last—hardly knows where to turn if he is to achieve the reproduction of his favourite sonata, his adored pop idol.

Manufacturers cannot halt this escalation toward technological perfection. Their production systems are dedicated to reaching the ultimate goal: a symphonic sound matched only by a concert performance. And, as their playback systems become increasingly sophisticated, they must, in deciding on their own strategy of communication, call on the art director and his writer to interpret the technology of their products for an audience largely bemused by the choices open to them.

In the middle period of the development of hi-fi, the required and accepted strategy was one of status: Own a good hi-fi system and you would be considered a trifle more sophisticated than your neighbour.

But times change, and the advertiser—and his art director—must change with them. Nowadays, despite a continuing feeling of confusion, the hi-fi consumer is more wary. He wants to know more about the product's technical capacity, its suitability to his home environment, and its ability to produce his kind of music. Thus, the advertiser has a different job to do. In simple terms, he must convince the consumer that, despite its apparent high cost, the equipment contains all that he asks for: fidelity to the original sound, reliability, good looks.

Several companies operating in the British market recognize this change of attitude. Others still cling to an older form of persuasion. It is not appropriate, here, to question the aptness of either approach. But we may examine the art director's approach—and his contribution—to the strategy of communication.

Hi-fi equipment is, in the long run, a mystery to many who use it. This stems much from the fact that most music lovers are not blessed with a good grasp of the complexities of microelectronics or transistorized technology. They have an ear for music without necessarily having an eye or a mind for engineering.

Thus, the art director will often either present the equipment in a way which suggests a kind of clinical perfection—a cold-eyed view of a cold-hearted prod-

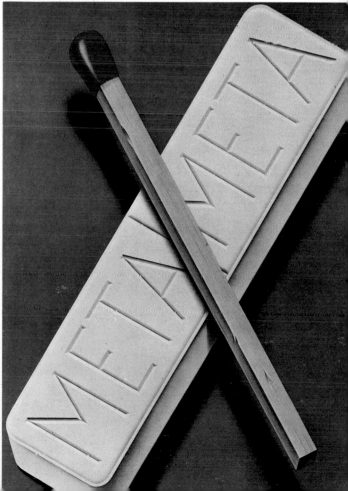

Above: Poster achieved through the visualization of one of the artist's personal sayings. By Raymond Savignac, c. 1950.
Right: Poster for a solid foodstuff. By Niklaus Stöcklin, 1941.

Why is the pretty girl smiling?

She lives in a country where everybody has a job and enough to eat,
where crime is practically nonexistent,
where there are no slums or ghettos
and there hasn't been a war in 150 years.

Is it any wonder that 80% of the people who visit Scandinavia wish they could
have stayed longer? SAS flies to Copenhagen, Oslo, Bergen, Helsinki, and
Stockholm (where the pretty girl lives). Leaving from New York, Los Angeles,
Chicago, Anchorage and Montreal. Within Europe, SAS serves more cities than
any other transatlantic airline. For more information, see your travel agent or
write: SAS, Dept. SX, 138-02 Queens Boulevard, Jamaica, New York 11435.

A Company for Your Travels

Opposite above: This picture for Air France is entirely worked out through the illustrative idea. By Michel Dubré.
Opposite bottom: An advertisement for Scandinavian Airlines extolling the experience of their services and the beauties of the country.
Above: Illustration for Air France. By Pierre Peyrolles.
Below: German poster for a Bremen navigation firm. 1930s.
Right: Poster for a Japanese tourist resort. By Yusaku Kamekura; photography by Susumu Hosojima.

General v. Steuben
in the track of Columbus

IORDDEUTSCHER LLOYD BREMEN

Naeba

ARE YOU IN THE MARKET FOR A HARDTOP?

Every Volvo has six steel pillars holding up the roof. Each one is strong enough to support the weight of the entire car.

Of course, this kind of strength isn't built into a Volvo just so it will hold up a lot of cars.

Volvos are built strong so they'll hold up a lot of years. Exactly how many we can't guarantee. But we do know that in Sweden Volvos are driven an average of eleven years.

Are you sure you're in the market for a hardtop? Or is what you really want a hard top?

Left: Sturdiness and long life are the characteristics emphasized in this advertisement for Volvo, put together with not inconsiderable difficulty. Art direction by John Danza; photography by Mike Cuesta.

Above: Poster for the Citroën 2-CV, in the spirit of traditional commercial design. By André François, 1970.

The new Fiat 132

Above: A wolf in sheep's clothing is the new model introduced in this poster for the British branch of Fiat. The picture speaks for itself, and does not need the backing of any text. By Neil Godfrey; illustration by Alan Brooking.

Left: French poster inspired by the futurist concept of dynamics and speed. By Moupot, 1926.

Our car the movie star.

You are looking at the romantic lead of a big new Hollywood picture.
Please, no autographs.
The picture is Walt Disney Studio's "The Love Bug." And our VW appears in all its real life splendor as Herbie, the main character.
Why would a big film studio want to make a movie star out of the bug?

Why not?
Signing one up for a lifetime costs only $1,799.* That's less than they have to pay other movie stars in a single day.
Once signed up, the bug won't suddenly start making crazy demands. (A gallon of gas for every 27 miles or so is all.)
No studio could ask for a less temperamental star. (It'll work in any weather.)

Or one with fewer bad habits. (It doesn't even drink water.)
Or one that ages so gracefully.
And of course, there isn't a performer around that's better known to the public.
Who else makes three million personal appearances on the road every day?

Volkswagen's unique construction keeps dampness out.

For years there have been rumors about floating Volkswagens. (The photographer claims this one stayed up for about 42 minutes.)
Why not?
The bottom of the VW isn't like ordinary car bottoms. A sheet of flat steel runs under the car, sealing the bottom fore and aft.

That's not done to make a bad boat out of it, just a better car. The sealed bottom protects a VW from water, dirt and salt. All the nasty things on the road that eventually eat up a car.
The top part of a Volkswagen is also very seaworthy. It's practically airtight. So airtight that it's hard to close the door

without rolling down the window just a little bit.
But there's still one thing to keep in mind if you own a Volkswagen. Even if it could definitely float, it couldn't float indefinitely.
So drive around the big puddles. Especially if they're big enough to have a name.

Volkswagen has for many years entrusted its press, cinema, and television campaigns to highly skilled advertising agencies throughout the world, which seem to find a common denominator in the amusing fantasy of gimmicks, making the product familiar and appealing to the public.

Above: "Our car the movie star," says this poster created in the United States.
Above right: Advertisement by Helmut Krone; photography by Wingate Paine.
Below: The Beetle, made into a sacred object. By Bob Kuperman.
Below right: Poster for the Swiss market. By Mathias Blatter and Jacques Lehnen.

Is nothing sacred?

VW

Welches Auto ist seit 20 Jahren das meistgekaufte in der Schweiz?

Right: Poster for Yamaha motorbikes. By Gan Hosoya, 1955.
Below and bottom left: Advertisements for tires with nail-proof treads.
Far right: Poster for the Italian importer of Triumph. By Alfredo Troisi; photography by Oliviero Toscani.
Bottom right: Japanese poster in which an unreal reading is given to the picture in order to emphasize its charm. By Gan Hosoya; photography by Saburo Kitai, 1959.

We put 100 nails
in the Sears Self-Sealing Tire.
And then drove it 100 miles.

And it didn't lose a breath of air.

Try that with the tires
you're driving around on.

Sears

Yamaha 250
Model YDS2
Sports Type

uct—or he will invest the product with an air of mystery achieved through the use of lighting techniques designed to cloak the product in that very mystery referred to earlier.

Of course, as with any other technical product, the art director's work has to appeal to the consumer on two levels: the emotional and the mechanical. His contribution to the strategy of communication will be concerned, in the main, with the emotional. His copy-writer will have the task of interpreting the technology of the product in a way both he and the consumer can understand. This calls for a thorough knowledge of the working of hi-fi equipment, which can be achieved only by studying the subject and by being correctly briefed by the client.

And, of course, their work will be influenced by the choice of the medium for the message. In most in-stances the press will probably be the major medium involved. This is as much because the consumer needs time to evaluate each brand against its competitors as it is because the static medium allows the art director to achieve the right kind of visual exposure for the product. The immediacy of television, and the shortness of its time scale, can do no more than allow the manu-facturer's name to be presented to the public. His products are too complicated for their worth to be fully appreciated in a medium that allows the viewer only seconds to assimilate messages of any kind.

Turning now to indoctrinated desires, we begin to encroach upon an area where art in advertising plays its most dramatic part. We are in the realm of propa-ganda, of created aspirations, politics, and propositions designed to encourage the sales of products, services, and ideas which, by their very nature, may have no value as necessities, no real desirability, but which are nevertheless an integral part of life in the latter part of the twentieth century.

The strategy of communication now faces the sternest test of its own sense of responsibility. The art director must here perform under the most demanding pres-sures; his professionalism and his integrity are at stake.

But first we must examine the nature of indoctrinated desire before discussing the ways in which strategically planned communication can be used to sustain that desire.

Put simply, indoctrinated desire exists because it has been created. It has its roots in the desire for material growth and for the projection of a stylized "good life." Mishandled, it can create pressures on individuals who, susceptible to temptation, strive for a degree of material success which is beyond their capa-bilities. It is concerned with ideologies, dogma, and doctrinaire teachings and is most prevalent in political

Serving Industry

Below: Poster for a manufacturer of industrial oils. By Jan Le Witt and George Him, 1934.
Bottom left: A public-interest campaign by Shell, inviting the motorist to keep clean not just the interior of his engine but also his country.

Photography by Jay Maisel; art direction by Richard J. Ende.
Right: Advertisement for a manufacturer of household products. By Paul Pracilio.
Bottom right: Poster advertising spare parts through the graphic intervention of photography. Warsaw, 1936.

Consider the egg. Dansk did. One of nature's most satisfying and useful forms, it signifies the beginning of things. The beginning of Dansk things was 10 years ago, when this first Fjord spoon was hand-forged. Its success egged us on to create a number of other fine objects. Tawny teakwood bowls. A candlestick crowned with twelve thin tapers. Dusky Flamestone cups. An enamelled casserole as bright as a sunflower. And linens with rainbows in their warp and woof. Today there are 493 Dansk designs. Every one made for daily use. And not an everyday piece in the lot. They all appear in a new 96-page book, a book with the good form to be absolutely free. Write Dansk Designs Ltd, Dept. O, Mount Kisco, N.Y.

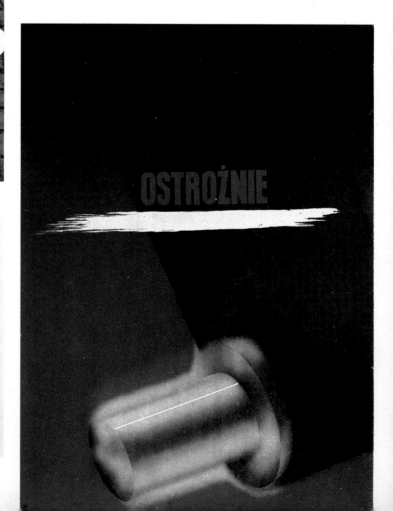

POSIŁEK DLA AUTA – OLEJE
GALKAR

What have you done to your country lately?

Cigarette butts. Gum wrappers. Candy paper. Don't drop them in all the wrong places. Like a sidewalk. Or the highway. Or on somebody's lawn. Or in the gutter.

Every once in a while, make a deposit in a waste can at your Shell station. It's a great way to save. The landscape.

Now you can visit your Shell dealer when your tank is empty, or when your ash tray is full.

That way, you not only keep a tidy car. You get a tidy country to drive it in.

Please keep this in mind; if we keep throwing trash away on the streets and highways, we're throwing something else away.

A nice place to live.

OSTROŻNIE

Ramset Fastening System

The world's most amazing stick-up. Whodunit?

New buildings seem to shoot up before our eyes these days. One reason is an extraordinary tool that actually shoots fasteners into steel or concrete with a powder charge. The Ramset® tool fastens steel to steel, wood to steel, steel to concrete and wood to concrete fifteen times faster than ordinary methods, with no wires, no drilling, no plugging — and with a powerful saving in human effort. With this new, completely portable power behind his skill, a worker can shoot a threaded stud into steel in a single second. He can secure a thousand square foot house to its foundation in ten minutes. He can fasten the miles of ducts needed for heating and cooling a skyscraper fifty stories high (ordinarily an eight-week job) in three days. Look! There's another new building! Another creative solution to a problem . . . from the Winchester-Western Division of Olin.

Olin

OLIN MATHIESON CHEMICAL CORPORATION, 460 PARK AVENUE, NEW YORK · CHEMICALS · INTERNATIONAL · METALS · ORGANICS · PACKAGING · SQUIBB · WINCHESTER-WESTERN

Above: Double-page magazine advertisement for a firm manufacturing mechanical utensils, demonstrating how to staple expansion nails onto any surface. Photography by Wingate Paine, art direction by Robert Gage.

Below: A Japanese manufacturer of containers tries to make a rather arid question seem appealing—that of goods transportation. Photography by Noriaki Yokusuka; art direction by Jun Kusakari.

Below right: A metaphysical advertisement in which the formal rigour of the Bauhaus is emphasized, created in the United States for the Container Corporation. By Herbert Bayer.

の日にシブヤヘ行きたい 4月19日金 西武渋谷店開店

SEIBU 西武

CONTAINER CORPORATION OF AMERICA

The advertising of cigarettes, tobacco, and alcohol is not controlled in the same way in every country, but even where it is more tolerated, a code of professional ethics is observed in order to keep it within the limits of minimum damage.

Below and opposite, bottom left: Two advertisements for a brand of cigarettes in which the blurbs comment ironically on the disadvantages of a cigarette that is too long. By George D'Amato; photography by Harold Becker.

America's favorite cigarette break.

Benson & Hedges 100's Regular or Menthol

ORE AND MORE PEOPLE ARE TAKING TO KENT.

Smokers like the rich taste. The micronite filter. Just the very idea of smoking Kent. Because it is one of the world's most desirable cigarettes... more and more people are taking to Kent.

KENT
KING SIZE

Roth-Händle

Left: Illustration for an American cigarette. By Tomi Ungerer.
Above and below: Two creations by Herbert Leupin: a poster for a German brand of cigarettes, achieved by means

of his singularly brilliant style of drawing, and an advertisement for a Swiss brand, made up of a realistic design, almost in imitation of macrophotography.

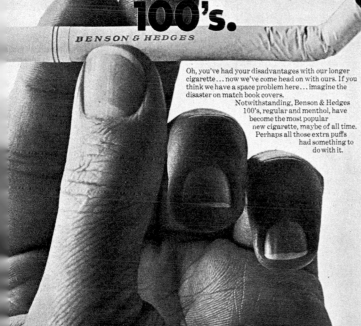

he disadvantages of advertising Benson & Hedges 100's.

BENSON & HEDGES

Oh, you've had your disadvantages with our longer cigarette... now we've come head on with ours. If you think we have a space problem here... imagine the disaster on match book covers.

Notwithstanding, Benson & Hedges 100's, regular and menthol, have become the most popular new cigarette, maybe of all time. Perhaps all those extra puffs had something to do with it.

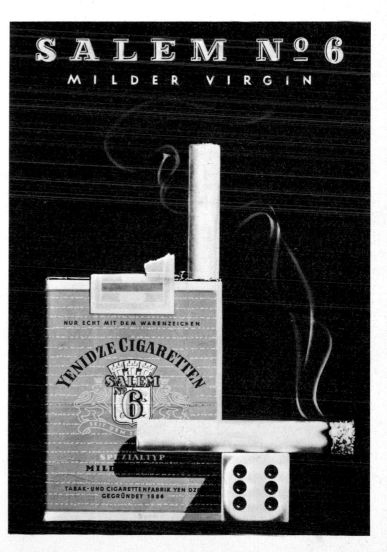

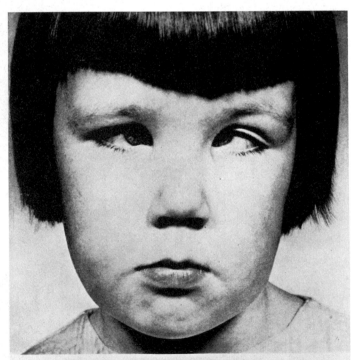

The Social Campaign

Can 70 million babies be wrong?

This is the long-stemmed American beauty that has unwrinkled the brow, stopped the tears, relieved the anxiety, brought out the dimples, satisfied the hunger and inspired the most celebrated burps of more American babies than all other brands of nipples combined.

It was designed 29 years ago and is still the most modern, scientific nipple you can buy. The Evenflo Nipple. Not a disposable. Just indisposable.

evenflo

THE IN-DISPOSABLES

Below: An advertisement to draw the public's attention to facing and curing sight problems. Art direction by Len Sirowitz; photography by Horn Griner; copywriting by Leon Meadow.

Above: An advertisement for a baby-bottle nipple. Illustration by Peter Shaumann, who has known how to place an essentially ascetic product into an unreal, dreamlike environment.

Why did Anne Flynn's parents allow us to use this picture?

advertising, or in advertising that sets out to persuade the consumer that by buying the particular product or service he will appear superior to those without it. In an era more conscious of consumerism, more sensitive to the needs of the people, the use of indoctrinated desire shows no sign of falling into disrepute, although it no longer commands the share of the advertising cake it once did. It is still practised in many countries where material growth is considered to be of primary importance. In the Western world, however, where the ethic of capitalism is not so much under attack but is, at least, viewed with suspicion, the concept of advertising that focuses on indoctrinated desire is one based on past principles which have less and less relevancy in contemporary society.

Yet, while desires that have been indoctrinated are still with us, the advertising art director will, for good or ill, find himself engaged in interpreting communications strategies that test his ability to the utmost. For, under these circumstances, it is his professional ability to create a myth or an ambience that will be on trial.

Let us consider, for the moment, political advertising.

All political parties are, of necessity and by design, as much in the business of promoting the future as they are in the business of managing the present. The strategic use of advertising techniques becomes vitally important here. The powerful imagery used in Russian political posters is designed to establish, in the minds of the people, the idea of a vast collective whose common goal is the growing strength of the motherland. Photographic imagery would be unlikely to achieve the same effect—the same sense of dynamic energy or the degree of idealized strength in the figures featured in the posters. The use of emotive slogans to add weight to this imagery is no accident of design, any more than is the choice of typeface used or the positioning of the slogan in relation to the figures. The whole concept is based on an ideology displayed with doctrinaire force. It compels the people to accept its message, as much by its sheer ferocity as by its strategic use of massive outdoor sites.

In the early years of the Russian Revolution, this thrusting propaganda had a vitality matched only by its necessity. The success—or failure—of the Revolution depended as much on its acceptance by the people as on their leaders' ability to manage its progress. Nowadays, with Russia's strength as a world power assured, its people need to be persuaded not so much of the validity of the overthrow of the czarist regime, or of the social benefits that would arise from that overthrow, but to be reassured of the continuing progress of their nation under the aegis of Communist rule. The indoctrination, having been introduced, must be continued. The art director working in this field must

Right: Two double magazine pages with the publicity campaigns of the Japanese insurance company Toray. By Koichi Tsuchiya and Katsumi Asaba; photography by Tadao Yoshida.

Bottom: Two advertisements which, by means of a slightly melodramatic montage, warn against the risks of certain professional activities. By Sidney Meyrs; photography by Melvin Sokolsky.

すわ、大地震。窓ガラスは落ちてこないか。

毎日毎日、1000トンもの油が海へ流れ出しています。

All these business risks can now be covered by one Continental policy.

We own Sylvania TV. We're worried about some of the shows you see on our sets.

hold fast to this principle, or fail in his work as an interpreter. He may not, in the case of political advertising, believe in the message in hand. He may not accept its value or even its moral rightness. But his interpretation must accurately reflect as well as perpetuate the original message.

Of course, there are occasions when degrees of indoctrinated desire can be challenged in ways that serve to reinforce them.

Some forms of cosmetic advertising, for instance, use this technique. In the main, cosmetic products are bought because the consumer has become accustomed to the idea that their use will, if not prevent old age, at least prevent its onset, and will also make them more alluring to the opposite sex. Their application is easy, the principles they rely on as old as beautification itself.

Capitalizing on the alternative methods, one British manufacturer of skin-care products ran an advertising campaign that cleverly showed how foolish young women would appear if they were to use old-fashioned methods. The art director was able to create not only the idealized result of using the product, but the inconvenience of the alternative. His contribution to the strategy was that of the interpreter who understands not only the benefits of the product, but, equally, the degree of resistance to the doctrine of prepared cosmetics and their usage. He and his copywriter perceived that many young women knew about skin-care products and were wary of their value, yet dismissed the usefulness of old-fashioned techniques.

In all these examples, one aspect of the art director's contribution to the strategy of communication remains constant. In his role as interpreter he has to be sensitive to both client and customer and to their respective needs and wants. On the one hand, he must be mindful of the client's self-image; on the other, he must be aware of the consumer's level of receptiveness toward advertising methods and alert to the shifting attitudes running through society's changing web. He must also keep a constant vigil over the stance of his product to ensure that his client is viewed not only as a responsible member of society, but is himself aware of his responsibilities.

It is the duty of the art director to avoid, so far as he is able, the use of exploitation in advertising. It would be irresponsible, for instance, to market an after-shave on the grounds that its use would endow the wearer with the kind of magnetic—and demonic—powers held by psychopaths and members of very powerful criminal organizations.

This issue is one of credibility as well as responsibility. While incredulous concepts—such as interplanetary visitors sampling instant mashed potatoes, or a talking lavatory cistern—have no connection with

People don't want to destroy prosperity. They want to be part of it.

When people see prosperity all around them, it's hard for them not to want to be part of it.

It's even harder when they see no hope of becoming part of it.

Faced with this, some people turn to destruction. For them, the want for more with no hope of getting more becomes bigger than laws. For them, life becomes war.

At IOS, we think it doesn't have to be that way. And we're trying to do something about it.

We feel that by giving a person the opportunity to share in the prosperity which surrounds him, he won't want to destroy it.

We're giving people that chance by giving them the opportunity to invest in business and share in the profits being made by businesses all over the world.

In other words, a chance to own a part of the prosperity which surrounds them.

Since we began 13 years ago, more than 650,000 people on six continents have invested more than one billion, five hundred million dollars of their money through us.

It's been profitable for us and profitable for them.

But equally important, for some of these

650,000 people, it's been their first chance to have a real stake in society.

Right now, IOS does business on six continents—in mutual funds, banking, insurance and real estate.

Our goal is to do business in every country of the free world, and to give more people than ever the opportunity to share in its prosperity.

IOS

The Eskimos used to freeze their old people to death. We bury ours alive.

Thinking of moving?

Find your ideal house in The Daily Telegraph

reality, their advertising value is quite acceptable. Such concepts must be handled with care, not only with the kind needed to preserve high standards of technical realization, but the kind, also, which stems from the art director's acceptance of his responsibilities to a responsible client and to the society that both advertising agency and advertiser serve.

In the strategy of communication, responsibility is the watchword. It determines much that is involved in the making of group decisions. It affects the implementation of those decisions. And, ultimately, it tests the art director's ability to exercise professional judgment in choosing the correct conceptual approach and the technique needed to realize that concept. Mistakes will occur—no one is infallible. But the good art director will learn from his mistakes. He will learn how his craft—his use of illustration, photography, or typeface and the arrangement of the elements of the message—can be used to play an increasingly important part in interpreting a variety of thoughts, ideas, propositions, and educational information held by the wise yet translatable to the crowd. In this way, and with this in mind, he will derive satisfaction from his work, in the full knowledge that his role as a go-between is essential in a society that becomes increasingly dependent on the clear and understandable use of the visual language of communication.

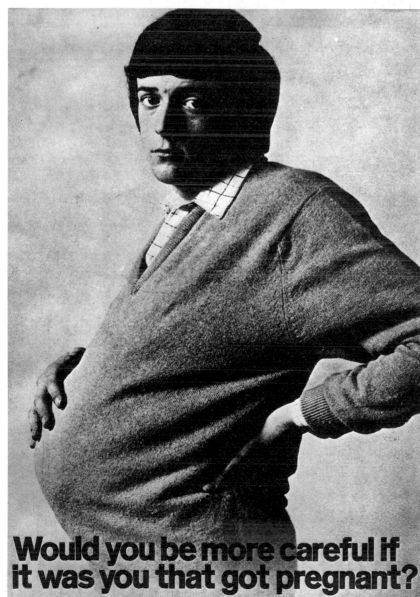

131

4. PSYCHOLOGY AND THE GRAPHIC MESSAGE

The graphic message imparts specific information by means of a written symbol. This symbol may be a letter or word, it may be combined, through ideograms or known objects represented as diagrams, into a calligraphic image, or it may be an abstract sign, such as a trademark. In all graphic communication, visual language is the common factor. It is therefore essential, if this process of communication is to be understood and utilized to its greatest effect, that the principles of perceptual psychology be applied in the design of the graphic image.

At the beginning of this century the scientific investigation of all aspects of seeing and perceiving gained momentum when psychological research was introduced into the field. This interest developed from the more philosophical study of aesthetics as it relates to the history and criticism of literature and all the visual arts. While Voltaire, Kant, Hume, and Ruskin are some of those who contributed ideas on these subjects, I. A. Richards in the 1920s was one of the first to apply psychological ideas to the appreciation and criticism of literature.

One particular school of psychological thought—Gestalt—has been of more fundamental importance than any other to the graphic designer. Gestalt psychology's main exponents were Max Wertheimer and his assistants Kurt Koffka and Wolfgang Köhler, who worked together in Germany and in 1910 conducted a series of experiments with a stroboscope on the organization of perception. Köhler used the analogy of the electromagnetic field to describe the relation of a figure to its environment. It is now an accepted physical law that in an integrated field—like the electromagnetic field around a charged body—a change in any single part causes a redistribution of energy and a readjustment of every other part.

The establishment of the Gestalt school reflects a changing emphasis in scientific thought. Until this development science had used mechanical models in order to see any structure as a combination of its constituents; now there was a shift to a more organic pattern, in which the entire system is considered as important as its individual parts and wherein the character and function of the parts depend on their context. Gestalt in German means a complete figure or pattern. A simple analogy helps to make the Gestalt theory clearer: the structure of a melody cannot be explained either by the qualities of its single elements or by the relationships between these elements—for instance, the pitch of the individual notes can be changed while the melody, which consists of the relationships of the notes to each other, remains the same. The notes represent the elements and the Gestalt, or whole pattern, is the melody.

Perception is an intrinsic part of the psychology of the individual. As Anna Berliner explains, "Seeing depends not only upon the environment but also upon the state of the person." Each person's perceptions are intimately linked to such factors as action, purpose, and expectancy, as well as to the total environment. A particularly revealing example of how perception can be affected is the case of the natives of New Guinea who were shown a photograph for the first time. Although they had been told it was a portrait of a known individual, they were still unable to read the photograph. They could not recognize this unknown image representing a familiar face until the salient features were pointed out, and even then they were disappointed in their expectations.

A well-known experiment by the American psychologist Adelbert Ames demonstrates that perceptions are not disclosures and that what we see is influenced by our expectations. In the Ames experiment, a distorted room containing proportionately sized figures is presented to the viewer. It was found that the brain selects the known form out of all the various possibilities, so that even when one knows that the room is distorted, the figures in it still appear to be the wrong size. The brain refuses to accept that the room is not rectangular. The exception to this is when the figure is intimately known to the viewer: a wife or a husband may deny the image presented to the eye—that of their spouse as a dwarf or a giant—and so realize that the room is distorted. Apparently, to the Zulus of Africa, who live in an environment free of rectangular buildings and parallel lines and therefore have no reliable measure of perspective, the people in the Ames experimental room look normal and the space is perceived as nonrectangular. This proves that the collaboration of the beholder is necessary for reading perspective images, and that empiricism is the key to interpretation.

Graphic means of representing perspective were discovered in the West only recently, during the Renaissance period, and probably were connected to the inventions of the first optical instruments and the camera obscura, in which objects are optically projected onto a flat surface. Filippo Brunelleschi, designer of the cathedral dome in Florence, made the first known perspective drawings. The crucial feature of perspective

A two-dimensional surface devoid of any articulation is an inert experience; it must become a pattern of references in the transformation of optical impulse into spatial force. The process of visual organization requires the participation of the beholder in order for an image to be perceived as a physiological and psychological fact. In this composition, entitled "Squares + Movement," a pattern of squares is crossed by diagonal lines. Against the background of a primary colour the artist combines a series of variations to alter the shape of the picture and confer upon it a sense of movement; he even changes the spatial field by nearing and distancing its chromatic values. By Toshihiro Katayama.

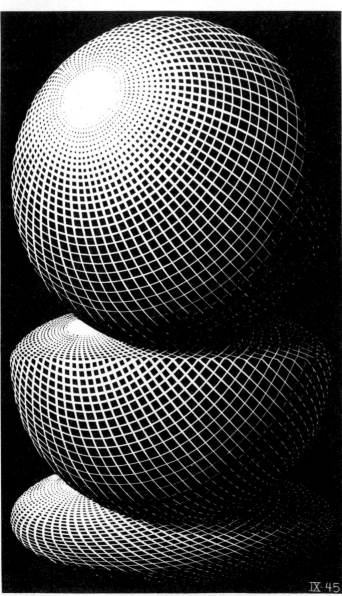

Above left: This picture crosses a series of figures with no background, thus making each side of the picture equivalent and enabling the spectator's eye to focus at random on either one or another figure. Woodcut by Maurits C. Escher, one of the artists who made the most inquiries into the ambiguity of the image, 1922.
Left: A progressive geometric projection from the sphere to the flat surface. By Maurits C. Escher.

a Pelican Original

New Horizons in Psychology

Edited by Brian M. Foss

Opposite, above right: A composite symbol that demands an attentive perception of the various parts that make it up. Japanese symbolic picture, nineteenth century.
Opposite centre: A line interrupting a collection of rays produces an action of interference and creates a marked sense of movement. From a test for the analysis of sensorial visual functions.
Opposite, centre right: An impossible shape illustrates the cover for this psychology book in the Pelican Original series. These shapes can be drawn, but they can find no analogous form in reality, neither can they exist as objects, precisely because they rely on illusory visualization.

Opposite, below right: Optical illusions should not be considered as mere banal effects but as useful instruments that give a better understanding of vision. Another drawing—more accurately, a study in structure—based on the ambiguity of perspective. By Josef Albers, 1955.

is that the eye cannot see around corners but only along straight lines, which accounts for the diminution of objects at a distance. We cannot judge the size of an object unless there is some gauge of distance, and vice versa. The brain must be able to measure between size and distance, and perspective is the means by which such an assessment is made.

The representation of perspective—or three-dimensional space—on a flat surface—or two-dimensional plane—is paradoxical. The eye is presented with two geometries: the picture is seen as flat and yet the illusion of depth is accepted. Richard L. Gregory, working in the Psychological Laboratory at Cambridge, noted that pictures "have perceptually a kind of double reality . . . common to all symbols." While images or letters are objects in their own right, as marks on a background, they are at the same time representations of things that are other than themselves. A drawing of a banana, for instance, is not a banana. And because marks symbolize something other or mean more than themselves, they have a special power. Cro-Magnon cave art, drawn over twenty thousand years ago, is the earliest record of humans taking this first vital step to symbolic language, which led eventually to organized, scientific thought. The graphic symbol—which makes use of the eye in a new way, freeing sight from immediate reality—held for primeval man the promise of formal language, and is, as Gregory has explained, what inevitably drew man away from his biological origins.

Certainly the experience of perspective is not an innate but a learned response to the environment. It is rather like the relationship of different maps to the same road system: the maps are broadly similar because the map and the terrain are broadly similar. According to Gestalt theory, we never have anything but maps of the terrain to indicate that it exists; what we think of as the terrain itself are merely the structural similarities in the repeating yet constantly varying maps of the terrain, and these serve to convince us that the terrain is real. What is real is not the terrain but the structure, the Gestalt.

As described in the catalogue to the Illusion in Nature and Art exhibit held in 1973 at the Institute of Contemporary Art in London, "the visible world is not immediately available. We gain access to it through our sensory systems and our brain processes. It is when we mistake the origin of the optical event that certain illusions occur." Wertheimer established the Gestalt framework in 1923 when he published his findings on the organization of perception, based on physiological aspects of the eye. Neurophysiologists like D. H. Hubel and T. N. Wiesel, who in 1969 collaborated on a paper for the journal *Nature*, have continued to explore how the brain is equipped to deal with vision.

Vision is a series of physiological events—a Gestalt happening. When a light pattern strikes the rods and cones of the retina, nervous impulses are fired that are transmitted down the optic nerve to the cerebral cortex at the back of the brain. These neural discharges are organized in a progressively complex system of columns to enable the different variables like colour, shape, and movement to be distinguished. Information from both eyes is integrated by the higher cells of neighbouring columns. There are two kinds of eye movement: tiny, involuntary tremors to locate an object, and larger movements to scan moving objects. The involuntary tremors produce the familiar moiré or shimmering effect when an image that consists of closely rayed lines is presented to the eye, as seen in the illustrations for the Mexico Olympics on page 138 and in the Mona Lisa image on page 142. These small eye movements prevent the visual image from fading, due to adaptation by the photoreceptors (which affects all sensory nerves apart from those transmitting pain and consists of the reduction of the firing rate when stimulation is continuous). This means that the firing of a nerve over a long period does not remain constant but falls off in spite of constant stimulation. New signals can be picked up from what might otherwise be a welter of distractions. Usually there is some compensation for these movements to give the impression of a stable image; when, in special situations, the tremors are not compensated, for reasons which are still unclear, an illusion of movement or dizziness is the result.

The crucial findings of the Gestalt school as they apply to design have been formulated by John W. Cataldo into a series of perceptual laws to "provide the graphic designer with a reliable psychological basis for the spatial organization of graphic information." The first is the law of equilibrium, and is based on the innate tendency of the cognitive processes of the brain toward simplicity and equilibrium and cohesion. This law involves the universal striving of all physical organisms for perfect balance, and is in operation when, for instance, a drop of water settles itself into a sphere, and the after-image of a square with sharp corners gradually takes on a rounded shape.

The second law, the law of closure, involves another aspect of perceptual structuring emphasized by the Gestaltists. Closed areas are perceived as more stable, so there is a natural tendency to close gaps or complete figurations that have been left open. Conversely, incomplete or broken images arouse hostility, which, if coupled with an emotional message, can be used to great effect in advertising.

The third law deals with the organization of visual perception, which is such that a curved line is likely to appear as part of a circle and a straight line to

135

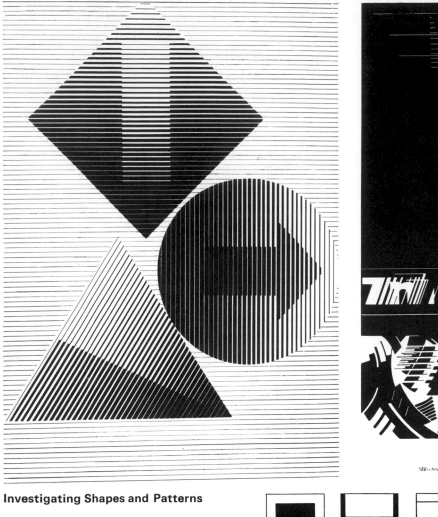

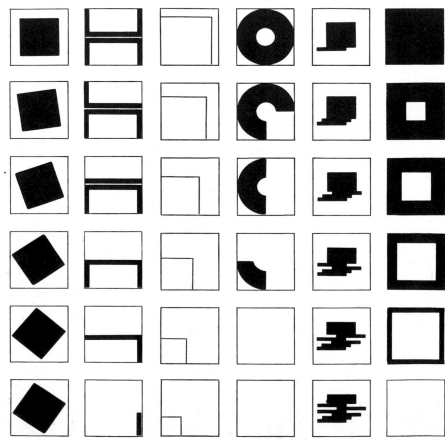

Investigating Shapes and Patterns

Above: Study for a poster. The use of the gradually strengthened lines emphasizes the effect of movement, while the background of equidistant strokes lends static support. By Armin Hofmann.

Above right: This drawing aims to demonstrate the possibility of a more articulate use of the same principles. By Armin Hofmann.

Below: Christmas wrapping paper. The design is created through a pattern made up of circles of different sizes. By Giancarlo Iliprandi.

Right: Study in spatial modifications of some shapes in relation to the limits within which they move and their kinetic progression. By Emil Ruder.

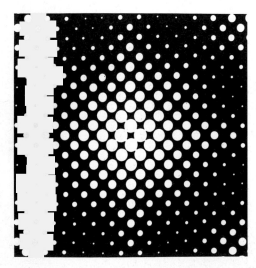

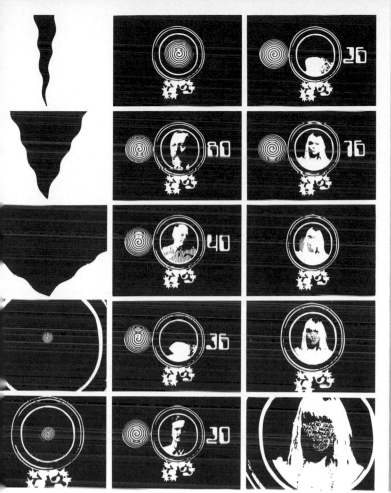

Kinetic Visualization

Above: Television graphics for a Munich broadcasting station. By Günther Griebl.
Above right: The stripes on the shirt are of the same intensity as those on the background, thus stimulating the picture—retina system of movement in this poster. By Elso Schiavo.

Below: Film stills for a television programme, created by means of the luminous impulses that design a nighttime metropolis. By Saul Bass.
Below right: The floor design of parallel stripes converges toward the point of escape, creating the illusion that the background figure is even farther away. By Koichi Tsuchiya and Katsumi Asaba.

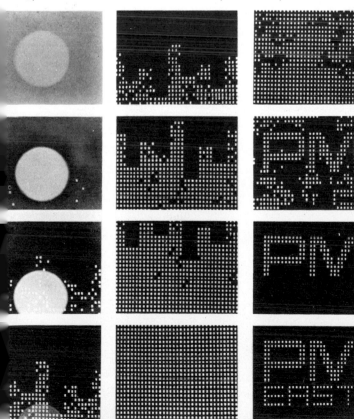

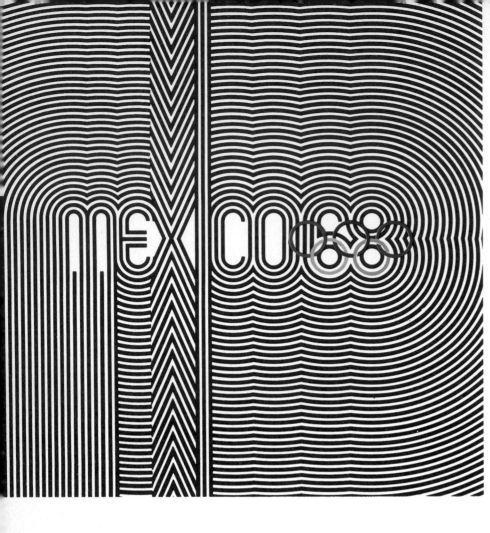

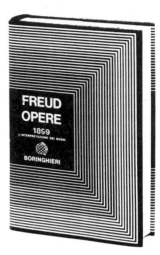

Left: Poster for the 1968 Mexico City Olympic Games, which exploits the lines of the letters and projects them outward in a centrifugal way, creating a dynamic optical effect. By Eduardo Terrazas and Lance Wyman.
Below: Book jacket achieved with a drawing of lines that are equidistant and of varying thickness. By Enzo Mari.

Below left: Book jacket in which the geometric pattern refers symbolically to the content. By Mimmo Castellano.
Below centre: Advertisement for a graphics firm. By means of a few lines curved around like a ribbon the artist creates a three-dimensional picture. By Franco Grignani, one of the most authori-tative researchers into the principles governing optical art, 1964.
Right: In this poster the artist superimposes and blends certain figures belonging to popular iconography, breaking up the images and reuniting them by rigidly vertical strokes. By Pino Tovaglia.

continue as a straight line even though alternatives are possible. This factor is known as the law of good continuation. Related to this law is the stroboscopic effect fundamental to film technology. If two visual stimuli occur in rapid succession but at a distance from each other, the image appears to move from the area of the first stimulation toward that of the second. Multiple images moving in sequence make up a film; when multiple images are static they can be combined to form a photomontage to give an impression of movement, as seen in the cover for the men's magazine *Now* illustrated on page 146.

Time-sequence ideas have become useful design elements and have introduced new concepts for page layouts. Multiple visual patterns can be intentionally used in graphic design to lead the viewer to a predictable behavioural response, and this potentially enormous power confronts the designer with serious ethical and social responsibilities.

The fourth law is the law of similarity and requires that "visual units which resemble each other in shape, size, colour, and direction will be seen together as a homogeneous grouping." This law is based on the tendency of the eye to organize visual stimuli into an ordered pattern, a tendency which is closely allied with the fifth law, the law of proximity.

Cataldo's fifth law, influenced by Gestalt findings, proposes that "in visual perception what is closest together tends to unite." Images of objects that are close to one another form groups and are seen against an empty space. This ties in with another Gestalt principle, which states that the nature of the perceived figure is dependent on the character of the surrounding field, even if this includes other figures. By definition, figures have a specific shape, whereas the background is shapeless. This factor has particular relevancy in typography, where words on a page are defined by the spatial relationships between the various parts.

Colour is regularly used in nature to disguise the three-dimensional appearance of animals in order to protect them from predators. Such camouflage has been successfully adopted during wartime to protect both men and machines. Colour is often regarded as mere decoration on a basic shape while in fact it can be instrumental in altering the perception of shape when the actual form is unchangeable. Colour applied in this way has become increasingly important for any designer involved in packaging or in designing a unified image for large corporations. Much of the research that triggered this renewed interest in colour was done by op artists (such as Vasarely), who based their theories on the well observed fact that colour values alter in relation to the adjacent colours.

Some interesting experiments on the effects that colour and pattern can have on the appearance of objects were made by Bob Hyde and his students at the

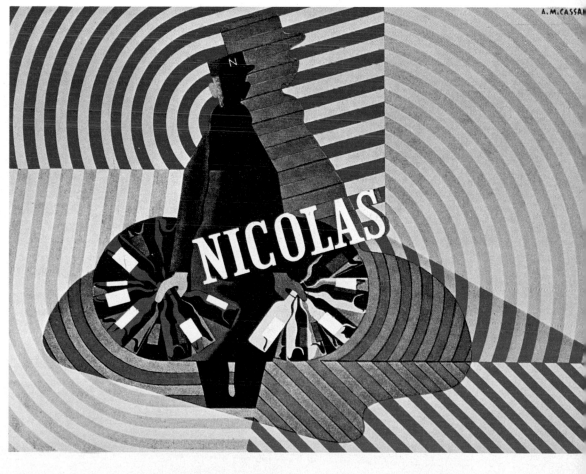

Above: Graphic interpretation of the structure pattern of a tire, made into an advertisement. By Pino Tovaglia.
Right: Poster for a wine merchant in which the artist projects around a late-futurist portrayal various strips of coloured lines onto the background, emphasizing the dynamic qualities of the composition. By Cassandre, 1935.

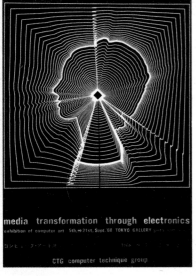

Perception and
the Spatial Field

The shape, position, direction, and dimension of an object are perceived by the eye and assimilated by the brain, always in relation to the background or at least to a visual field; if one of the two juxtaposed parts is heightened, some fascinating graphic results can be obtained.

Top left: Poster for an industrial design conference in Kyoto. By Yusaku Kamekura.
Top right: Poster for Nikon, also by Kamekura.
Bottom left: An electronically created picture. By the Computer Technique Group (CTG), 1968.
Bottom centre: Poster for an art exhibition. By Yusaku Kamekura.
Bottom right: A visual field of cosmic references appears in this poster created for an exhibition. By Kazumasa Nagai, 1974.

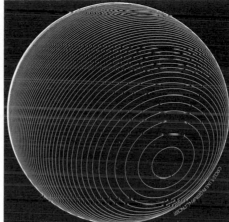

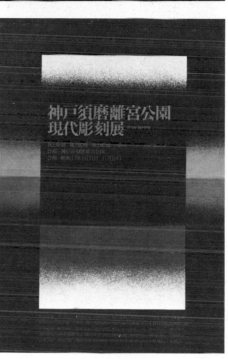

TOSHIHIRO KATAYAMA

stedelijk museum
amsterdam

SM

Far left, top and bottom: Magazine pages in which autonomous graphic elements are grafted onto a photographic background. By Kazumasa Nagai.
Left: Sleeve for a pop music record. By Eiko Ishioka, Yoshio Nakanishi, Seiya Sawayama, and Masao Koomura.
Centre: Poster for an art exhibition. By Ikko Tanaka.
Below: Advertisement for an exhibition of the graphic design of Toshihiro Katayama.
Bottom right: Poster for a series of exhibitions at the Stedelijk Museum in Amsterdam. By Wim Crouwel.

141

Colour and the Limits of Psychic Balance

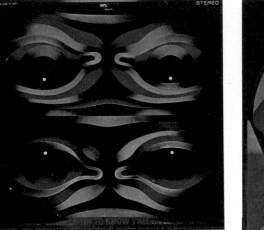

Left: Negative superimposition of McKay rays onto Leonardo's Mona Lisa alternates its visual effect in this exhibition poster. By Makoto Nakamura and Shigeo Fukuda.
Below, centre and right: Two record sleeves. By Wolfgang Baumann.

Wimbledon College of Art at the beginning of the 1960s. Because human vision is selective, and to give his ideas the severest test, Hyde chose as his model the human figure, as this is the form most easily recognizable to other humans.

Many tribes throughout the world have used body paint when performing rituals in which they imitate the spiritual manifestations of traditional customs, and so must submerge their personal identities. The designer uses the same means—colour—to alter shape, but for the opposite effect of creating a new identity for the client's product. In one of Hyde's most dramatic experiments the spectator's eye perception is thrown off balance because the usual points of reference are lost in the black and white lines that are painted over a face, obliterating the main features. The simplest example of such optical illusion is the familiar cosmetic device of the use of paint to heighten or lower the cheekbone.

Because of their movement and the obvious difficulty in painting over them, the eyes constitute a focal point in the face and make it recognizable. Hyde conducted an elaborate experiment to see if this recognizable facial feature could be eliminated. He removed eyebrows and eyelashes from several faces and then painted new shapes around the eyes in the same pattern as the clothes so that they became incorporated into an overall dominant pattern and the customary distinction between body and clothes was lost.

Ballets organized by Hyde have exploited the influence of overall pattern by using multiple projections combined with painted body stockings to accentuate different movements of the body. In a similar way, psychedelic projections onto a dance floor alter the emphasis in perceiving the dancers. In 1966 Rediffusion filmed a ballet of Hyde's that showed how dancers and environment are visually interchangeable when the

unifying pattern from two projectors matches the costumes worn. Parallel ideas had been explored much earlier by the Bauhaus painter-dancer Oskar Schlemmer, who tried in various projects to redefine the relationship of man to total space instead of using traditional figures against painted backdrops.

An interesting example of the commercial use of shape alteration through colour is the way different airlines, by applying colour in various patterns, make the same aircraft look unlike each other. Hyde has shown on model planes that a nose coloured in contrasting stripes achieves an elongated appearance while one striped in closely related colours looks more compact. Hyde also visually isolated the tail from the nose by painting the wings and fuselage the same colour, which produced a lengthened appearance; for the opposite effect—visual compactness—he gave the terminal features the same colours. These effects are the bases of important design principles for controlling the appearance of products as well as for drawing attention to special features, like control knobs and switches.

During the 1950s and 1960s psychedelic colours were part of a wider movement in revolt against analytical thought and the formality of symbolic language as used by scientists. Exponents of the counterculture sought sensory stimulation of the most intense kind (often enhanced by drugs) in all artistic fields. The Vietnam War was seen as an expression of a cold, mechanical attitude by those involved in a movement that probably started with the Beatles, had developed into full flower with the hippies of Haight-Ashbury in San Francisco, and was described in the jargon of the period by Abbie Hoffman in his book *Woodstock Nation*. According to Marshall McLuhan, the Beatles provided the soil from which developed

The hippie generation of the 1960s inspired the creation of posters that were destined for an underground circuit chiefly comprised of young people and artists—mainly American—who were looking for alternative expressions to official art. The posters rapidly reached a more widespread public.
Below: Art poster. By Jacques Richez.
Right and bottom: Psychedelic posters. By Victor Moscoso. Psychedelic art was inspired by a culture that adopted drugs, such as marijuana, mescaline, and LSD.

Right and below: Two posters for rock concerts. Although a fantastic and flaming lettering prevails, the text is difficult to read and is considered a pretext for the purpose of impressing a visually psychedelic effect onto the whole. By Wes Wilson.
Far right: A calmer composition; here the large vermillion-coloured flowers stand out thanks to the complementary green colour, which also functions to create an illusory raised effect. By Victor Moscoso.
Bottom right: Solar symbols and signs of the zodiac are the ingredients of this hippie poster. By Sätty.

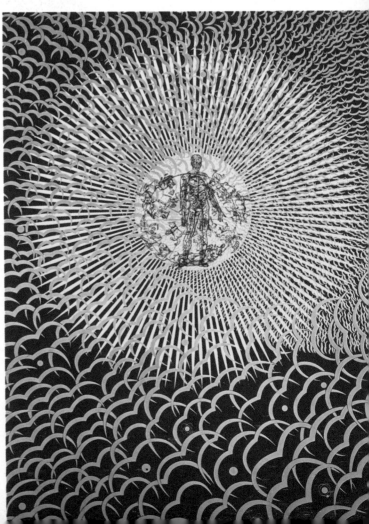

Below: Posters featuring Paul McCartney, George Harrison, and John Lennon,
three members of the pop group the
Beatles. By Allen Hurlburt, who has
worked on photographs of celebrities
taken by Richard Avedon, liberally
manipulating the images to make the
stars even more mythical to their fans.

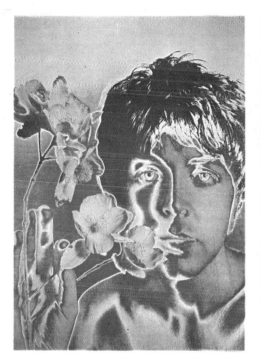

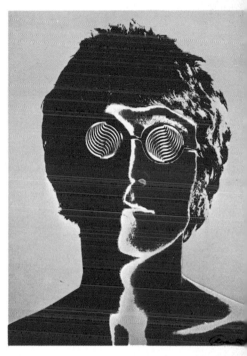

Above, left and centre: Two other posters created with the young hippies of San Francisco in mind; decoration that recalls art nouveau is interposed on a style that evokes fairy tales and dreams. The artists belonging to this movement have never denied their predilection for three great names in the art of the past: Hieronymus Bosch for the fantastic, William Blake for philosophical mysticism, and Aubrey Beardsley for graphic qualities and eroticism.
Above right: Poster inspired by the spiritual life of the Indian deities. By Victor Moscoso.

145

Adaptability of Shapes

Left: A photograph, created along the lines of conceptual art, in which the artist, aided only by a mirror, modifies reality, and thus obtains a virtual image. By Gan Hosoya.

Below: A montage of disparate elements surrounds the human figure, in a context that is deliberately humorous and delicate. By Tom Daly.

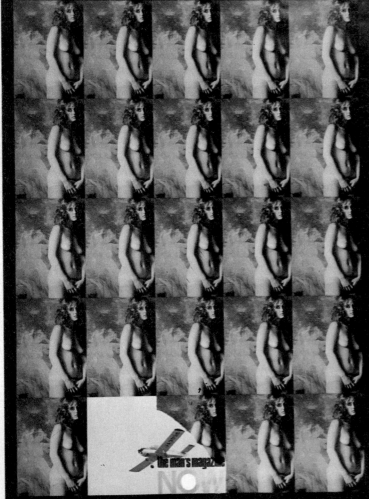

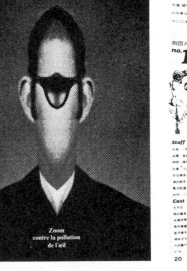

Zoom
contre la pollution
de l'œil

20

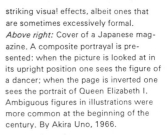

Left: Cover of the Japanese magazine *Now.* The figure of the model is presented in a repetitive sequence, producing a sense of movement and multivision. Art direction by Tamotsu Ejima; photography by Taiho Yoshida.

Above left: Poster against "optical pollution." By Roman Cieslewicz, who has often used photographic and technical devices to manipulate the features of the human figure in order to obtain striking visual effects, albeit ones that are sometimes excessively formal.

Above right: Cover of a Japanese magazine. A composite portrayal is presented: when the picture is looked at in its upright position one sees the figure of a dancer; when the page is inverted one sees the portrait of Queen Elizabeth I. Ambiguous figures in illustrations were more common at the beginning of the century. By Akira Uno, 1966.

the later, more radical movement known as punk (meaning rubbish). With typical irony McLuhan stated: "The 'yellow submarine' of the Beatles was their idea of the garbage machine, or disposal unit. The Beatles, a very creative group, understand garbage thoroughly. In fact, they use little else in their operation; the old sounds, old rhythms, old tunes suitably archetypalized by new electronics. They use these contrived units, or submarines, to submerge and explore the depths of the cultural unconscious, retrieving all sorts of strange fruit. It's like an 'inner-space capsule'—a completely contrived and programmed human environment for retrieving the junked past as art." Although seeking to distort normal perception through the use of psychedelic colour, the posters produced at that time do not manage to convey the excitement of an important mass movement in America as it was envisioned by Charles A. Reich in *The Greening of America*: "There is revolution coming. It will not be like revolutions of the past. It will originate with individuals and with culture and it will change the political structure only as its final act. It will not require violence to succeed and it cannot be successfully resisted by violence. . . . It will be 'revolution by consciousness.' "

Communication is the major function of written letters made up into words. The patterns of letter forms allow for artistic expression independent of verbal meaning, although the most successful calligraphic art is usually the one that relates the optical elements to the verbal ones (examples of which may be seen on page 144 and in the cover illustration for *Beards* on page 156). Ideograms are an especially expressive form of a typographical design that incorporates the concept of the text. They appeared first in the seventh century and again at the beginning of the twentieth century with the futurists and dadaist writers and artists of Germany, France, and Italy. In Guillaume Apollinaire's poem "Il Pleut" the type appears to rain down the surface of the page. The futurists preferred an evocative, abstract form for poetry rather than a literal translation into typographic form, since they recognized the Gestalt idea that the reader supplies an important element to the message by his understanding of it as it relates to his personal situation. This emphasis on words as removed from the standard sentence structure had a particularly great effect on the American poet E. E. Cummings, and among such other writers as Edgar Allan Poe, James Joyce, and Walt Whitman.

The illustrations in this chapter all show the influence of Jan Tschichold's ideas about typography, incorporated in his *Elementare Typographie* of 1925, which sold an unprecedented twenty-eight thousand copies throughout the world. Another important contributor to constructivist typography, which this new typography is often called, was Karl Teige of Prague. He drew up a list, the influence of which is

still apparent in graphic design today, of the basic formulations concerning this approach to typographical problems:

1. Freedom from tradition and prejudice; overthrow of archaicism and academicism and the rejection of decoration. No respect for academic and traditional rules unsupported by visual reason, which otherwise means lifeless form.

2. A choice of type that is more perfect and more legible and cut with more geometric simplicity. Understanding of the spirit of suitable types, which should be used in accordance with the character of the text. Contrast of typographical material to emphasize content.

3. Constant appreciation of purpose, and the necessity of its fulfillment. Differentiation in special aims. Advertisements meant to be seen from a distance require different treatment from a scientific work or a volume of verse.

4. Harmonious disposition of surface and text in accordance with objective visual law; surveyable structure and geometric organization.

5. Exploitation of all means which are or may be offered by present and future technical discoveries; conjunction of illustration and text by typephoto.

6. The closest cooperation between typographers and experts in the composing room is desirable, just as the designing architect cooperates with the constructional engineer. Specialization and division of labour are as necessary as close contact.

The clearest example of this approach is to be found in telephone directories, with their large amounts of information arranged within a rectilinear design system of varying sizes and compositional elements consisting of carefully selected and precisely placed typefaces, point sizes of type, white spaces, and margins.

The impetus to the new (sometimes referred to as architectonic) typography came from the Bauhaus and its architects' concern with "virtual volume," or space. Equally important influences came from the constructivists and the de Stijl group as well as from the futurists, the manifesto of whose spiritual leader Filippo Tommaso Marinetti had been published as early as 1909 in *Le Figaro*.

Typographical discipline was revolutionized when, in the 1950s, new machinery was introduced and offset printing was replaced by photocomposition processes used in conjunction with computers. Such recent technological innovations as lasers and the ink-jet system have had as shattering an impact as the replacement of the hand-scribed book by Gutenberg's metal typography in the fifteenth century.

These electronic changes did not stem from any desire among compositors but arose in response to an immediate need in the American space programme in 1957: its researchers were unable to deal with the

Rhythm and Dynamics of the Layout

Left: Example of an illustrated-book layout prepared, according to a graphic trend of the Swiss-German school, on a nine-square grid. The grid is the element of unity for both the text and the various formats of the pictures. Presented in Emil Ruder's manual *Typographie.*
Below, left and centre: Composition demonstrations using typographical shapes. By Emil Ruder.

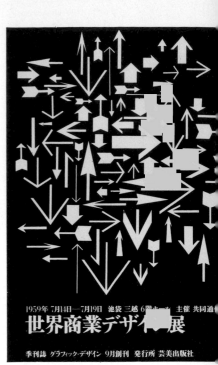

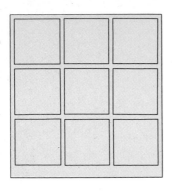

Below and centre right: Three double pages, the result of a typographic and photographic interpretation of an Ionesco play. These experimental shapes demand a wholly pictorial reading that includes

the texts. Type design by Massin; photography by Henry Cohen.
Bottom, left to right: Three layouts for a photographic feature by Richard Avedon; the effect is both classical and modern,

with spaces and breaks assuming a major role. By Alexey Brodvitch for the periodical *Observations*, 1959.

Above: Exhibition poster achieved exclusively with conventional typographical elements in a fairly considerable range of variants. By Ikko Tanaka.

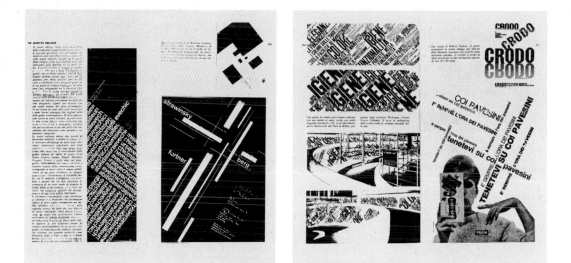

Above and below: Three double pages of printing compositions. The reproductions above show instances of graphics still bound to constructivist patterns, the legacy of historical avant-garde tendencies of the 1920s; those below show more daring experimental possibilities. Nowadays, with the gradual disappearance of a more traditional school of printing and the concurrent rise of the multitalented graphic artist, the positions of type designer and lettering specialist are also beginning to disappear. Composition with inscriptions by Herb Lubalin (below), Raymond Gfeller (top right), and Bruce and Pegge Hopper (top left); presented in Giancarlo Iliprandi's book *Linguaggio Grafico* (*Graphic Language*), of 1966.

Above: Announcement of a show put on by the Directory of Advertisers in which the artist takes advantage of the opportunity to play on the initials, recalling the celebrated mark of Albrecht Dürer. By Herb Lubalin, undoubtedly one of the most sensitive interpreters of letter designs and of the various aspects of lettering as a whole.

The Legacy
of the Bauhaus

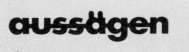

Above left: Poster for an international
exhibition held in Cologne in 1928 that
reveals the influence of a total renewal
brought about by the Bauhaus, even in
the field of printing.
Above right: Poster for an exhibition of
American graphic designers held in
Tokyo. By Gan Hosoya.

Below left: Swiss poster for an exhibition
of Brazilian architecture. By Josef Müller-
Brockmann, 1954.
Below, centre and right: Pages from a
publication printed in Switzerland in
1972 entitled *Kompendium für
Alphabeten,* edited by Karl Gerstner.

Right: Typographical poster for a concert, with a layout according to the neoplastic canons of Josef Müller-Brockmann.
Centre left and bottom: Two symbols created for Olivetti, the communications firm. The first is by Walter Ballmer, the second by Giovanni Pintori, who for many years looked after the company's image.
Centre right: Visual inquiry into the gradual reduction of a logo to a monogram. By Pino Tovaglia.

vast quantity of data processed by teleprinters. The Mergenthaler Linotype Company came to the rescue by devising the Linofilm machine, which was capable of transcribing computer data into ordinary type.

Edward Rondthaler, a pioneer in commercial photosetting, founded Photolettering, Inc., in New York in 1936 and caused a sensation in 1960 when he showed three thousand alphabets in his *Alphabet Thesaurus*. For the five hundred years following Gutenberg's invention, typefaces had been designed by printers and made in foundries. Often founders became the exclusive manufacturers of the entire output of engravers and designers. In an earlier age the process of casting a type took months and even years and involved heavy financial investment. Today a typeface can, in a short space of time, be designed and redesigned any number of times to suit various typesetting systems. Specialized studios now exist to draw or adapt new faces to sell to the maximum number of manufacturers of typesetting machines. Rondthaler and his associates Aaron Burns and Herb Lubalin are still members of the Association Typographique Internationale (ATYPI), founded in 1957. Through their own International Typeface Corporation, founded in 1970, they have been instrumental in the augmented creative graphic technology resulting from all these fundamental changes in typographic art.

Alan Fletcher, writing about trademarks in the book *Pentagram*, suggests: "The company emblem might be specially designed to reflect the business or occupation; it is also often developed from heraldic sources, or haphazardly evolved from inauspicious and humble beginnings. Bibendum, the eighty-year-old trademark of the Michelin Rubber and Cartographic Company, was conjured up from a heap of old tyres by the Michelin brothers, who created the image and made a world-famous figure. The unlikely name of Shell, so the story goes, began in the days when shells were used as ballast by ships returning from trading in the East until oil took their place, and the company adopted the name and design. Sometimes marks and meanings even become part of our spoken symbology. The term 'private eye' is said to be derived from the emblem of the famous Pinkerton National Detective Agency, whose trademark was an eye embellished with the slogan 'We never sleep.' "

Fletcher continues: "Emblems and insignia used for commercial marks can be labelled according to form, purpose and function. The designer's terminology, although not altogether precise, generally defines symbols as pictorial or abstract devices, logotypes as signatures, and monograms as intertwined or connected letters. Specialized occupations also have their special terms, and publishers, for example, refer to their imprints as colophons, while clubs have badges, and

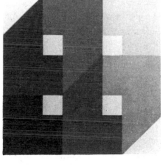

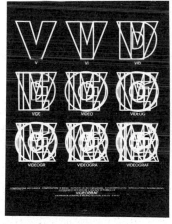

151

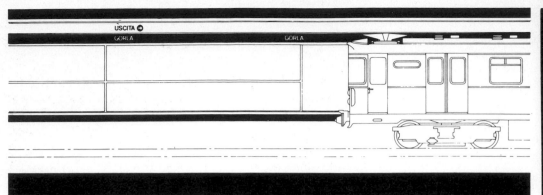

Graphics for Public Transport

Left and above: Study plans for the Milan underground's sign posts. With the station's urban exterior, devised by the Albini-Helg Studio, these sign posts constituted the first example of corporate identity to be created by an Italian public body. The choice of colour, vermillion, has proved fortunate even at a distance, transforming the various elements into characterizing symbols. By Bob Noorda of Unimark International, 1962–63.

Below: Signs for the New York subway. The Transit Authority had requested a project that, without involving structural changes to the existing parts, would bring order to the 480 stations comprising the city's subway with constant coordinations. Shown here are a few of the direction signs. By Bob Noorda of Unimark International.

Below: Research project that takes a text to the limits of legibility and perception in the connection between the various words made up as an outline, without the break of any spaces. By Pino Tovaglia.

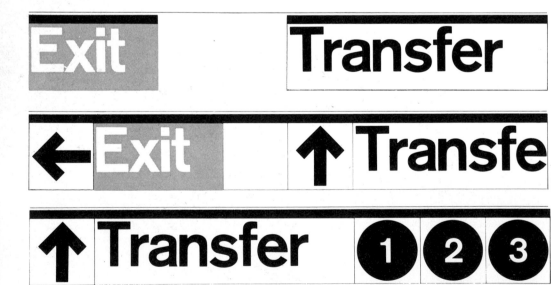

the aristocracy coats-of-arms. However, the term 'trademark' is generally used to describe all those marks concerned with commerce."

In his book *The Corporate Personality* Wally Olins criticizes designers' use of abstract symbols for corporation logos and describes the not uncommon, embarrassing situation that arises when two totally unrelated concerns end up with the same logo because "the differences between some abstract symbols are so small as to be barely visible." Tom Wolfe has also written on the general attitude that contributes to, if not results in, poor design, in an article that was published by *New York* magazine for a second time in the July 17, 1972, issue after a particularly glaring example of company logos clashing. Wolfe is typically scathing in his remarks: "These abstract logos, which a company . . . is supposed to put on everything from memo pads to the side of its fifty-story building, make absolutely no impact—conscious or unconscious—upon its customers or the general public, except insofar as they create a feeling of vagueness or confusion. I'm talking about the prevailing mode of abstract logos. Pictorial logos or written logos are a different story. Random House (the little house), Alfred Knopf (the borzoi dog), the old Socony-vacuum flying red horse, or the written logos of Coca-Cola or Hertz—they stick in the mind and create the desired effect of instant recognition ('identity'). Abstract logos are a dead loss in that respect, and yet millions continue to be poured into the design of them. Why? Because the conversion to a total-design abstract logo formation somehow makes it possible for the head of the corporation to tell himself: 'I'm modern, up to date, with it, a man of the future. I've streamlined this old baby.' "

Peter Gorb, another contributor to *Pentagram*, says that communication can be divided into two principles: the designer conveys "information" and also signals "identity." Designing an identity for a corporation does not stop with the creation of a logo, abstract or otherwise. All aspects of the groups of people involved in a corporation must be taken into consideration and the "complex social and economic systems which govern their organizational behaviour" accounted for in creating a suitable identity. "The designer's concern with information," writes Gorb, "is to present it efficiently, to simplify the complex, suggest the subtleties behind the obvious, to enlarge the 'micro' and reduce the 'macro.' Furthermore, the work stretches along a spectrum which at one end may be concerned with objective descriptions of the technology of products and environments and at the other with the highly emotive and persuasive, the advertising and sales promotion of these products and environments."

The pictorial treatment of information is now being applied more than ever. Charts, maps, menus, and cartoons help to clarify and interpret information

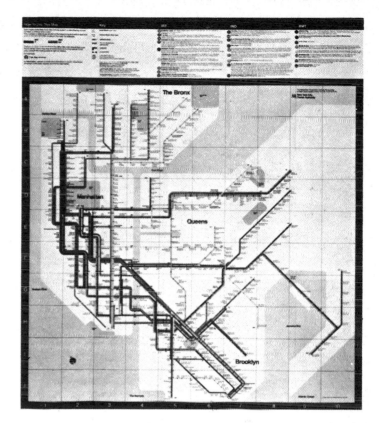

Above: Map of the New York subway, graphically reworked into a coordinated system that is easily understandable even to those unfamiliar with this kind of printed material or, for that matter, with the New York subway. By Massimo Vignelli.

Below and bottom: Two examples of optical illusion, achieved with degraded lines that emphasize the sense of depth and relief, light and darkness, and metallic glint. Logotype for Harlech Television designed by Bob Gill and Robert Brownjohn; the intersecting of squares forms the pattern designed by Alfredo Troisi for an invitation to a cultural event in Milan.

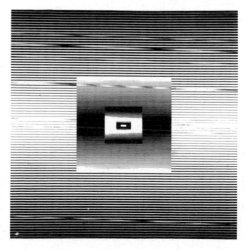

The Trademark

Below: Advertisement for a prize-winning competition sponsored by a television programme for the design of symbols. By Pino Tovaglia.
Bottom: Study of graphic symbols for the Pirelli Tire Corporation. By Theo Crosby, Alan Fletcher, and Colin Forbes.
Right, from top to bottom: IBM trademark, designed by Paul Rand; various representations of the Westinghouse Electric Corporation logo; the Olivetti typewriter logo (left), designed by Marcello Nizzoli in 1956, and the new word logo that accompanies it (right), designed by Walter Ballmer; variations of the Coca-Cola trademark.

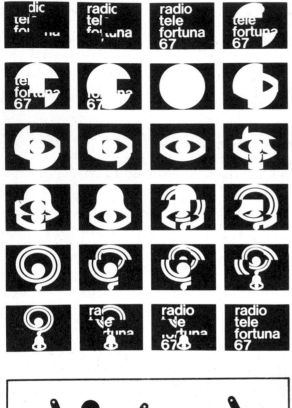

The designing of the modern trademark has always been one of the most attractive ambitions of anyone working within the field of graphic design, but this is also one of the reasons why it is becoming increasingly difficult to represent a company, a corporation, a range of products, or a cultural activity with a symbol that should be at once simple, memorable, and strongly characterized without resembling any other existing ones. Here are a few examples of graphic compositions considered to be of particular interest today.
Above: Graphic symbol created for the Teatro Popolare Italiano. By Albe Steiner, 1959.
Below: Logo designed for the Macfadden-Bartell Corporation. By Roger Ferriter.
Bottom: Logo designed for *Vista* magazine. By Hess & Antupit.
Right (from left to right, top to bottom): Crosby, Fletcher, Forbes for the Conference for Islamic Solidarity; symbol by Gerard Miedinger; Vance Jonson for Steelcase; Eskil Ohlsson for Kroma Lithographers, Chermayeff & Geismar Associates for Chase Manhattan Bank; Keith Bright for Clover productions; Francesco Saroglia for Pure New Wool; George Nelson & Company for U.S. Information Agency; Michael O. Kelly for Audio Archives; Romek Marber for Ferguson Research Laboratories; Tor A. Pettersen for Scandinavian Bank; Damien Harrington for National Parks and Monuments of Dublin; Saul Bass and Don Handel for Alcoa Aluminum; Giulio Confalonieri for St. Andrews of Milan; Giulio Confalonieri for Boffi Arredamenti.

Reginald Reynolds

The fascinating history of beards through the ages.
"First-rate entertainment." — San Francisco Chronicle

The Portrayal of Type

Above left: A face sports the word "beards" on this cover for a book of the same name, accentuating waves and curls to simulate an actual beard. By Herb Lubalin.

Above right: Eric Gill, one of this century's most sensitive type-design artists, is famous for having drawn two series of letters for the Monotype Corporation, which are still used frequently today: examples of the Perpetua and the Gill Sans, with italicized capital letters, are reproduced in this illustration designed by him.

Below left: An experimental alphabet worked out according to the principle of reproduction of the cathodic line, on which the television picture is formed. By Wim Crouwel.

Below right: Collection of initials that make up the symbol of the studio of Sudler, Hennessey and Lubalin, Inc. By Herb Lubalin.

carried by the accompanying text. And an increasing number of diagrams, charts, and so on are now being drawn by computers. The designer of the London underground map, Henry Beck, chose to disregard the street pattern (which does not correlate with the tube lines anyway) and instead devised a form of stylization that treats the rail network as an independent system. In New York City, which has a rectangular grid of streets, the subway map follows the street pattern and is easy to read.

The first time that the power of symbolic thought was utilized as a tool was when pebbles were laid out to represent numbers. Calculation derives its name from the Greek word for pebbles, *calculi*. Mechanical aids transformed thinking, and as Richard L. Gregory has suggested, they perhaps to a large extent determine what is thought about. Even so, however complicated and efficient they are in handling symbols, machines cannot perceive the world. So far it has been impossible to teach computers to recognize surrounding objects or even the simple handwritten letter A.

Computers cannot function without their human programmers, although the machine can manipulate symbols with increasing subtlety, process information, and even learn by experience, like the two computers that improved their chess game by continually playing against each other. "Nevertheless," as Jasia Reichardt has written in the July 1968 issue of *Studio International*, "the computer is not capable of making abstractions and is devoid of the three prime forces behind creativity—imagination, intuition and emotion. Despite this, the computer as a budding artist has been making its appearance since about 1960."

The discovery of the silicon chip within the last few years has revolutionized the computer industry and has had as great an effect on human life as the creation of the first hand tools or the development of the steam engine. The silicon chip, only six millimetres (a quarter of an inch) square, has the same calculating and information-storage capacities as a room-sized computer of twenty-five years ago. The microcomputer is now so small, so versatile, and so economic that it will soon become as common a household device as the telephone or television. In taking over much of the daily drudgery of human life, as optimistically predicted in the February 20, 1978, issue of *Time*, the microcomputer can expand the mind in ways that are only beginning to be explored.

At present, access to one of the large commercial computers (the first of which was marketed in 1950) is necessary before anything creative can be undertaken. Before long, however, microelectronics will be accessible to everyone and also available as an artist's tool just as the airbrush is now. In much the same way that an artist must acquire mastery of the techniques for con-

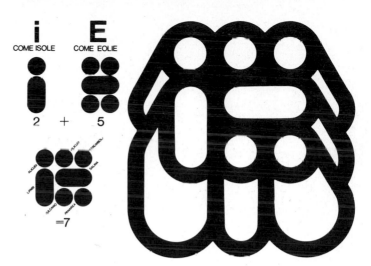

The Codification of Services

Above: The structure of the sign and some examples of symbols that make up part of a study of signs to be used in tourist centres (the pilot experiment was carried out in the Aeolian islands). By Mimmo Castellano.
Below: Visualization of the symbols referring to the various athletic competitions held at the 1972 Munich Olympics.

trolling an airbrush, so will learning how to make use of the full potential of the computer be further explored.

The term "computer graphics" was coined in 1960 by the airplane manufacturing company of Boeing. Computer graphics were used as visual aids for such complex information as is necessary to assess the landing accuracy of a plane viewed from the pilot's seat and the runway. The use of computer graphics for utilitarian purposes constitutes one of its functions, the other being in the area of aesthetic design or pure art. Included in the first category are the isometric view of neutron distribution in a reactor created as a research aid for physicists at Westinghouse Electric Corporation in Pennsylvania and perspective views for architectural designs or entirely computer-designed dimensional systems as used in 1968 by the architects Llewelyn-Davies, Week, Forrestire-Walker, and Bor for a hospital building in northern London. In the field of fine arts, computers have been used to programme not only drawing and painting but also sculpture, music, choreography, and poetry. Computer animated films—such as IBM's *Permutations* by John H. Whitney—have been produced and are playing an increasingly important role in education and research. Also in this vein is Paul Resch's work at the University of Illinois in Chicago, where his Programmed Logic for Automatic Teaching Operations, otherwise known as PLATO, is a much-praised teaching aid in a wide range of subjects. The student communicates directly with the computer by means of a typewriter keyboard.

Computer graphics are made by one of two methods. The first includes either computer-driven plotters that produce ink drawings directly onto paper, or a typewriter that is automatically operated by the computer and prints out drawings made up of letters and figures. In the second method, computer graphics are composed on a cathode-ray tube and an electron beam is electrically deflected across the phosphorescent screen to produce the image. As Reichardt has explained, "whether the pictures are made for analytical purposes or just for fun, the computer graphic is a visual analogue to a sequence of calculations fed into the computer."

The earliest electronic abstractions obtained from the analogue computer were shown by Ben F. Laposki in 1956. One popular computer graphic which has been circulated as a poster by Motif Editions is *The Snail;* made by Kerry Strand and Larry Jenkins for Californian Computer Products, it takes four and a half hours to plot. Further developments were encouraged by the editors of *Computers and Automation* magazine of Newtonville, Massachusetts, who

organized the first competition for computer graphics in 1963 at which prizes were awarded for aesthetic standards. At about the same time, the Germans Frieder Nake and Georg Nees and the American A. Michael Noll had their first exhibition in 1965. In 1968 the Cybernetic Serendipity exhibit was mounted by Jasia Reichardt at the Institute of Contemporary Arts in London, and in 1969 Kathe Schroder exhibited computer art in Hanover, Germany. Numerous computer graphics groups have been established, such as the Computer Group in Japan and Ars Media in Vienna. Important work in computer graphics has also been accomplished by artists in Madrid, Spain, and in Argentina, by Manfred Mohr in Paris, and by Auro Lecci now in Amherst, Massachusetts.

The field of cybernetics was officially established by Norbert Wiener in 1948 with his book *Cybernetics,* the subtitle of which is the best definition of the subject— *Control and Communication in the Animal and the Machine*. In a second, less technical book of 1950, *The Human Use of Human Beings*, Wiener states that "society can only be understood through a study of the messages and the communication facilities which belong to it; and that in the future development of these messages and communication facilities, messages between man and machines, between machines and man, and between machine and machine, are destined to play an ever-increasing part." Wiener goes on to claim that "it is the purpose of cybernetics to develop a language and techniques that will enable us indeed to attack the problem of control and communication in general, but also to find the proper repertory of ideas and techniques to classify their particular manifestations under certain concepts."

The computer revolution is part of Wiener's programme for cybernetics. Dr. Herbert W. Traube, another cybernetician, has written in number 161 of *Graphis:* "The special feature of computer graphics is the fact that a machine also helps in the conception, the creation of the figures produced. It is not told exactly what it is to draw, but is only given a skeleton plan. . . . The individual results cannot be foreseen even by the person who writes the programme."

Two examples of the wide influence that computers have had on graphics are illustrated by the poster *Pierre and Paul* by Hans Hillman and by Alwyn Clayden's collage project for the *Radio Times* cover, both from *European Illustration 78/79*. The possibilities opened up by computer graphics and computer control in typographic areas are among the most exciting developments in the history of graphic design.

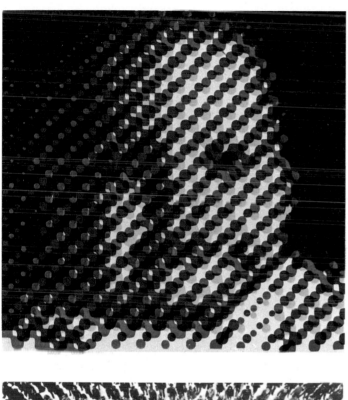

Left: This three-colour print as greatly enlarged shows up the chromatic structure and forces one to observe the object at a distance greater than usual. By Rudolph de Harak for the magazine *Perspectives*.
Below: A cover for *Radio Times* created by simulating the cathodic lines of the television screen. By Alwyn Clayden.
Bottom left: Film poster in which a multitude of people, caught in a zenith projection that moves in a centrifugal direction, forms the shape of a man's head. By Hans Hillmann.
Bottom right: Graphic pattern of the shape of the United States which, by its use of chromatic tones, produces an effect similar to that of a luminous sign: a board with digital lettering. By Rudolph de Harak.

Regie: René Allio
Mit Pierre Mondy,
Bulle Ogier,
Madeleine Barbulee
Kamera: Georges Leclerc
(Pierre et Paul)
Pierre und Paul

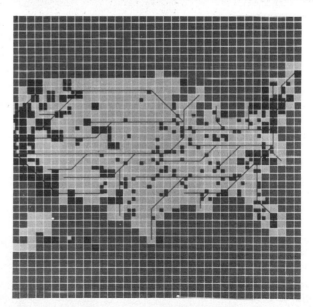

Graphics and Electronics

Over the years the computer has been shown to be an excellent instrument for producing pictures and constructing new shapes, or at least to be capable of changing them according to both man-made and haphazard rules. As IBM experts put it, the artist is credited with the concept, the computer with the execution—that which is devised by the artist is subsequently developed by the computer, with the aid of certain graphic devices such as the printing press, the plotter, or the television screen.

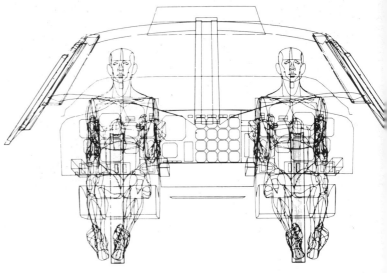

Above: The computer provides the designer with the possibility of mathematizing shapes; in designing the body of a car, one can automate the drawings, thus producing not only actual scale drawings but mathematical models as well. The Alfetta-GT drawings were achieved with the DACAR computerized system, which is automatic.

Right: Studies of the piloting position of a Boeing cabin (top) and the simulation of a head-on collision, with the driver wearing a seat belt.

Left: Variations on the spheric shape. By Paul Resch.

Below left: The Vitruvian man by Leonardo da Vinci, transformed. By Charles Csuri.

Below, centre and right: Two art creations programmed on a graphic computer, reproduced on microfilm, and printed as lithographs. By Aaron Marcus.

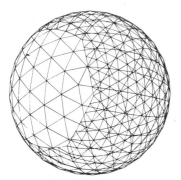

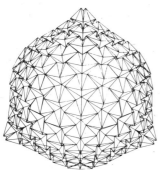

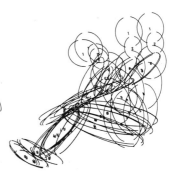

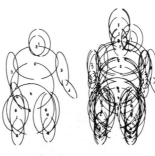

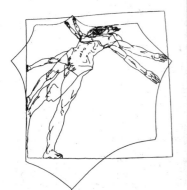

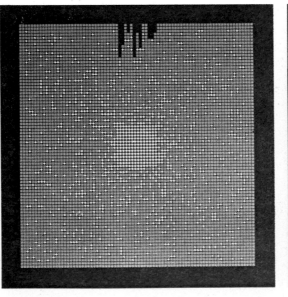

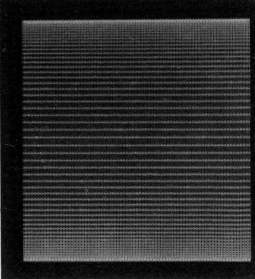

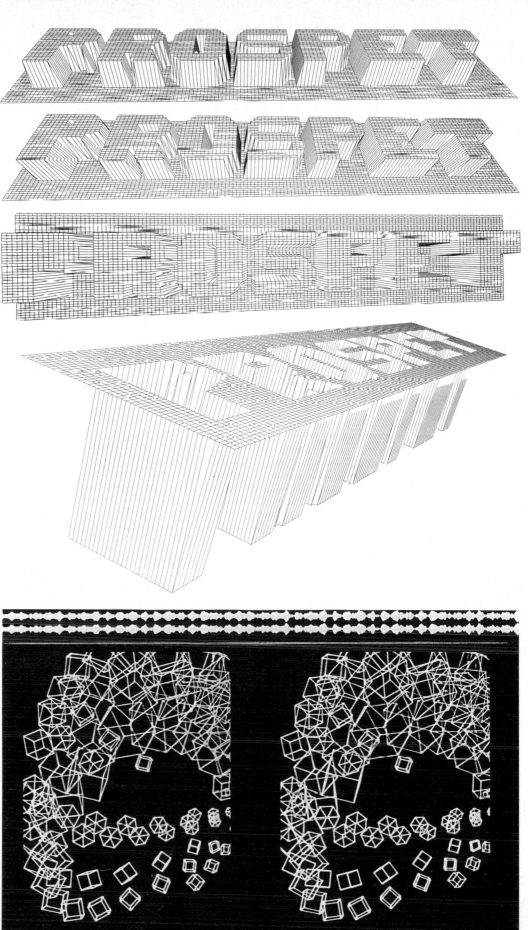

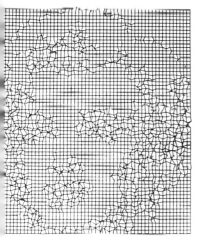

Top left and above: Portraits of John F. Kennedy and Marilyn Monroe. By the Computer Technique Group.
Top right and right: Construction of the letters making up the word "prospet" according to the programme of the same name, which designs perspective or stereoscopic projections of surfaces, working on the numerical values in relation to the intersection of a screen.

Below: Variation and transformation of a screen. By John Roy.
Right: Two pictures from the film *Permutations* by John Whitney, one of the pioneers of the art of creating film with the aid of a computer, who has given a rhythm to the pictures, programming them in harmony with the musical sounds of a symphony.

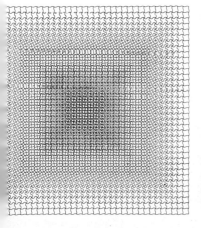

5. THE GRAPHIC OBJECT

Love my label like myself.
JAMES JOYCE

For centuries man has labelled himself, has created an identity within which he can live and be known as he would like to be known. It is not a new phenomenon, but rather an ancient ritual, designed to express the differences between one group of humans and another. It began, perhaps, with increasing wealth and better education, as a way of displaying material achievement. Thus the rich man's sophisticated clothes and jewelry immediately identified him as a man of material subtance, while the monk's simple habit was a mark of his humility and faith, his unpretentious belief in a life lived closer to spiritual values than to material ones.

Today this process of self-identification continues, and has, in many ways, been refined. Partly this is due to the increasing complexity of the multifaceted society in which we live, be it Italy, Japan, the Americas, or Australia. Though we are of one race, we are, nevertheless, members of minute groups within that race. And as such we all need to identify both ourselves and others around us. Who would recognize a policeman were it not for his uniform? Or, in the corridors of hospitals almost anywhere in the world, how would one know who of the many people in the building were the doctors and nurses were they not wearing coats or dresses somewhat identical in colour and style? In restaurants or on station platforms, we recognize those who serve by their initial identification: their uniform. And by the same criterion can those who serve recognize each other: military troops identify friend or foe by the shapes of their helmets or the coloured flashes on their shoulders.

Uniforms then, but not uniformity, present us to each other in a way that enables us to identify each other's function in society.

But what of the self-selected uniform? Is this a case of mass marketing overkill? Do people grow to look alike because their choice of clothes has been reduced? The reverse is probably true. For, while many men join a branch of the armed forces to be "in uniform," many others, of all ages and both sexes, choose their clothes to match their own idea of self-identity. They create their own uniform and in so doing create their own uniformity. The influences are many. Some, like the bikini of the 1950s and the miniskirt of the 1960s, are the products of fashion designers. Others, like the "denim revolution" of the late 1960s and early 1970s, are the result of sociological changes that, in the age of satellite communications, have had global impact.

But whether the uniform is imposed or self-selected, the sense of purpose is the same. Both are concerned with visual identity; both are designed to achieve as near to instant recognition as can be expected within their particular context.

In the field of visual communication as it relates to industry, this need for an instantly identifiable personality is nowhere more important than in the packaging and presentation of products. For, by the careful use of visual communications techniques, through the intelligent use of the visual language of communication and graphics, every product—good, bad, or indifferent—can be cloaked in an identity which, to the consumer, will establish that product's desirability, its function, its value. And its personality.

Many of the best examples of packaging are to be found in nature. The egg, for example, in its natural state is packed in a shape that virtually cannot be improved upon. Designed for easy production, built to provide protection for its contents, an eggshell is more than a neat piece of nature's packaging. For humans it is a symbol of new life, of food and nourishment, as well as strength and durability. Place an egg end to end between the palms of your hands. Its strength is apparent as soon as you try to crush it. Or place an egg on the table. Its natural form will cause it to roll until it takes up the position designed for an easy birth for the chick it might hold.

Look at an orange or a banana. Their skins are their packs. Vibrant and warm colours seem to confirm their inner goodness. We see them for what they are— sources of nourishment provided by nature.

In historic terms, the Japanese were among the first to appreciate the natural beauty of leaves: they used them as wrapping paper, along with rice grass as an extra, protective packaging material, for the humble egg. And for the Japanese, with their ancient traditions

Charles Eames, the American designer and architect, who worked in various fields during his career—the building trade, product design, and the setting up of fairs and exhibitions—created this card house in 1956. He reproduced on both sides of every card many of the attractive images he had collected over the years, thus providing the child with an educational pictorial panorama as well as an active building game.

The product label has always had the simple role of stating the contents of the package, from the denomination to the ingredients, but visual operators have turned this to advantage, seizing on the chance to express an idea, to draw attention to the quality of the product, to show off refined or amusing graphic formulas—the chance, therefore, to impose an individual mark of distinction. These pages show a few period labels, now of historical value.

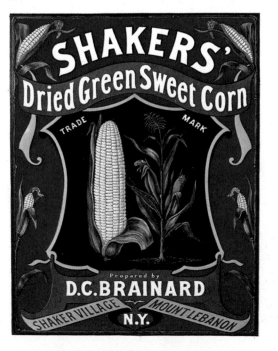

Distinguishing the Product : The Label

Above left: English label for haberdashery goods.
Above centre: Turn-of-the-century label for a box of matches.
Above: Label for a Japanese beer. 1897.
Left: A wraparound label for tins of preserved fruit. Printed by the Shaker community of Mount Lebanon, New York, the most famous of the collectives founded on utopian ideology, whose members lived in a self-sufficient way, developing agricultural and craft activities to the maximum. Early 1900s.

Far left: Two other matchbox labels, printed in Japan toward the end of the nineteenth century.
Left: Food label from the Shaker community in Mount Lebanon.

Above: Two other tin labels, part of a series created by the Shaker community in Mount Lebanon.
Above right: Floral-design label for toiletry goods. Printed in Japan.
Right: An elegant label with art deco references. Printed in Germany, 1928.

Above: An illustrated label serves as lining for a box of vegetable seeds. This is a rational approach to tackling packaging problems because, besides the compartments inside the box that function to separate the contents, there is an internal label that enables one to check instructions for use. This trend in devising practical solutions to even the most minor of everyday problems was a typical feature of the work of the Shakers, who after collectivizing all the production tasks went on to cultivate specialists in various fields, from furniture manufacturing to the tinned-products industry.

Natural Packaging

Left: An ancient Thai system for wrapping fruit, still commonly used today, entails the making of small baskets with flexible canes to encase the fruit.
Right: Food products wrapped in banana leaves and packaged with a paper label. Printed in Thailand.

Left: A box for sweets made of a sheet of thin wood onto which the script is directly impressed. United States, 1906.
Right: A portion of a type of French cheese that to this day still comes wrapped in wood to enable the product to keep its freshness.

Right: A container for agricultural products transformed into a gift, ennobled by the wood it is made of. By Laura Advertising & Marketing, Denmark, 1970.

Above: Another Thai food product wrapped in banana leaves.
Below: A small basket, made of woven tree bark, for Ceylon tea.

Above and below: Two other packages made of thin sheets of wood for French cheeses. Despite the passing of time, these have never been replaced even by materials more congenial to modern manufacturing technologies.

Soft Wrapping

of art and craft, packaging became an expression of their basic philosophy, that nature is a friend of mankind, not an enemy, that a person's life can—and should—be lived in harmony with nature, not in conflict with it.

Traditional Japanese packaging constitutes a world in itself—a world made up of a complex jigsaw of many distinct sources of inspiration and application. First and foremost it has a utilitarian source, a kind of crystallization of the wisdom gained from centuries of day-to-day life. The rice grasses are an example of this, as are the rope wrappings once used for dried fish. While the rice grasses protected the eggs—and, as perhaps subconsciously felt by the Japanese, enhanced the natural feelings of freshness and warmth inherent in the eggs—the rope wrappings afforded the right amount of ventilation, thus preserving the fish for more than six months and allowing the package to be unwrapped a little at a time—as much as was needed, in fact. Other similar wrapping materials once in wide use are oak leaves (for wrapping rice cakes), the

edible leaves of the beefsteak plant (for wrapping pickled plums), and magnolia leaves (for rice balls or bean curd).

Each of these examples reflects the Japanese ability to see beauty in the simplest forms of nature. They also teach us that wisdom and feeling are especially important in packaging because these qualities—or the lack of them—are always immediately apparent in every form of packaging. And what use is any pack if it shows no feeling for the product or the consumer?

The second clearly recognizable source of Japanese inspiration stems from the nation's natural development of handicrafts. Departing from the purely functional aspects of packing and wrapping, Japan's craftsmen turned their attention to the refinements of what to them soon became an art form in its own right. For these craftsmen the act of packaging came to have important meanings of its own quite apart from the contents of the package. The package came to have a symbolic value distinct from its practical function. And as techniques became more sophisticated, the art

of packaging became professionalized. It was a profession taken up by artisans working in old, long-established shops, men dedicated to developing their techniques, to making packages more and more beautiful until they achieved a level of competence so high as to constitute a new apex in design and decoration in the history of packaging.

This was the beginning of packages viewed as works of art, as products which often had more charm and value than the actual contents themselves. Packaging had become an end in itself, and the motivation of these artisans was entirely personal. They simply could not resist the desire to perfect their craft, a craft which was, by now, an art. They were driven by two considerations: an aesthetic philosophy holding that everything could and should be made beautiful, and a value system declaring that all objects—large or small, expensive or cheap—were of real intrinsic value.

Of course, industrialization has changed much of this, even—if not especially—in Japan. Yet there are

still examples in the older shops in and around Kyoto of this dedicated approach to the beautification of every packaged object. This is in part because Kyoto was for almost a thousand years the political and cultural centre of Japan, and as such gave its name to a particular style of Japanese packaging: kyofu (that is, Kyoto style).

In the Western world, where society's philosophical approach to nature is one of conflict more than harmony, the earliest forms of packaging were, if not similarly natural, then similarly utilitarian. They probably began with the humble paper bag. Then, because some forms of dry goods, like flour and talcum powder, are physically alike, those paper bags became first more informative, later more decorative, and finally more concerned with advertising the product's excellence or value.

With the advent of mass-production techniques in almost every walk of life, the business of packaging became more sophisticated, for not only were products coming off production lines more rapidly, but packaging

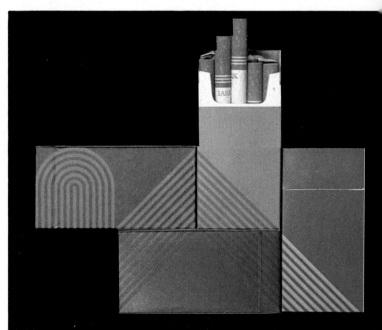

Even with the heavy consumption of cigarettes and tobacco it is difficult to establish, as it is with other products, how much a label or a wrapping influences sales, but one thing is certain: the smoker grows attached to the picture of the product he considers is to his taste, and makes it a statement of personal style.
Above left: A box of Egyptian tobacco in which the characteristic Egyptian look has been retained.
Above, centre and right: A Swiss cigar box in a nineteenth-century style.

Centre left: The packet of a refined Russian product, which even today retains a marked 1930s flavour.
Left: Two examples of original and revamped packaging for a Japanese brand of cigarettes; the exotic birds, which in the 1920s packet represented tobacco-producing countries, are in the modern version transformed into a single dove, the symbol of peace, more in keeping with the name of the product. Graphic interpretation by Raymond Loewy.
Above: Packaging for an American brand of cigarettes that relies on graphic and geometric patterns in a series of compositional and chromatic variations, thus avoiding more traditional pictures of labelling. By George Tscherney.

Above: The characteristic style of French poster design of the 1930s—a cross between neometaphysics and art deco— is presented on the Gitanes box, still in its original design by M. Ponty.

Above right: Modern packaging for a Greek brand of cigarettes that evokes the ancient wonders of Hellas, translated here in black and gold into a *Pierrot Lunaire* stage set.

Left and bottom, clockwise: The somewhat spontaneous metamorphosis that took place over the years in the packaging of a famous American brand of cigarettes: the printed tin of tobacco from the early 1900s; a Christmas gift box from the 1930s on which the Lucky Strike logo, still used today, is prominent; the modern version, in which extraneous decoration has been obliterated and the label translated into an imprint.

Packaging of Boxes

Top: A series of wrapped goods packaged in a geometric design that develops into a series of compositions when the pieces are brought together. By Yoshimasa Kawakami and Akemi Kajima.
Above: Printed prism cardboard wrapping for a French iron.
Left, above and below: Two examples of a kind of packaging, made of double, decorated cardboard, in which the receptacle has a purely ornamental function and becomes desirable for itself as well as for the product it contains. By Katsu Kimura.

Containers for Objects

Very often the characterizing element in the industrial wrapping of an object is the portrayal of the object itself on the exterior of the box, using more or less traditional techniques of reproduction. *Below:* Two boxes containing household accessories, created for a company in Finland.

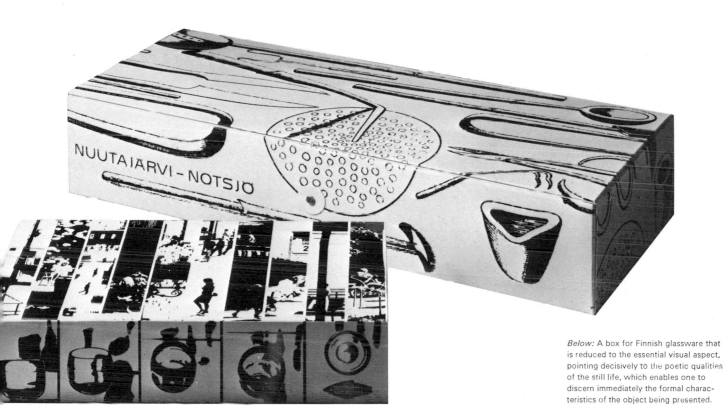

Below: A box for Finnish glassware that is reduced to the essential visual aspect, pointing decisively to the poetic qualities of the still life, which enables one to discern immediately the formal characteristics of the object being presented.

machinery had improved, too. It began to be possible to produce new shapes, with endless variations, in huge quantities.

With this proliferation of products and their packs came a certain amount of confusing similarity of design. The demise of the human touch in both production and packaging had created a feeling of distance between producer and consumer, a polarization of the relationship between those who manufactured goods and those who used them.

Into this environment was born the contemporary packaging designer, a specialist so skilled in the language of visual communication that he could alter the personality of a mass-produced product to give it the feel and look of human touch and proportions, or who could, under other circumstances, take a handmade product and, with the aid of mechanical packaging techniques and equipment, change its surface identity so that it had, to the unwary or untutored, the look and feel of a product produced in huge quantities.

And this is the function of contemporary packaging design: it is concerned with telling the customer something about the product—something about its background, its use, and its value—and it is equally concerned with selling that product.

KIPPO on kulho herkkusuille. Siitä maistuvat jäätelö ja jälkiruuat, karamellit, pähkinät. Kekkereihin Kekkerit.

Kekkerit, dessertskål för finsmakare till nötter, karameller, glass och efterrätter.

Kekkerit means 'party', and these bowls make ideal party pieces filled with ice cream, fruit, dessert or nuts.

Schale Kekkerit für Eis, Dessert, Konfekt und Blumen.

Kekkerit i

But how does the designer go about his job? How is he to achieve his objectives? And what are the pitfalls involved?

Much like a beauty consultant, the package designer has one function to fulfill: he must make the product as attractive as possible. The beautician, by the careful application of lipstick, eyeshadow, toner, and mascara, can make the plainest of women more attractive; but, like the package designer, he can overdo it, transforming a face into a mask, a personality into a caricature.

On another level, the designer must dress the product in an informative way, giving the consumer as much information as is necessary to evaluate the product's worth at the time of purchase rather than at the time of use, when it may be too late to do anything about

wasted time and money spent in buying the product in the first place. And in concerning himself with the surface design of an individual pack, the designer must take into account how its overall identity is to fit in with the corporate image of the manufacturer or retailer, if the product is one of a range.

Let us consider a few examples of contemporary packaging in Britain with an eye to how the designer solved the problems with which he was set: the identity of the product, its value to the consumer, and its attractiveness or visual appeal as a pack that will have to fight for attention on the crowded shelves of a department store or supermarket.

Sainsburys is one of Britain's largest retail grocery chains. Its slogans "Where good food costs less" and "Where good food sells fast" reflect its attitude

Below: A powerful graphic design was devised for this slipcase containing folders for loose-leaf material. By Hans Peter Weiblen.

Right: This box with a handle was made to present and sell this Japanese television set, the packaging being illustrated by a series of pictures inspired by television programmes. By Minoru Honda.

Left: Box for a cut-glass dish; visual information on uses for the plate is given inside the flap. Sweden.

Opposite: A curious wood package, like those normally used to preserve cheeses, for a set of plates. The graphics on the label and on the plates themselves are of the same design, one inspired by botanical illustrations of the nineteenth century.

Below: Toy box. The large letters and vivid colouring identify for the child the product intended for him. By Clement Meadmore.

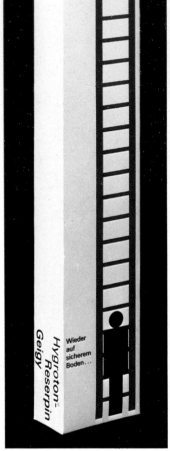

Above: The structure of a box designed for a traditional oriental product, sake. By Yuji Sato and Kumiko Yokoyama.
Above right: Medicine packet designed for the Swiss firm Geigy. By Max Schmid and August Maurer. In the field of pharmaceutical packaging, the Swiss graphic school has in the postwar years established a style that has become a model for many other nations.
Below: Chewing-gum packets designed in Japan in recent years.

Below: Some medicines for the various forms of arthritis, packaged for the American branch of Geigy. A technique reminiscent of radiography is employed onto which the graphic element is superimposed to emphasize that part of the body for which the treatment is intended. Art direction by Fred Troller; design by Markus Low.

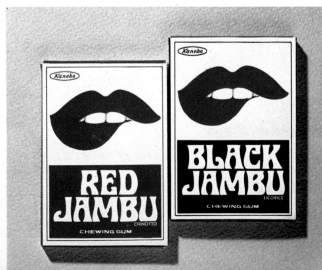

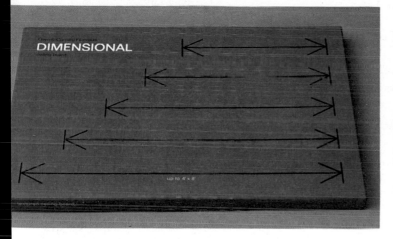

Above left: A box achieved by means of a graphic pattern for the Owens-Corning Fiberglas Corporation. By George Tscherney.

Above: Packages for tablecloths, created exclusively around the design of the product's name with a highly sophisticated lettering that is not easy to read, but is graphically very effective. By Walter Landor Associates, a group of graphic designers specializing in corporate identity.

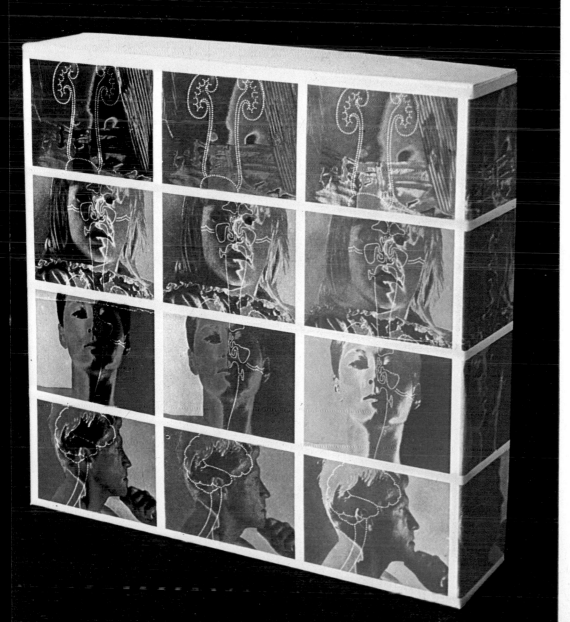

Left: On this packet of medicines various ailments are visualized through an elegant photographic composition and emphasized by the superimposition of a graphic relief. By Frank Wagner.

The Bottle

Above, left to right: A bottle of Riesling wine with the traditional long neck—label by Walter Landor Associates, 1958; French red wine in one of its classic bottle shapes—label by Chermayeff & Geismar Associates; a bottle of Brazilian wine, protected by a traditional multi-coloured straw covering; a flask of Madeira with a basket covering that not only protects the wine from light but functions as decorative packaging as well.

Left: A bottle for a Swiss fruit liqueur with a somewhat affected shape but one that is undoubtedly functional.
Right: One of the beautiful nineteenth-century engraved bottles, used for bitters; even the label, which reveals the printing taste of the end of the century, is perfectly in harmony with the design of the bottle.

toward the customer: it is dedicated to providing high quality at a sensible price. Of Britain's grocery businesses, it was among the first to introduce the "own label" approach to retailing, either producing its own or buying processed foods from other producers and packaging them in a uniform house style. In a retail business where keeping costs down is an article of faith, the designer has to work within strict budgetary limits. He cannot afford richly decorated packs, which are expensive to produce. So, when Sainsburys first designed a consistent style for its own-label products, it was intentionally clinical. This was to distinguish it from the hodgepodge of colour and nondesign then common on supermarket shelves. But it was also designed to reflect the competitive pricing of the business; Sainsburys' own-label items have always been a few pence cheaper than the equivalent brand products. In recent years Sainsburys' packaging has become less austere, a little more colourful than it used to be. Nevertheless, Sainsburys still stands by its original approach to the problem—and its original attitude toward the consumer—and believes that the elimination of everything but essential information reflects the honest, value-for-money philosophy of the company. Certainly in the company's own estimation, about 15 percent of the attraction of Sainsburys as a place to shop is believed to come from the clarity of its packaging.

Sainsburys' approach to its own particular problem has been echoed by many other grocery businesses. Another British chain—International Stores—recog-

The Refined World of Perfume

Above and opposite left: A Russian perfume inserted into an ovoid-shaped box clearly inspired by the precious jewels created by Carl Fabergé for the last czars.
Below: Another irrational object that could be part of a kitsch review is this eau-de-cologne dispenser for men designed in the United States.

Above: A range of cosmetic products designed for Biba of London. By John McConnell.

Below: A package for an eau de cologne, achieved with the photomontage technique. By Sioma Schönhaus.

Right: Two perfume bottles designed in France between 1910 and 1920 that herald the art deco taste to be in vogue some years later.

Above: A modern container for a cosmetic product clearly showing the contrast between an industrial material not yet fully assimilated by contemporary culture, such as plastic, and a strict formal design as required by the better trends of the modern package. By Marco del Corno.

Right: Several ranges of cosmetic containers, all of them with a spherical shape of more or less phallic connotations, designed by graphic designers from various parts of the world. Range on top left by Murray Jacobs, Cay Gibson, Wayne Stettler, and John Alcorn; that on top right by André Courrèges; the one bottom right by Shunsaku Sugiura and Masaki Matsubara.

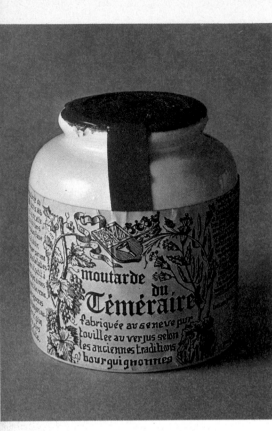

Jars and Tins

Above left: An earthenware jar for French mustard, still packaged according to tradition and with a label that is meant to state its artisan manufacture.

Above centre: Ordinary airtight tin for an extra-strong tomato concentrate produced in Italy.

Above right: A glass jar for Indian-produced chutney revealing the influence of a traditional English culture, inherited during the lengthy colonial period.

Below and opposite left: These French tins of paint were designed in such a way as to allow for the visualization of a pleasing, continuous pattern when the tins are stacked together. By Jean-Philippe Lenclos.

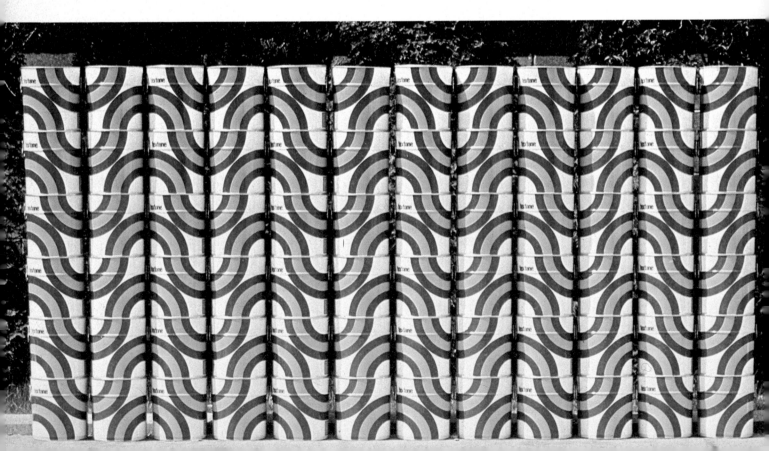

Right: A Hong Kong-produced peanut oil comes in tins that have the formal appearance of industrial containers, scarcely appropriate for domestic use. Graphics by Henry Steiner.

Right: Tins of herring appearing to show their contents through a transparent panel on the front, an effect created by a photographic still life. By Jacques Richez.

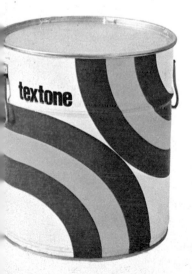

The Shopping Bag

Right: A shopping bag created for a promotional campaign in Milan; the graphic motif's main feature is the X of Arflex. By Giancarlo Iliprandi.

Far right: The bag given away to the customer who buys a particular make of jeans features the motif devised for the entire publicity campaign. By Ida van Bladel.

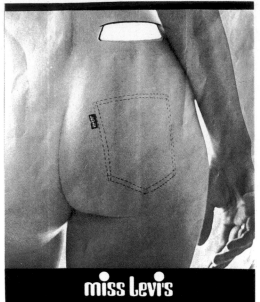

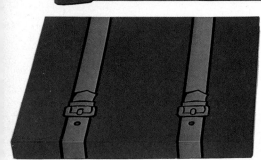

Above: A sophisticated range of paper bags to contain fashion articles. The bags are part of a series in the Roberta di Camerino trademark packaging that features a traditional luggage pattern of wrapped belts. Created by Giuliana Coen.

Right: Shopping bags for a Canadian drugstore, created by means of logotype treated in positive and negative. By François Dallegret.

The highly inventive designs of some record sleeves create other problems for the graphic designer, not the least of which are those of an editorial nature, particularly as regards the visualization of the contents.

From left to right, top to bottom: A record by John Lennon and Yoko Ono presented as a newspaper, with references to the songs it contains; a record of music by Stravinsky (art direction by John Berg and Ed Lee; design by Henrietta Condax); a record sleeve in the shape of an envelope, faithfully reproduced and labelled with the musician's name; an RCA record (design by Acy R. Lehman and John Morello; photography by Nick Sangiamo); a double sleeve with a combined flavour of surrealism and pop mixed in with cultural references to ancient Japan (by Tadanori Yokoo).

The Display Rack

Above: A counter display rack for ink bottles. By Seymour Chwast.
Right: A study for shop display racks that are highly colourful and most suited to the product to be displayed, namely, Clarks shoes. By Pentagram of London.
Below: Boxes for teaching aids. By Chermayeff & Geismar Associates.

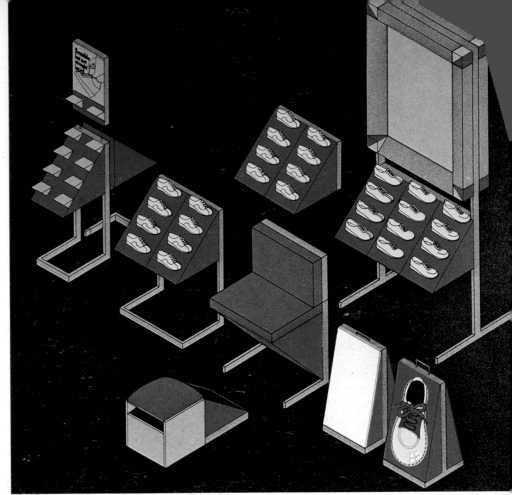

nizing the consumer's search for especially good value for money, has introduced a new line of basic foodstuffs under the banner of Plain & Simple. Here the packaging has been reduced to minimum essentials. No other information is given beyond the contents, weight, and price of the product. To enhance the idea of simplicity, the packages have been designed with a strong typography set in a single colour. As with the Sainsburys exercise, the intention is to demonstrate in a visual and practical way the retailer's concern for the customer's pocketbook without in any way detracting from the essential quality of the products.

Both these examples of grocery products sold in high-volume supermarket outlets demonstrate that a clean, simple approach to packaging can be extremely effective when the products in question are to be sold in an environment that more often that not is cluttered, confusing to the customer, and frequently full of brand goods of every kind, each competing with the others for attention. They show that the cool approach often works.

But not all manufacturers would agree, for not all manufacturers face the same problems. They have one common objective: sales. Their selling environments, however, differ as much as their products.

Windsor & Newton is one of the world's leading suppliers of artists' materials. Their goods are sold through specialist outlets in competition with a limited number of rival products. For many years all their products had been packaged to conform with a corporate image as projected in the letters WN. It is not unkind to say that their packaging was dull, or that for a range of products concerned with the creation of art they were fundamentally drab. The original packaging had been designed at a time when austerity was the overriding mood of the age.

A few years ago Windsor & Newton recognized the need for a radical change of policy. Their products are supported by very little, if any, advertising, and thus the packaging must do all the selling it can if the company is to maintain its position in the market. And that position has become increasingly difficult to maintain as more people have more leisure time to devote to hobbies and handicrafts. So, Windsor & Newton, in collaboration with their design consultants, took a bold step and not only redesigned their package surfaces but, in the case of their drawing inks, completely remodelled the containers. It was thus that a new range of bottles as well as boxes for the bottles was developed.

This project, handled by Michael Peters & Partners, brings us into the area of "added value." Peters recognized the sales task inherent in all packaging and saw that each product should be capable of expressing not only its value as a drawing medium but also its potential as a tool for creativity in the hands of the artist. He understood as well the need for a kind of

package that would catch the artist's eye by reflecting the artist's aspirations as a craftsman. The solution to the problem was expensive—especially so when viewed against the examples quoted earlier. Not only was it proposed that the four-colour printing process be used on the packs but it was also recommended that each bottle of ink be treated as a separate, but linked, item within the total range.

The results were spectacular, both in commercial terms and in terms of pure packaging that was similar to the ideals of the ancient Japanese crafts.

Peters's solution was to create an illustrative framework within which each coloured ink would be boxed. Drawings were commissioned from nearly a dozen illustrators whose style and approach reflected various aspects of commercial and fine arts, with the accent on the former. The subjects used to illustrate each box related to the colour contained within—for example, a stylized sunburst illustration for sunshine-yellow ink, three red-coated militiamen for vermillion, a portrait of Nell Gwynne (King Charles's favourite orange-seller) for orange, and a delightful drawing of two bluebirds for blue. Twenty illustrations in all were commissioned, and what resulted was the creation of a range of inks designed to bring out the hidden promise that lay within each bottle, a promise of a product which, excellent in its own right, would assist the artist in his own search for excellence.

As for the commercial value of this exercise, the sales speak for themselves. Within a year or two of the launch of the newly designed range, sales had increased by 600 percent.

This example of adding value to the product through packaging has been repeated over and over again by many different manufacturers. Windsor & Newton, naturally pleased with the results that packaging obtained for their coloured drawing inks, later extended this approach to include poster colours and acrylic paints. Their poster-colour range now features works by some of the most celebrated commercial artists of this century, each one related to the particular colour and augmented by an entertaining description of the work. Posters by such artists as Henri de Toulouse-Lautrec and John Hassall, and even Joshua Reynold's *Bubbles*, have been modified slightly and featured on the packaging. Alkyd, another company that manufactures artists' materials, has repackaged their line of paints on the theme, again, of added value. Each tube features a pastiche of the works of a famous painter—Pablo Picasso, Lawrence Stephen Lowry, George Stubbs, and René Magritte, for example—whose art is almost instantly recognizable.

More usually, this added-value approach to packaging can be seen in the cosmetic industry. Here the promise of the package must reflect the promise inherent in the product. Cosmetics—with the exception of a very few—are produced with one aim in

The Promotional Package

Above left: The packaging of a portable typewriter, intended to emphasize the suitability of the item as a Christmas gift, with the elegant script and the green and red colours contributing to the psychological suggestion. By Milton Glaser.

Above: The design for this Italian fountain pen is consistent throughout, even including a cylindrical metal container for refills. By Marco Zanuso and Richard Sapper.

Far left: Original packaging devised in France for a set of fondue cutlery that allows the pieces to be stored after use with a minimum of clutter and a great deal of sense.

Left: Two promotional wooden boxes, created by a French china firm for egg-cup sets.

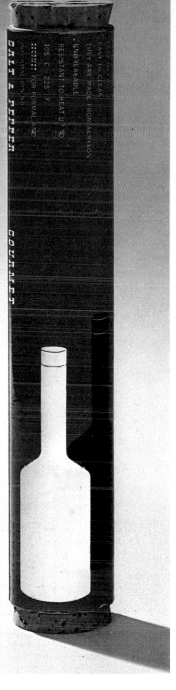

Right: A complex package of printed cardboard created with three prisms that combine to form a hexagon in their wrapped appearance and serve as holders when the product is being used. The packaging is thus an integral part of the object as it constitutes the base for an educational chemistry set. By Ryoichi Yamamoto, Yoshio Wakui, and Tateaki Kiriu.

Above: Salt and pepper set, made from acrylic material, is packaged in a single vertical tube; both the packaging and the product are Danish. Since World War II, strong industrial activity has flourished in Denmark, chiefly in the fields of glass, china, and wood objects for household use, together with serious and deep research into the fields of product, package, and graphic design.

mind: to beautify the consumer and in so doing increase her—or his—attractiveness to the opposite sex. Thus, to offer the promise of greater appeal, the package must speak to the consumer in just such terms, and it must suggest that that promise will be fulfilled. The package must not, however, become more beautiful than that promise, nor must it step outside the boundaries of the market in which it will be sold.

Take, for example, the packaging for Chanel No. 5, or that for Christian Dior's Diorissimo line of toiletries. Both these packaging programmes have a timeless quality about them that suggests itself well to women who may take little or no interest in the ephemera of day-to-day fashion but who rather see themselves as part of an ageless, near-indestructible section of a society that has for centuries led the world in taste and refinement. The clean, uncluttered surface of the Chanel line, with its simple, classically proportioned typography, is well matched against the Dior range, which, though a little more fussy, retains the basic elements of simplicity.

Not all cosmetics packaging can be judged in this way. But neither are all cosmetics sold in such an elitist section of the market. Many are aimed at younger women, and some at teenagers. Again, the packaging design and concept must reflect the promise of the product as well as the lifestyle of the consumer. Staid, timeless design will have no great appeal to the young woman whose life is one long round of disco parties, dinners for two, and nights on the town, any more than the same classic approach is likely to work on the woman who likes to spend her weekends on a country ramble, or sitting by the fire making macrame jewelry.

The message here is that added value must have relevant value. The package design must relate not only to the product itself, but also to the market into which that product will be sold. The designer must be as aware of this as he is of the practical considerations of his craft and his client's needs.

On the practical front there are those who will argue that today's shops are too full of overpackaged goods. True, the elderly and arthritic face far greater difficulties than many manufacturers realize. Yet, as with many aspects of contemporary society, they simply cannot be allowed to influence production, if only because the economies of scale will not permit it. Here it can be in the hands of the designer to alter the consumer's perception of the product. Careful attention to the details of package construction can, in some cases, override prejudices which may exist against the product. And a good designer can achieve some degree of positive response to a product through his interpretation of the way in which people see the product and the way in which it might or could be seen.

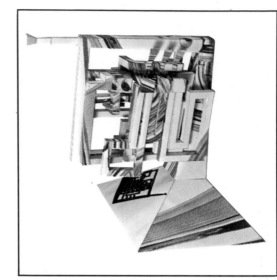

Above and right: The transformation of an object into a portrayal on a flat sheet of paper, with the possibility of the object's returning to its three-dimensional origins —albeit in approximate form—can open up extraordinary possibilities for graphic design. Here, printed on a sheet of paper, in superimposition and with no structural relation to each other, are a horn and an outline in fifty-seven parts, all to be cut out and pasted together. By Shigeo Fukuda.

This, too, is connected with the concept of added value. And perhaps it can work for the elderly, just as it works for children, who, more often than not, will keep an attractive box long after the toy it held has been outworn or broken.

The ultimate expression of added value remains, however, in the hands of the retailer—and, in a sense, in the hands of his customer. Nowhere is this more apparent than on the shopping streets of the world's capital cities. Here one may see shopping bags of every colour, shape, and size. Some are well designed, others are not. Most reflect the standing of the store and, in many cases, act as a status symbol for the customer.

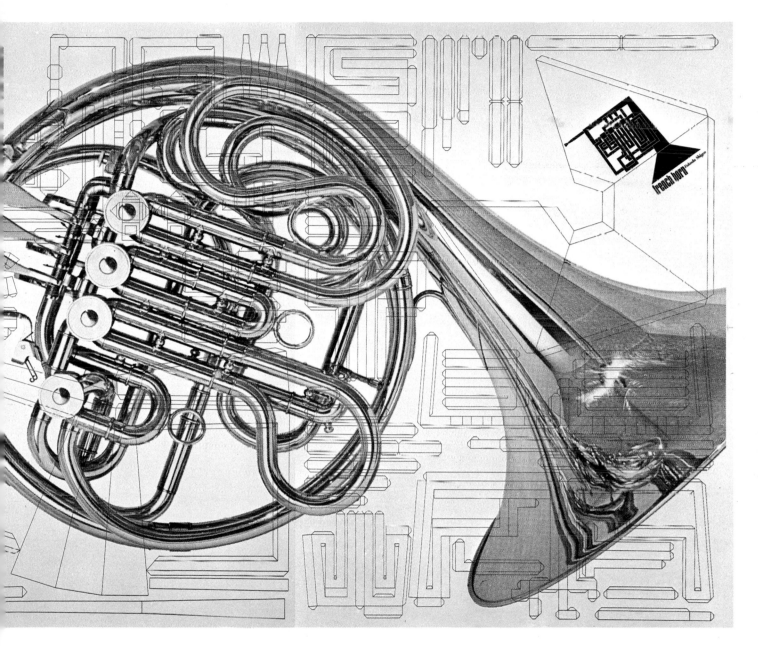

In London, Harrods still rises well above every other department store in the city as being *the* place to shop. For those who visit the store regularly there is nothing unusual about owning one of their shopping bags. But for the thousands of tourists who visit London, and for the equally numerous British who may make only one or two trips to London during the course of a year—or even a lifetime—a Harrods bag spells out a sophistication of taste that is also reflected in the store's apt slogan "Enter a different world." On a lighter note, Fenwicks of Bond Street wraps all their customers' purchases in paper or bags bearing the message "Carried away at Fenwicks," a clever phrase implying

that not only has the shopper bought something in the store, but because of the Aladdin's-cave style of the store's interior, he or she has been unable to resist the temptations on offer.

Beyond adding value to a product, effective packaging can change the consumer's perception of that product. In his recently published book Wally Olins, a partner in the British design-consultant firm of Wolff Olins, discusses this aspect of packaging in some detail, illustrating his argument with an example worked up by Michael Wolff.

Wolff's idea was to take two dissimilar products and exchange their packaging concepts. The two products

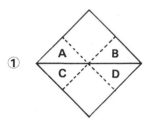

①

②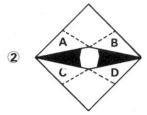

③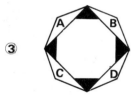

Origami and Other Folds

Origami is an ancient art very popular in the traditional Japanese world. Practised mainly by women and children at home, it is a pastime in which shapes are created by folding and re-folding coloured pieces of paper. In the hands of an artist these folded pieces of paper can become highly individual objects.

Right and centre: A strip of patterned cardboard, correctly manipulated, assumes shape as a solid object with spatial variations. By Wallace Walker.

④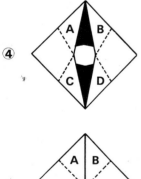

⑤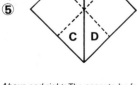

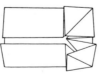

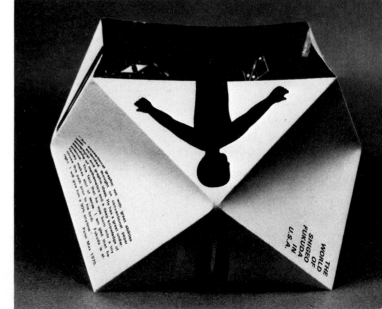

Above and right: The paper to be folded provides illustrations printed on a flat surface with three-dimensional movements. The encounter between contemporary graphics and origami forms the basis of these objects. Graphic design by Shigeo Fukuda.

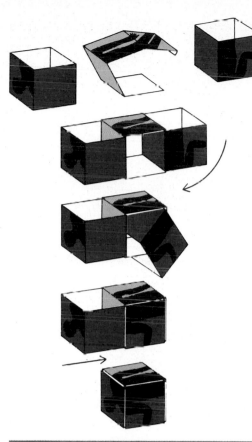

Above and below: Examples of puzzles based on a structure of small cardboard cubes linked together in threes, allowing for numerous figurative combinations. The picture can develop lengthwise or can concentrate itself on the normal six-sided cube. By Shigeo Fukuda.

**The Product Assumes
an Identity**

To make a product more popular and
desirable, particularly if it is intended for
children, advertising often invests it with
an identity as symbolized by an imaginary
character. This leads to anthropomorphic
packages and personified boxes.

Below left: A can of foam in the shape
of an aggressive-looking toy figure. By
Shulton's Art Department.
Below right: The figure of an inebriated
old gentleman constitutes the packaging
for a wine sold in the United States.

used were Chivas Regal, a twelve-year-old Scotch,
and Nobrium, a tranquilizing drug. Chivas Regal, in its
recognizable bottle and with its rightful labelling, can
easily be seen to be a whisky of some distinction, an
expensive Scotch bought by those who can discern,
and appreciate, the differences between brands of
spirits as well as types. The rich golds and browns of
the label reflect the rich, golden flavour of the drink.
The drug, on the other hand, is labelled in the simplest
of styles. The typography is no more than neat, with the
number of colours—and their tonal values—reduced
to a minimum. The effect is, appropriately, clinical.
With some minor alterations made in the style and
content of each label Wolff demonstrated how our
view of each product would be changed if the labels
were transposed. Chivas Regal became, instantly, a
cheap-looking drink—in fact, it could have even passed

for a disinfectant. Nobrium, on the other hand, though
still in the correctly shaped druggist's jar, took on the
appearance of an exotic condiment, an oriental spice
or seasoning, or even some sort of succulent sweetmeat.
And this transformation occurred despite the introduction
of a product description that read: "The tranquillizer
for active patients."

One fundamental principle of packaging design is
emphatically illustrated by this single example, which
is that much of the way in which a product is perceived
by the consumer is influenced by the atmosphere
surrounding it, by the ambience given it by its
packaging.

Consider another example—the elaborate packaging
of Havana cigars. The decorated wooden box, the
layers of thin paper, the band around the cigar, and the
complications involved in opening the box in the first
place all add to the feeling of luxury and connoisseur-
ship associated with Havana cigars. Yet how much of
this feeling would there be if those same cigars were
shrink-wrapped in plastic and sold from a dispenser
beside peppermints, chewing gum, or packets of safety
pins? It is the packaging, then, that defines the product
and creates its aura. It even, in the case of the
Havana cigar, suggests its aroma.

Colour, too, is important in packaging, just as it is
in many other areas of applied art. There are people
who would not have their bathroom painted blue
on the contention that blue is a cold colour and reflects
nothing of the luxurious feelings associated with the
relaxing qualities of a hot, perfumed bath. Similarly,
because metallic colours bear no relation to the colours
of nature few would consider buying green peas that
were wrapped in gunmetal-blue paper. And who would
be attracted to a package of soap that was decorated
with pictures or symbols rendered in grimy colours?
Certainly the soap will be used to cleanse away grime,
but in our mind's eye we want to see the results, not
the "before" aspect of the before-and-after argument.

Colour plays a part on a national level, too. In some
parts of the world—most notably in those with a trop-
ical climate—bright, almost harsh colours are part of
the environment. In the Caribbean islands, the
bougainvillea and poinsettia blaze from the under-
growth, their vibrant presence screaming against a
background of rich, dark greens and browns. In Europe
the tonal values in nature are less abrasive, more
muted. Thus, for those living in these differing environments there are different levels of perception connected
with each of the everyday colours of life. And so, in
an age when some brand goods are marketed on a
multinational basis, the packaging designer must be
aware of ethnic reactions to various colour values and
their understood meaning within different national
groups.

Crazy Foam
the toy that cleans

Right and below: Animated packages containing sweets. Designed for the enjoyment of younger children, such items are deliberately directed toward play and consumption.

Right: Another packet of sweets, in the shape of a clown whose large shoes act as rockers. Sometimes the two-dimensionality of the paper makes it possible to create objects that do not have the same logic as a normal dimensional structure.

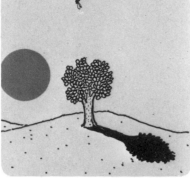

Instructional Games

Opposite above: The green apple tree
turns gradually to red; the sun rising in
the east sets in the west, projecting a
shadow which is always different. These
cards show eight views of an environment that changes with the passing of
hours (the sequence is to be seen in a
clockwise direction). The games have
an educative function: they favour
observation in younger children, and emphasize a sense of logic—if they were not
put in the correct order, absurd effects
would be created. By Bruno Munari.
Opposite below: Cut-out paper animals
that with a few perpendicular elements are
ready to fly, as though they were all
birds or aeroplanes; that a zebra or a
hippopotamus can be made to fly
stimulates a child creatively. By Shigeo
Fukuda.
Above and right: Silk-screened images on
cardboard squares portray a fantastic
forest to be shuffled freely among itself in
order to achieve different backgrounds
that suggest new stories. By Enzo Mari.

But what of packaging design in the future? How will it develop? What new problems will be faced by the designer? And how, once the problems are recognized, will he deal with them?

One aspect of life in the latter half of the twentieth century is becoming increasingly felt in the world of packaging design: man's greatly expanded ability to travel at will from one side of the globe to the other, from east to west or north to south. And this mobility is no longer the prerogative of the cultured few. Indeed, many of the world's most mobile peoples are migrant workers or refugees. Few have a common language. Fewer still have the educational background needed to interpret signs and slogans, messages and information, as relayed in an alien tongue. Yet these people need—and must have—information. They must have directions, instructions, and facts if they are to understand anything of the new society they have entered, no matter how temporary their stay may be.

Designers have, in recent years, recognized this situation. Their work can be seen in railway stations, in airport terminals, and on cartons containing goods for shipment abroad. Simple signs have been developed to indicate direction, to warn of hazards, and to inform travellers where they can change their money or find the lavatory.

The most serious area where the language of visual communication can be expressed to good effect is in the medical world. The misuse of common drugs is one of the frequent causes of accidental death. Often it is a case of misunderstanding in which the patient—a foreigner in an alien country, perhaps—simply was not clear about the drug's use, or was ignorant of which pills to take or how many or how often. Here designers can, and should, be involved in interpreting instructions in a way that makes them clear, concise, and understandable.

One such designer, Michael Peters, has developed a system he calls "logoptics." Like all good ideas, it is a simple solution to a difficult problem. And it is likely to have an important effect on packaging, not only in the medical world but in all areas where potentially hazardous products are marketed on a global scale.

Logoptics employs a series of graphic symbols and time scales to display information that covers the way in which drugs should be taken and how often they are to be used. For example, a cough medicine would bear a label illustrated with a spoon and a head, which is a clear indication as to how the drug should be administered. The accompanying time scale allows the druggist to indicate the measure and frequency of the dosage; one teaspoonful three times a day, for example. Other examples include eye drops, and tablets or capsules that are to be taken with meals or in water. Again, the time scale indicates the frequency of administration.

Peters has already extended this logoptic scheme to include other areas where products are likely to be used by immigrants or the illiterate. Other design groups have applied similar techniques with the use of symbols to indicate storage times for various refrigerated products.

The basic idea is not entirely new. Step-by-step illustration has been included on convenience food packs for some time. And the use of stylized symbols for "This way up" and "Handle with care" goes even further back in the world of international freight and shipping.

But Peters's work with pharmaceutical products may well presage a fundamental change in the principles of packaging design. We may yet see a time when the barriers of verbal communication are broken down completely, a time when symbols and diagrams will tell us all we need to know about a product, its use, its value, and what we may expect to gain from its purchase. Will we then be able to love the product as its label? In this century it is unlikely. Verbal language still serves an important function in the composition of our national identities. It still plays a part in subdividing those identities and in creating ethnic groups on both a national and an international level. And there is still a fascination with the form and structure of a foreign tongue, its letter shapes and accents, which is unlikely to be completely broken down in the application of packaging design, which uses the language of visual communication to do all the work thus far handled by both pictures and words.

In this respect alone, package design is the same art and craft today as it was so long ago in the hands of the earliest Japanese practitioners. And it is likely to continue as such, as a craft which, handled by a sensitive, intelligent designer, can express as much—or as little—of the true nature of a product as is required. And one which, practised with love and care, will produce a sincere yes in response to the proposition "Love my label like myself."

Right: A construction with corrugated cardboard walls, "The Play Place" can be put together to make screens, houses, little forts, and other places of children's fantasies, creating a space in which to play games. By Enzo Mari.

Below: Simulated animal skins in paper which stimulate children to make up new games; the style of portrayal of the animals is very free and in it prevails a sense of graphic decorativeness. By Fredun Shapur.

Graphic Clothing

Printed clothing fabrics are by no means a novelty, but the investigations of graphic art have shown that, even in this field, there is a different way of looking at things.

Left: A scarf with a vivid graphic pattern. By Isao Iwasaki.

Right: A one-piece dress, printed as though it were made up of a skirt and a sweater tied with a belt. It is this last feature that, being so out of proportion and charged with an ironic meaning, gives the game away. By Giuliana Coen for Roberta di Camerino.

Right: Designed for the waitresses at New York's Yankee Stadium, this uniform with printed decorative writing doubles as a restaurant menu. By Jun Kanai.

Far right: The traditional kimono is possibly the earliest historical garment to be conceived of as a graphic concept.

Below left: Three examples of ties printed with graphic patterns that have no analogy in ordinary silk designs. By Isao Iwasaki.

Below right: Graphic designs on canvas. When the umbrella is opened and looked at from the inside, it appears that a piece of cloth is gathered up, while on the exterior everything seems held together by a large belt. By Giuliana Coen for Roberta di Camerino.

The Furnishing Object

Above left: The life-size figure of a woman sitting on a cushion is reproduced as a printed fabric cushion; the cushion's stuffing modifies the flat aspect of the photograph, creating in it a marked three-dimensional effect. By Yu Shinoda.

Above right: A plastic tray. By Tadanori Yokoo, who created many such graphic objects.

Left: A sculpture table created in primary colours and black, in a geometric and balanced colour partition of the surfaces. By Hiroshi Awatsji.

Opposite above: The coffee cup with musical notes and the accompanying record-shaped saucer were created in the wake of American pop art, as part of a trend of artistic inventions that were sometimes turned into gadgets. By Shigeo Fukuda.

Opposite, below left: Plates with surrealist designs. By Piero Fornasetti, a singular artist who for some decades—and outside of any particular fashion trend—has developed his own highly individual language through the use of conventional materials like china, and on sets of items for household use.

Above and below: More examples of portrayal, applied here to ordinary decoration on the edges of coffee china. By Shigeo Fukuda.

6. THE ENVIRONMENT AND GRAPHIC ART

> The purest and most thoughtful minds
> are those which love colour most.
> JOHN RUSKIN

The modern movement in architecture was born after a number of social, technical, and economic factors happened to coincide in about 1925. The fundamental tenet of its philosophy was that art could contribute to social change. This conviction was based on such ideas as "form follows function," Adolf Loo's belief that "we have outgrown ornament," and Ludwig Mies van der Rohe's "less is more"; extended by Le Corbusier's view "architecture would transcend even politics—architecture or revolution"; and influenced by the Russian constructivists, the Bauhaus designers, the dadaists, and the surrealists. Not for nothing is the modern movement also well known as the international style, a designation coined by one of its main exponents, Philip Johnson. Its influence can be seen in all parts of the globe—a tribute to the success of this style.

The enormous expansion of our cities as a result of the continuous influx of people, combined with the potential of modern building technology, made the modern movement in architecture irresistible. Its constructional logic and natural austerity satisfied an increasing pressure to build, and appeared as a solution to wipe out slums and create a new world for millions of people.

The earliest signs of this architecture appear with a series of reformist movements in the nineteenth century. These began with John Ruskin's writings on aesthetics and received a great boost when William Morris advocated honesty of material, the value of hard work, and the joy of craftsmanship as a process for releasing individual creativity and also promoting spiritual maturity. Ideas like these were in conflict with the industrial system and were partially abandoned by Morris's successors. C. R. Ashbee, W. R. Lethaby, and Walter Gropius came to accept the inevitability of machine production.

The style of the twentieth century, dominated as it has been by industrial interests and government bureaucracy, has obviously altered our cities and landscapes. As Ruskin predicted, the adoption of a machine aesthetic has led to an acceptance of both the imperatives of the production process and the economic priorities guiding industry. Functionalism, which has become the most important consideration, accurately reflects industry's concern with the organization of large quantities and an ascetic attitude toward luxurious details.

Architecture is the sociological art; paintings or sculptures are looked at, but people live and work in a building. Architecture, because it is so expensive, is one of the slowest art forms to change—ironic, because it is also the most immediately visual of all the arts. Buildings can be seen to shape the environment, while paintings and murals adorn it. This means that although architectural changes occur less frequently than those in the graphic arts, they are more immediately noticeable.

In the United States a new wave of architecture has developed over the last ten years—postmodernism. This movement has neither a common style nor a unity of ideology comparable to that of the Bauhaus. In his book *The Language of Modern Architecture* the English critic Charles Jencks wrote that "any building with funny kinks in it or sensuous imagery" has been labelled postmodern. This movement shares with architecture only a fascination with architectural linguistics—ironic allusions to the history of architectural styles which approach unwitting parody. Another verdict on recent building styles was passed by Peter Blake in his *Form Follows Fiasco*: "After a run of a hundred years or so Modern Dogma is worn out. We are now close to the end of one epoch and well before the start of a new one. During this period of transition, there will be no moratorium on building . . . there will just be more and more architecture without architects." This can be seen today not only in the United States but also in Europe, the Middle East, Africa, and Japan. Private dwellings and office blocks are designed with economy, not creative imagination, in mind.

The controversial design for the American Telephone and Telegraph (AT&T) headquarters in New York City (as yet unbuilt) by Philip Johnson has caused much comment. Paul Goldberger of *The New York Times* described it as "the most provocative and daring skyscraper proposed for New York since the Chrysler Building." *The Village Voice* called it "the architecture of appliqué . . . the Seagram Building with ears." Today there is no real avant-garde, and the ideas related to the modern movement—which no longer exists—have become historical notes for students.

The interior of an apartment where graphics form an integral part of the fittings. The alternations and successions—of walls, strips of colour, and triangles—in some cases break and in others enhance the natural harmony of the architectural structure. Design by William Tapley.

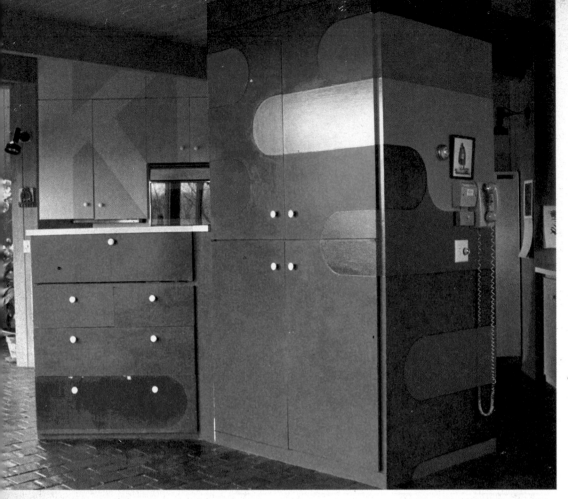

Superdecor for the Home

Shown on these pages are a few examples of the intervention of graphics in furnishing, the fruit of research developed by Charles W. Moore together with some of his students. Moore believes that the use of graphics must be handled not just in a purely decorative sense but also in an ideological sense, and that this same standard be applied to all other household objects.

Left: The interior of the Klotz residence, in Westerly, Rhode Island, 1970. Graphics by Charles W. Moore and William H. Grover.
Opposite: Interior of the holiday complex Sea Ranch Condominium in Sonoma County, California, designed between 1965 and 1969 by Charles W. Moore with the collaboration of Lyndon, Turnbull, Whitaker. Graphics by Barbara Stauffacher.

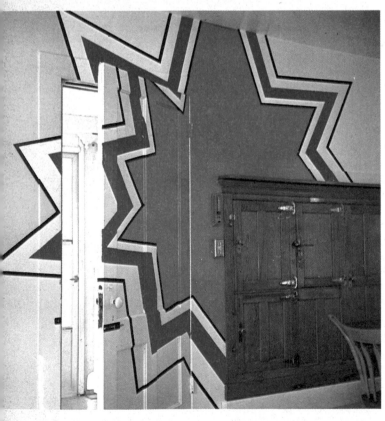

Above: The Grover residence, in Essex, Connecticut.

Right: The Murray residence, in Cambridge, Massachusetts, 1972. Graphics by Charles W. Moore and Mary Ann Rumney.

Please
do not
wear
street shoes
above the
ground
floor.

Left: The walls of a Tokyo office. The coloured stripes, equidistant from each other and turning occasionally into semicircles, contribute, albeit with a two-dimensional optical effect, to changing the banal plan of the place. By Takao Doi.

Interior designers today must also be sociologists and environmentalists. One of the problems confronting the designer is the steady increase in the population's mobility. As air transport becomes faster and more and more people spend a greater amount of time travelling or waiting in airport terminals, these public areas become like a home for many people since so much time is spent in them.

A certain kind of interior design, then, has become ubiquitous, and it is connected with this particular lifestyle. There is little difference between one airport and its surroundings and another; aircraft interiors are virtually indistinguishable from each other and the food that is served in them also looks the same. This lack of variety extends to many hotels in almost every major city one cares to visit—identical decor and similar menus tend to be the rule rather than the exception. Huge chain enterprises like the Hilton Hotels or McDonald's are found on every continent. Even office blocks and interiors show this same lack of imagination. It is possible to travel around the world and feel that one has been nowhere, since the environment rarely changes. Marshall McLuhan's "global village" is close to being realized in this general loss of national identity. Even the clothing worn in public places accents uniformity. Prestigious labels—such as Gucci—for dress and travelling bags are internationally recognizable.

The desire of manufacturers to inform the public of their products has led to the development of exterior advertising. From the middle of the Libyan desert to every city centre, signs such as those for Coca-Cola have become part of the landscape. The history of murals to date must consider the role that posters, billboards, and shop fronts have played in developing as mediums for advertising, which currently uses neon lighting and lasers to emphasize its message.

The development of the railways in the nineteenth century and the adoption of the car in the twentieth encouraged manufacturers to spread their signs not only in the cities but also, for the first time, over the countryside in the hopes of reaching the growing number of travellers and with an eye to the opportunities that an increasing consumer orientation lent itself to. In many areas of the world these advertisements may be judged as eyesores, but they are, nevertheless, part of the landscape. They have even been the subject of a pop song by Bob Dylan: "Advertising signs, they con you into thinkin' you're the one that can do what's never been done, that can win what's never been won, meantime life outside goes on all around you."

The neon sign, however, has developed into a real art form, with work of high quality having already been produced by many creative people. Advertising may therefore be considered in a more positive way, as a gracious kind of urban decoration, especially when it disguises building construction or covers up ugly slum areas. Nevertheless, it is interesting to note that the neon light has the effect of giving all city centres the same look—Tokyo, Paris, London, and New York all use the same means to emphasize or disguise their

Below: The Staff Leuchten factory at Lemgo, West Germany. Not only the wall surfaces but also the doors are painted according to a colour code that indicates the function of each place. Graphics by Gerhard Wollmer.

Above: A highly decorated entrance. By Jean-Philippe Lenclos.

Above: A corridor of the USIS of the American embassy in Tokyo, where graphics have an informative function. The aim of supergraphics, according to Ray Komai, the creator of the project, is to establish an environment of communication, to introduce an atmosphere of surprise into an area that has become too habitual.

Above: Entrance and staircase of the Kyoto American Center. The graphic element introduced is decidedly daring, bearing in mind that this is an official government building, and shows that even an environment serving a sombre function can be made more attractive and less dull. By Ray Komai.

**For the Better Reception
of the Customer**

Above: The Metamorphosis beauty salon, designed by the American architect Alan Buchsbaum. The panels dividing one area from the other are made up of walls moulded into female profiles, like giant mannequins. A strip of deep pink runs along the perimeters of walls and floor, dominating the paler shades and at the same time drawing attention to all the equipment, with a chromatic jerk.

Left: A conference room in Switzerland's Hotel Zürich, with walls devised by Müller-Brockmann & Company. Examples of supergraphics, which are often extemporaneous and ephemeral in relation to other art forms, reveal elements of a detailed study in the creations of Müller-Brockmann. He operates within the sphere of research into the scientific use of colour, which has been carried out for many years, chiefly by Max Bill and Richard P. Lohse.

Below left: A highly original way of indicating the gentlemen's lavatory. By Ray Komai.

Below right: A kiosk created in the interior of a room in the County Federal Savings Bank in Westport, Connecticut. Graphics, which clearly evoke images of the American flag, by Mary Ann Rumney and William H. Grover.

Above: Another wall devised by Josef Müller-Brockmann for a retirement home in Switzerland, a remarkable example of optical art as applied to the environment; an innovative probe into colour use.

Below: A luminous sculpture in a Westport, Connecticut, residence. By the working team of Charles W. Moore, Mary Ann Rumney, William H. Grover, and Peter Soroos.

buildings. A department store like Harrods looks like an amusement arcade or a casino and the monolithic M of McDonald's is seen everywhere. As Theo Crosby says in his book *How to Play the Environment Game,* "At night the electric tubes of neon, argon and xenon discharge their messages in intense pools of light which focus our awareness of a new space and time. But they are no longer illusory worlds which might confuse with our own, but a real addition."

Lasers are one of the most exciting developments of this century. Their importance extends far beyond optical science to many different areas, especially those of art and communication. In July 1960 the American scientist and inventor Theodore H. Maiman first demonstrated the principles of laser, which derives its name from its operating principle: light amplification by stimulated emission of radiation. Ordinary white light, composed of many different colours with varying wavelengths, is "incoherent," whereas the "coherent" light of a laser is much more intense, consisting only of identical waves that produce beams of a regular frequency. There are two main types of lasers: continuous-wave gas lasers and pulsed lasers. Ionized argon (emitting blue and green beams) and ionized krypton-argon (producing all colours of the spectrum) are the most powerful, but the helium neon laser is the most commonly used, as it is the cheapest. None of these continuous-wave gas lasers is as powerful as a pulsed, such as a synthetic ruby laser, but all produce more coherent light and are therefore more versatile.

The potential of laser beams was initially seen only in militaristic terms—like the death ray of science fiction. However, countless applications have been found for laser in the twenty years since its discovery, in fields like missile guidance and satellite communication; as a means for telecommunications over glass-fibre cables or for creating direction-finders like the gyroscope; as drilling tools able to burn through steel or diamonds or weld the retina in the most delicate eye surgery.

Unlike the light from an electric bulb, which spreads out to flood an area with a generally intense level of illumination, light from a laser remains finely concentrated along the entire length of its constantly narrow beam, which appears infinite. The colours depend on which type of laser is used and are, if within the visible part of the spectrum, absolutely brilliant. Commercially used lasers often emit light in the infrared or ultraviolet range, for instance those used by printers in the four-colour separation process for illustrated material.

The development of the laser furthered research into an earlier discovery—the hologram. This is a kind of photographic process for reproducing an object in three-dimensional form. The word "hologram" is a combination from the Greek, meaning complete picture,

A restaurant on top of the World Trade Center in New York. The construction separating each area consists of three-dimensional letters that make up the word "kitchen," providing a visual reference and an amusing game for the customers. Decor by Milton Glaser.

Above: Op art's most authoritative painter, Victor Vasarely, was called upon to design the graphics for the Montparnasse train station, in Paris. He devised the front of the main hall with chromatic and formal elements that tend to emphasize the dynamic quality of the environment.

Left: A two-dimensional sculpture in painted metal, created as a contrast to the rough cement of the place, to give a sense of composition to dead ground; it stands outside a Westport, Connecticut, residence. By Charles W. Moore.

Signboards and Illumination as Advertising

Right: Luminous advertising board in New York City. Electric architecture, which originated with the neon-sign trend of the 1930s, tends to transform the urban layout, superimposing itself onto it until finally the environment takes on a completely altered image during night hours.

Right: The Chinese pagoda in the Tivoli Gardens in Copenhagen, illuminated by night. In amusement parks, such as Disneyland in California, the tendency is to point to the spectacular and exceptional architectural shapes, while relying also on totally falsified perspective visions (as is the case in many gigantic advertising posters), to produce astonishment in the spectator.

and was used by Dennis Gabor for his discovery made in Britain in 1945. His invention was not acknowledged with a Nobel Prize for physics until 1971, since until the advent of the laser no light source had existed that was strong enough to make the hologram viable. In the future, holograms are likely to revolutionize techniques used in films and television. If sets and backcloths were holograms, the camera would not have to remain stationary, as it presently must. Michael York acted inside a hologram of his own head for *Logan's Run*, a movie about life in the twenty-third century.

The laser has been used to add a new dimension to rock-music entertainment, although at present only the more successful groups can afford such expensive equipment. The laser beam can be split to produce a bright shaft of pure colour that gives an almost solid appearance, especially if woven into a pattern with several other beams. The perception of space can be altered by moving such screens of coloured light either horizontally or vertically or both. By placing oscillating mirrors in front of a laser, light sculpture can be projected onto clouds or smoke, and has already been demonstrated at open-air rock concerts. These unique qualities were successfully exploited by pop groups like Paul McCartney and Wings in an event organized in 1976 by John Wolff for UNESCO in aid of the Venice in Peril Fund. The Who were the first group to use laser light for its visual drama; they now own eleven lasers, which they are careful never to

employ for more than a few ninety-second bursts during any one performance in order not to diminish the mysterious and mesmeric effect.

Colloquial or public art can be related to architecture, fine art, sociology, politics, commerce, and town planning. Such art dates back to prehistoric times—to before the written record—as witnessed by the Cerne Abbas hillside giant. Public art can be found in such disparate examples as cave paintings, Greek friezes, medieval churches, and Renaissance frescoes. It originally served a social or religious purpose, as it informs by simple images an often largely illiterate audience.

Within the development of fine art, there has been a move away from easel painting to, as Fernand Léger put it, the "adaptation of colour to architecture." The increase in murals now noted in cities can in part be ascribed to this change in emphasis. Far from the storytelling function of previous large-scale public art, murals became an extension of abstract art. As late as 1954, in *Problèmes de la Couleur*, Léger wrote, "In my opinion, abstract art is perfectly suited for large mural decorations"; and many murals of the 1950s and 1960s were indeed decoration.

For Léger murals were a collaboration between architect and painter in the interest of mutual social goals. In 1902–12 Léger and Robert Delaunay led the "battle for free colour." Colour was regarded as a thing in

itself without being closely tied to the sky, a tree, or a flower. "It has an intrinsic value like a musical symphony," said Léger. For him colour was not structural when used with architecture, but rather like a noble symbolic decoration.

Léger advocated a return to the spirit of the pre-Renaissance in which architecture would be dominated by public buildings but adapted to the main orientations of the twentieth century—a marriage of machinery and urbanization. He was careful to stress that a mural "can either be an accompaniment to the wall or a destruction of the wall." This statement dates from about 1924, when architects freed the wall from its art nouveau decor. Le Corbusier sums up the mood of many architects at the beginning of this century who wished to escape from the earlier decorative styles: "We have also applied a completely new conception of polychromy in pursuit of a purely architectural objective: using the physical quality of the colours . . . just as we had used the architectural forms to shape urban space. This was an attempt to incorporate architecture into town planning." It was also an attempt to incorporate the individual into the collective, an aim that recurs in nearly all public art.

Le Corbusier's approach was paternalistic. "One could build beautifully designed houses, always provided the tenant was prepared to change his outlook," he contended. Much institutionalized public art displays this patronizing attitude. One has only to look at the numerous bureaucratically planned mural decorations to see how uncreative and dull they are.

Opposite: Two nocturnal views of Las Vegas, Nevada. The architecture of Las Vegas is different, born of free combinations of exteriors and interiors, of facades that anticipate surreal buildings—an architecture that peremptorily rejects natural light and that establishes a condition of equal quality between all the ingredients of the buildings.

Right, above and below: Two gigantic signboards advertising hamburgers seen against the Los Angeles sky. Open-air advertising is closely bound up with the problems of urban traffic. The driver's reading speed can become extremely fast with practice and experience, but certain basic standards can never be ignored—hence the need to channel information into a formal simplification of figurative elements. The product is thus presented in a realistic but also idealized way, and it is for the success of the latter that it is remembered.

Graphic Art and Propaganda

Right: A human tapestry forming a portrait of Mao. Seldom in the past has a sportive-gymnastic decoration for propaganda purposes reached such a level of perfection.

Below: A wall in a Chinese factory papered with posters—the voice of the people and the revolution.

Left: Placards in Moscow's Red Square to mark the celebration of the Communist victory. Their large size is proportional to the depth of the available area of the facade.

Right: A gigantic portrait of Fidel Castro dominates the scene of a demonstration in Cuba.

Hoardings

Today paternalism is left over from the functionalism of the modern movement, epitomized in the de Stijl group's philosophy that one serves mankind by enlightening it. As M. Foucault said, "It is useless to try to describe the things that one sees, for visual objects can never be expressed in words." And yet the de Stijl group's concern with purity may be looked at in a different way when we realize that the Dutch word for beautiful, "schoon," is the same as their word for pure. The de Stijl group used primary colours as a symbolic way of stating purity, whereas the cubists' palette was monochrome.

The development of constructivism in Russia and de Stijl in Holland had to do with the general consciousness, or Zeitgeist, of the age, which emphasized the relationship of the individual to the collective. Relationships between painting, sculpture, and architecture changed as painters became concerned with abstraction and the rejection of literal reality. It would be a mistake, however, to assume that the modern movement did not contain internal dissent or disagreement. The translation of their theories into a design process caused considerable conflict. El Lissitzky identified two design philosophies which emerged from the theories of Le Corbusier and the de Stijl group. The first was that the world is given

through vision, through colour, and the second that the world is given us through touch, through materials.

In 1925 Léger had said of colour, "It is the end of obscurity, of chiaroscuro, at the beginning of the state of enlightenment. Too bad for those with weak eyes." The need was finally felt in the 1950s and 1960s to carry out Léger's prophesies as set forth in his *Derrière le Miroir*: "I believe that the acceptance of these large mural decorations in free colour, which is possible very soon, could destroy the cheerless soberness of certain buildings: stations, large public space and factories." He accused architects of rushing ahead, of going too far, and challenged them to the kind of urbanism that is socially involved. He believed, then, in a return to "intelligent and sensitive collaboration" as in the Gothic cathedrals that showed collective achievement, but he was emphatically against copying the Gothic style. As the Russian constructivist Alexander Rodchenko had said, "Work for life and not for palaces, temples, cemeteries and museums. Work among everyone, for everyone and with everyone, down with monasteries, institutes, workshops, studios and islands. Art which has no part in life will be filed away in the archeological museum of antiquity."

The value of a work of art no longer lay, then, in its execution, but in the creative idea from which it grew. It freed the artist from the privately owned canvas into the world of murals as public art. Léger epitomized this attitude, according to Edward Fry, "not only in his insistence on the social function of his own art and that of his fellow artists, but also in his instinctive sense of the need to communicate to the world at large by whatever means lay at hand—a painter in search of an escape from the social limitations of his art."

During the turbulent 1960s there was a rebellion against the colourless urban environment which coincided with a cultural rebellion against the affluent materialist society. The architectural style that grew out of all this was a mixture of collective planning, a watered-down modernist style, and individual enterprise. We have been witness in the 1970s to an erosion of the traditional boundaries, established at the time of the Renaissance, between disciplines. Artists have not been rebelling against anything in particular, but there continues to be a movement to break out of any restrictions and to recognize the limitations put on growth if strict boundaries are adhered to. Brian Clarke, a contemporary public artist, explained in *Omnibus* the relationship between the painter and the work: "Painting activity is introvert, but the expression is extrovert. You can't afford to compromise: collaborate but don't compromise. If you're making a statement, it's an absolute, therefore anything less is a lie." In a sense, this is why many painters turn to mural

A city street, or better still, the pavement, which is a man-size space created to safeguard man's existence, is to be viewed as a relative space, which ought to favour creative interventions. The high wall that gives the impression of weighing on passers-by, the yard's provisional hoarding, and the asphalt-black pavement are elements that are frequently transformed into instruments of dialogue.

Top: A series of pictures painted along the hoarding of a yard belonging to students at Harvard University, Boston, Massachusetts.
Centre: "Tribal" decorations lining a Monte Carlo street.
Left: A semipermanent wall exploited to an advertising end by an Italian restaurant in Copenhagen.

221

Graffiti and Murals

Left: A large placard created for an
exhibition for the victory of Hanoi in
1973. The pictorial technique aims to be
popular and easily communicative, but
it is actually a skillful use of the sign, not
without some degree of elegance, and
one in which the black outlines that
enclose and simplify the pictures
seem derived from comic-strip techniques.

Opposite below: This San Francisco shop
has dedicated the blind side of the lower
part of a building to the creation of a
comic-strip story in which the protag-
onists are characters by designer
Robert Crumb, one of the latest, most
fashionable cartoonists in America.

Left: Graffiti on the walls of a New York City primary school. In the early 1970s a singular phenomenon in nonfigurative mural art exploded in the United States. It was a veritable graffitomania, which also spread to means of transport.

Above: The facade of this old house in New York City served as a signal to draw attention to the shop contained within it, playing on echoes of the American flag and the name of a then-candidate for the American presidency.

Right: A Paris fence painted by children. In the detail of the foreground (near right) a language that is an alternative to that of traditional drawing is expressed by an "art brut," or very primitive technique. It is considered a liberating influence not only for most younger children but for art students as well, as it affords them with the opportunity to express themselves on large surfaces and, above all, to escape from everyday conditioning.

Right: The reconstruction of a Chilean mural on the walls of a house in Murano, Italy, created by muralistas of the Salvador Allende brigade during the 1974 Venice Biennale. The South American mural, which evolved as an instrument of clandestine fighting—and as a message of revolution and denouncement—was the poor man's means of spreading the thoughts of the party; it found its greatest popular participation and its poetic apex in the Chile of Allende and Unidad Popular. Unlike the cultural examples offered by the Mexicans Rivera, Orozco, and Siqueiros, the Chilean murals were an immediate expression of the historical context of the time.

Murals undoubtedly have a different premise in America, where they serve more as street art than as tools for propaganda. Even so, there is an impulse, inspired by the heights of buildings, to break down the codes for communicating information, even if one sometimes notes the reuse of signs seen elsewhere in advertising or painting. According to critic Mark Treib, two schools can be distinguished in America that are different from one another in style and content, and that are represented by the contrasting cultures of the West Coast and the East Coast, with Los Angeles and New York as points of reference. The realistic expression that is heightened by suggestion is typical of mural painting—also known as photorealism or sharp focal realism—in Los Angeles, and has as its aim complete technical perfection in imitating reality.

Right: Cinema-style picture on the wall of a Los Angeles house. Graphics by Kent Twitchell.

Opposite below: A detail from the exterior of Detroit's fruit and vegetable market. *Life* magazine has observed in an article on this market that the inhabitants of Detroit have found again their old market in which they walk through a kind of open-air art gallery consecrated to countryside products. Graphics by Alexander Pollock, who created over thirty similar works.

225

The Hyperrealistic Wall

Opposite above: Pig anecdotes are related with a wealth of detail on the enclosure to this meat factory in Vernon, California, creating an evocative display. Graphics begun by Leslie Grimes, a Hollywood scene-painter, in 1960; completed after her death by Arno Jordan.

Above and centre: This picture painted on a wall in Santa Monica, California, looks as though it were crystallized on a cinema screen.

Below and opposite below: A city view that appears in another corner of the same city can create disconcerting optical illusions, as can a highly realistic representation of an imaginary catastrophe employing the trompe l'oeil technique. Examples shown here are typical works by such groups as the Los Angeles Fine Arts Squadron. The aim of such art, according to some American psychologists, is to substitute the nightmare produced by the metropolis with a dream.

painting—it is a means of escape from the isolation of working on a canvas. It is also a way of regenerating creativity. Sfoerd Manhema, writing about stained glass, confirms this need to explore new ground: "The [stained-glass] technique, currently enjoying a renaissance (1970), has encouraged the undertaking of large enterprises by such artists as Matisse, Chagall and John Piper. A painter like Chagall has almost certainly warded off the possible drying up of his creative powers by taking up this new medium."

One of the reasons for the uniqueness of the Mexican mural during the revolutionary period between 1920 and the late 1940s was the desire of its various creators to reach the people by using popular imagery. Although the murals developed alongside the political and social movements revolutionizing the country, they were never dominated by narrow political ide-ologies. By using familiar traditional idioms of communication, the subject matter expressed a general concern with the human condition. Many of the painters were anarchists, and indeed there was always a strongly anarchic element in the Mexican Revolution.

In Russia, Communist ideology insisted that the painter concentrate on social realism. This influence is evident in all countries that have undergone similar social upheavals, such as China, Spain, Iran, and Portugal. The same images of family groups looking up at the sky are seen in the paintings of all these countries, with the exception of Mexico, where "these men could express the social urges of their time in a public manner, and yet remain free as painters to follow their own experiments." Rare in the history of art have been the occasions when painters were so publicly encouraged and left so free.

Playing Fields

Above: The outside wall of the Robespierre School in Aubervilliers, France. Graphics by Jean-Philippe Lenclos. *Opposite:* Painted silhouettes on the outside walls of a New York community centre's gymnasium. The presence of colour in a child's world is very important for a visual education. A new type of primary school has evolved in recent years that is orientated toward the "open plan," the intent of which is to overcome the traditional concept of space and allow the child a free choice by providing him with a variety of architectural structures.

It is very difficult to assess the current mural movement, especially as it is on such a worldwide level. The message behind the monumental scale of graphics goes deeper than the first impression of cheering up a derelict area or a drab piece of urban landscape. "They can go far beyond that, and really call our attention to the things which our modern cities ruthlessly deny us, dominated as they are by profit motive by which respect for the individual succumbs meekly, ignored and crushed by a power without logic and reason." The muralist Mel Pekarsky had complained, "Cities aren't being built for human beings but for dollars per square foot. In the end that's not even economic. It causes an explosion of urban decay. We don't seem able to act on the implications of the fact that we receive more information through our sight than through any other sense. We refuse to recognize the effect of an ugly environment, of ugly walls." This new wall art, then, constitutes a revolutionary medium; whether it is an heroic Mexican mural or a "tapestry of political messages of protest" given by the youth of Harlem to the local authorities of New York City, these murals express a desire to participate in shaping an environment over which individuals have otherwise little control. On a local level, murals raise the collective consciousness by accentuating areas of urban distress. According to Jason Crum, "The walls act as a catalyst for community spirit and action. The surrounding environment of the Bronx or Brooklyn is so sour that a painting seems to give an area a community focus. In the city planner's jargon, it's a Community Totem and the community takes pride in it." In some cases the mural is done to upset traditional complacency. "It is the job of the enlightened to rebuild

Left: The Mikimoto Pearl Shop in Tokyo was "wrapped up" during Christmas of 1972. The technique is not pictorial, yet it differs from other examples of super-graphics: in this case the package was made with a large strip of cloth. By Masahiko Sakamoto.

Below: The O'Farrell Theatre, created from an anonymous building in San Francisco, was decorated on the exterior with this ecological painting.

The Personalized Hangar

Opposite above: The front of Detroit's Eastern Market was painted with unmistakable visual signals relating to the contents of the interior. By Alexander Pollock.

Below: One of the various hangars of the Sierra Pine Tanning Company in Vernon, California, decorated with prairie scenes imagined before the white man's conquest. By Arno Jordan.

with the tools of creativity what the hateful with their weapons of oppression have destroyed," reads a quotation from a mural in New York's Lower East Side.

In the last few years mural painting has taken an even more bizarre direction. It has been used as a remedial camouflage by most artists, including Brian Clarke, rather than as part of the building—a far cry from Clarke's statement that art should be part of (both in and on) the building, instead of spending money on "chandeliers and marble facades." This new application of mural painting is part of a movement that attempts to redefine the role of the artist as a contributor to urban life in a more dynamic way than is possible within the confines of commercialism. There are a great variety of areas where this mural art is happening with more or less public participation. Some, like the scenes painted on the outside of a meat-packing factory in Los Angeles, are sponsored by businesses or corporations for publicity purposes. In other cases the individual is making a statement to the community by painting the

exterior of his or her house. There are also groups of professional artists who undertake mural projects, such as the Fine Heart Squad in Britain and City Walls, Inc., in the United States. These groups sometimes involve members of the community as assistants.

As the spontaneity went from the Mexican murals after the Revolution ended so may the current wave of mural paintings lose its impetus. As John Willet commented in *Art in a City*, "The difficulty facing public art (in Liverpool) is that when it is more or less traditional in style nobody will notice it, while when it is not, it is noticed all right but it is liable to be taken as a personal affront by the public." Generally the public does not like change, but there is some evidence that they can identify with murals in a different way than to commercial posters or billboards. "I'm not sure I like it but I sure like it being there," commented a car-parking attendant to Stacy Marking of *The Guardian*, the leftist newsweekly, about the mural overlooking the car lot.

The Mimetic Facade

Left: A Manhattan snack-bar, surrounded by an attention-getting collage of pictorial references that have nothing to do with food.

Above: To make the entrance to their shop on London's King's Road more visible, the owners of the Granny Takes a Trip boutique have modified the architectural typology, inserting this old American Buick into the building's facade.

Left: A row of flats in Manhattan's Upper East Side, a traditional area now replete with singles bars and restaurants, was freshened up in a highly original way, with colours that harmonize with those of the Adam's Apple restaurant beneath it.

Bob Wiegand, one of the City Walls, Inc., artists, is optimistic: "I don't want to relegate the artist to role of teacher or social worker—that's not a useful way to use him—nor make generalizations about bringing Art to the Masses. But each wall involves showing a large work of art to the people. As it goes up they see how it's put together, and that's the biggest, most public art education there could be. The process leads to understanding."

The graffiti phenomenon really exploded on the subway trains of New York. As *New York* magazine put it in 1973, "The Graffiti movement is a lot like Rock and Roll in its pre-enlightened phase . . . it announces the first genuine teenage street culture since the fifties." The city fathers condemned it while the environment designers condoned it. Intellectuals said that it was a great art form and a social expression of the times, due to the poverty of the ghettos which did not otherwise allow its youth to express themselves. Slogans were sprayed in the subway, often accompanied by a signature like Lollipop 135 or Iceman 73. One muralist known as Mike 171 informed *New York* magazine, "There are kids all over town with bags of paint waiting to hit their names."

Norman Mailer taps the pulse of this phenomenon in *The Faith of Graffiti*: "Perhaps that is the unheard echo of graffiti, the vibration of that profound discomfort it arouses, as if the unheard music of its proclamation and/or its mess, the rapt intent seething of its foliage, is the herald of some oncoming apocalypse less and less far away. Graffiti lingers on our subway door as a memento of what it may well have been, our first art of karma, as if indeed all the lives ever lived are sounding now like the bugles of gathering armies across the unseen ridge. . . . Graffiti is the expression of a ghetto which is near to the plague, for civilization is now inimical to the ghetto. Too huge are the obstacles to any natural development of a civilized man. In the ghetto it is almost impossible to find some quiet location for your identity. No, in the environment of the slum, the courage to display yourself is your only capital, and crime is the productive process which converts such capital to the modern powers of the world, ego and money."

Of course, all revolutionary periods come to pass and in the 1950s mural painting in Mexico seemed conservative, "a style of dully heroic realism dominated by historicist sentiment in the work of men like Cueva

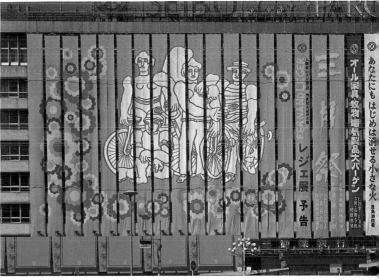

Left: In this piece of environmental art gracing the Tokyo Department Store the figure of a young Hawaiian girl was enlarged and reproduced on sheets of cloth that were then draped over the front of the building; thus another ulterior technical possibility is introduced into the domain of supergraphics. By Tadanori Yokoo, one of Japan's major graphic artists, internationally renowned since the 1960s.
Above: A similar idea, and one which focuses on a design with clear allusions to Léger, on the facade of the Seibu Department Store, also in Tokyo. By Tomoyuki Tobo and Yoshiro Kojima.

Walls and Abstractions

Shown on these two pages are some examples of pictorial mural creations carried out by organized groups of artists, whose aim is the participation and management of collectivity in the building of a city and the environment that surrounds it.

Above: The walls alongside a staircase in Echo Park, Los Angeles.
Below: Neo art deco in Paris.
Right: Side wall of a New York City building.

There are various groups of painters working in New York for whom contact with the reality of the streets means a liberation from the frustrating art gallery–collector relationship that conditions them. John Davidson of the City Walls group maintains that some mural paintings are to be understood as banners in the fight to change the environment and help re-create the city in relation to man. Harlem was the favourite field of action of a group called the Smoke House Associates, which included among its ranks not only painters but also town planners, architects, graphic designers, and sculptors.

Above left: 340 East Ninth Street in New York. By Allan D'Arcangelo of City Walls, Inc.

Above right: Third Avenue and Seventeenth Street in New York. By Jason Crum.

Right: Houston and Crosby streets in New York. By Mel Pekarsky of City Walls, Inc.

Below: Twentieth Street and Twelfth Avenue in New York. By Knox Martin.

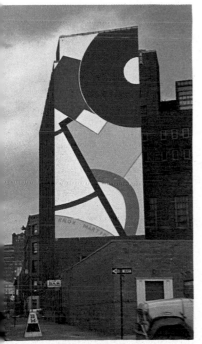

Colour in the City

Above left: The parking area of the Philadelphia Museum of Art, painted with stripes of colour. This was undoubtedly something more than just an attempt to capture the attention of someone arriving by car—it was a large project that altered substantially the optical effect of the environment. By Gene Davis.

Above right: This Milan pavement between Via Manzoni and Via Montenapoleone underwent a facelift and became this floral sidewalk. Some artists, speculating on urban decor, maintain that pavement space exists in relation to the people who walk on it, and that supergraphics, which can modify its appearance, can communicate through it by coming up with pleasing ideas.

Right: The entrance to a tunnel, through which the federal highway passes, in a Los Angeles suburb. Painted like a rainbow, it has the effect of an ambiguous signal for anyone seeing it from a distance. Here, too, the artistic mould belongs to the trends of environmental and land art.

The effects created by supergraphics in recent years have reached new heights of visual and psychological expression in the city, leading to a reconsideration of the use and function of certain buildings. But if it is possible to make an architectural construction more attractive with a layer of colour, transforming, for instance, an abandoned church into a theatre or an ex-garage into a bank, it is also possible to go further. The environment can accentuate its potential as a communications medium through more coherent planning, one in which the potential use of graphics in the architecture—sign and space—colour relationships is borne in mind. Significant examples of this are these coloured towers in Mexico City, which—in an urban setting and in an updated version—replace the traditional and rhetorical monuments of the past.

The Structural Value of Colour

Two examples of cultured architecture, in which the colour is an integral part of the structure.

Above: Decorated by Otto Wagner in 1898, the Majolika Haus had a great influence on the Vienna Secession groups.

Right: A detail of the Centre Pompidou in Paris, better known as the Beaubourg. Designed by Renzo Piano and Richard Rogers, completed 1977, the building reflects the factory spirit of communication intended by its promoters.

Opposite below: A housing block in San Cosme, Argentina, repainted with rhombic designs. When graphics are not in direct relation with the preexisting construction, the appearance and the meaning of the building automatically become equivocal.
Right: A factory near Gerona, Spain, reduced to a surrealist object, the facade of which depicts an emblematic chain of production.

Below: A house in the Eridania quarter of Bologna, Italy. The superimposition of a pop-art-style Greek temple onto a middle-class block of small flats creates an effect of disorientation, produced by those architectural trends that have as their objective self-irony and the demystification of dogma. By the architects Lorenzo Cremonini and Riccardo Merlo.

The use of colour in architecture, in a structural sense, was experimented with as early as the 1920s, chiefly through Theo van Doesburg, Piet Mondrian, Gerrit Th. Rietveld, and Cor van Eesteren, all belonging to the Dutch de Stijl group. *Above and left:* Two buildings belonging to a school complex in Cergy Pontoise, France. Graphics by Jean-Philippe Lenclos.

Below: The Karioka Building in Tokyo. Here one can actually speak of an architectural object rather than a mere building—of a design product, also, because of its simplified stereometry, the strong presence of colour, the absolute lack of obvious elements, such as windows, in the architectural composition. By Shiro Kuramata and Haruyasu Iwasaka, 1971.

Below: Primary school in Bergamo, Italy. By architects Walter Barbero, Baran Ciagà, Giuseppe Gambirasio, Jr., and Giorgio Zenoni, 1972. It is another attempt to fuse graphic design with architecture—to make an enlarged object out of the building. In this case it is a very apt solution, as it serves to eliminate the oppressive image the traditional school held in the past.

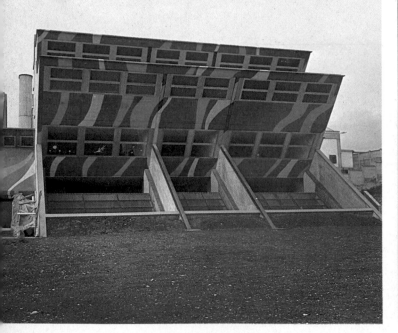

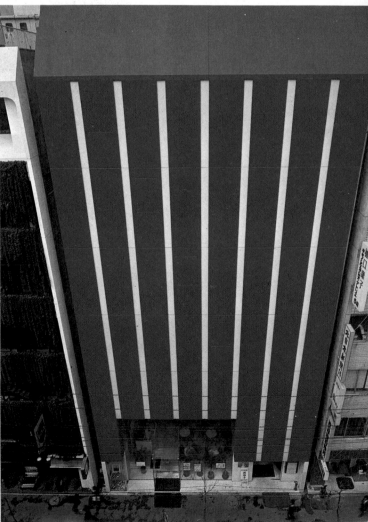

Above: Block of flats in Aubervilliers, France. Industrialized architecture, chiefly when prefabricated, can anticipate the colour element already in the project stage, as is the case with certain materials intended for interior design.

Below: Entrance to Kyoto University. In contrast with the example above, here the colour literally covers the entire surface of a traditional Kyoto building.

Left: A large Japanese printing-ink firm, Dainichi-Seika of Tokyo, commissioned the task of decorating two factory chimneys (the photograph shows only one). The chimneys have become a landmark, a signal, in the vast countryside surrounding them. By Ryoichi Shigeta.

Above: The abstract composition on this liquid-gas-containing tank, 46 metres high, links itself to American action painting. In 1972 the city of Boston awarded a gold medal to Boston Gas for this public-spirited project. By the painter Corita Kent.

Below: Chromatic patterns on the main area and facade of the Kagome Food factory in Ibaragiken, Japan.

Supergraphics in the Industrial Landscape

del Río and Gonzales Camarena." "A wall painted by an artist of standing gives tone to an expensive hotel, to a chic apartment block; it sets the pictorial seal on a politician's pretensions. In such circumstances the old hope, which so many of the early muralists cherished, of speaking to the people through a public art derived from popular sources has proved an illusion."

Buildings do have the potential, however, of becoming intrinsically more colourful with the rapid transformation that building materials are undergoing. In the immediate future colour and shape could be designed into the structure of the building. The Centre Pompidou in Paris or the Sainsbury Centre in England show the direction in which design and architecture are pointing. But empty walls will be with us for a long time yet. When empty walls run out, it would seem that the mural revolution as we know it must end. Or will the revolution, having slowly lost its original meaning in assimilating into the society that provoked its rage, run out of steam before then?

Above and top: At Port Barcarès, a seaside resort in the Languedoc region in southern France, the Gondolys shipyard is an enormous hangar for boats that stretches between the sea and the motorway. The two facades were designed with a festive decoration. By Jean-Philippe Lenclos.
Left and right: The road signal which leads into the Kagome Food factory in Ibaragiken, Japan, and a detail of the same factory.

Means of Transport

Till now we have looked at situations where supergraphics were projected onto immobile, static elements, which had a contemplative effect. In the graphic design of transport vehicles a different phenomenon comes to the fore: the dynamic element, which forces a perception of movement.

Left and centre right: A bus and two tram cars in the streets of Hamburg.
Centre left: A London double-decker bus, totally sponsored by advertising.
Bottom left: An old English car, with a bottle-shaped body.
Bottom right: A personalized Volkswagen Beetle in Hamburg.
Opposite above: A Japanese ferry, disguised as the sun on the horizon. Previous experiments in redesigning old ships had been carried out in the United States.
Opposite below: Aircraft belonging to Braniff International Airlines in Dallas, Texas, codified by means of different colours; even the cabin crews wear coordinated uniforms. Graphics by Mary Wells.

7. ILLUSTRATION IN EDITORIAL AND PUBLICITY COMMUNICATIONS

Whatsoever thy hand findeth to do,
do it with thy might.
ECCLESIASTES 9:10

Saul Steinberg, one of the great illustrators of our time, in commenting on his own particular brand of art, said: "My strength comes out of doing work which is liked for itself, and is successful by itself, even though it is not always perfectly accessible. I have never depended on art historians or the benedictions of museums and critics." It is only recently that illustrators, whose job by definition is to elucidate or explain someone else's message, have begun to be acknowledged as artists in their own right, and to receive some of the benedictions that Steinberg mentioned. In contrast to only a generation ago, when commercial artists were considered second-rate and distinctly inferior to the so-called creative artist who conveyed no one's message but his own, today's mass-media illustrators—whether working on magazines, newspapers, or books or in advertising, television, or film—are now recognized as producing some of the most creative and imaginative work in contemporary art.

Of course, prejudices against commercial art and its creators still exist. Because illustration is functional (it is commissioned by someone else for a particular purpose), and because it is ephemeral (its lifespan may be only that of a daily newspaper or a weekly magazine), many people, including some art critics, feel that it somehow cannot be taken seriously. Yet the genius of the illustrator lies precisely in his ability to transcend the limitations imposed on him. He is given a brief, but he conceives his work with originality. He is given a deadline, but he executes his work with the care of any craftsman. And, most important, although the newspapers, books, or posters in which his work appears will be discarded, the best illustrator will have captured, expressed, even helped to shape, the mood of his time.

The work of the conventional creative artist may hang on the walls of various galleries for several lifetimes and still only be seen by a small minority of people, by those who go out of their way to look at art. The work of an illustrator, on the other hand, comes to millions of people; it is part of their lives; it is the colloquial art of

our time. The mass media are the living galleries for this art, in contrast to them, the great national museums are no more than cemeteries for the genius of artists past.

Because illustration plays such a vital, organic part in modern life, those involved in its commissioning and execution bear an enormous responsibility. It is easy to see that some illustrators maintain the highest possible standards, which is clearly revealed in the *European Illustration* annuals, or in any of the anthologies published in America and Japan. At the same time, we can see examples of bad illustration all around us—bad in the sense that they are commonplace or derivative in conception, do not fulfill their purpose, or are poorly executed. Such work is inexcusable; it is a kind visual pollution that contaminates our environment just as perniciously as industrial waste. The companies, the art directors who commission the work, and the artists who carry it out must be made to realize the harm they are doing; but the public, too, has a duty to insist on good art.

Whereas originality is one of the modern illustrator's greatest virtues, his earliest predecessors were often employed to reinforce tradition. The artists who illustrated manuscripts for medieval Bibles or Psalters, for example, were expected to reproduce the conventional patterns and images to which their audiences were accustomed. For these artists there were three types of illustration: narrative miniatures to follow the text; ornate initials to mark the beginnings of chapters or sections; and marginal drawings often bearing no relation to the text. Often three separate illustrators were at work on one manuscript; individual style, or unity of style, was not considered important. The characters in the holy stories would always be portrayed in the narrative pictures in a conventional way—in certain attitudes or garments—and the illustrations would incorporate symbols—the lamb representing Christ, for instance, or the lion, the angel, the calf, and the eagle representing the Evangelists—that would be instantly recognizable to the medieval reader.

Of course a large part of the function of these illustrations was to illuminate as well as decorate the manuscript, and to some extent they helped to tell the story they accompanied. But in providing a familiar set of images, heavy with symbolic and traditional meaning, they also reassured the reader of the unchanging doctrine of the church, and of his own place in the symbolic world picture that was crucial to medieval thinking and social organization.

Drawing, in that it is a communicative entity, is the oldest means of expression after the spoken word. Modern advertising was born of illustration, and the first great affiche artists were in fact some of the major painters of their day. In Jacques Debut's 1897 poster, a gleaming new bicycle is offered to the sport consumer by a radiant fairy.

Above: A lithograph for one of the many covers created by the artist for *Harper's* magazine. By Edward Penfield, who was art editor of the magazine and one of the most brilliant American designers of the early 1900s.

Above right: A modern illustration in a fantastical vein; the dominant figure and the print are clearly of revivalist origin. By Seymour Chwast of the Push Pin Studios.

Below left: This gentleman, lost in thought and pedalling forcefully away, has been captured as if in a snapshot, with the pictorial technique of hyperrealism, for a medical print. By Will Rowlands.

Below right: A pen-and-ink drawing with black and white backgrounds. By John Sloan, an American artist of the early twentieth century.

The Passion for Sports

Right: Poster for a men's wear firm. By
Ludwig Hohlwein, 1908.
Below right: Poster for the Audi automobile company. By Ludwig Hohlwein,
1912.

Below: Bicycle poster. By Will Bradley,
who of all American graphic artists was
the closest to the Anglo-Japanese
aestheticism of Aubrey Beardsley, with
the addition of a few concessions to
art nouveau trends, 1899.

The first printed books, like the early manuscripts,
were illustrated by hand; Albrecht Pfister, working in
Germany in the 1460s, introduced the woodcut into
book printing, which revolutionized the profession.
From then on, book illustrations were mass-produced,
and the illustrator was to some extent alienated from
his work: instead of executing his design directly on the
page the illustrator would carve it out of a wooden
block (leaving the design in relief), and the printer
would transfer it to paper. Sometimes there was even
more intervention: an engraver would be employed to
copy the illustrator's design onto the block, and a
colourist would fill in the illustration after it had been
printed. These intermediary processes altered and often
spoiled the illustrator's original image.

This alienation has become even more extreme in
modern times, as there are all sorts of expertise now
involved in the reproduction of a piece of artwork: the
choice of paper and printing ink, the separation and
register of colours, the operation of printing machines—
all these affect the image that finally reaches the
audience. The illustrator, then, is not entirely responsible
for what the audience sees of his work, which is another
reason why some critics are reluctant to consider
illustration as a legitimate art form.

Albrecht Dürer, one of the greatest engravers of all
time, was working in Nuremberg, Germany, when this
separation of functions began. From 1486 his vigorous

drawings were being produced not only as illustrations for books but as collections of prints without text. He exploited the medium of the woodcut to the full, and was the first engraver to use cross-hatching to obtain tone. Although, like his contemporaries, he allowed copyists to cut his blocks for him, he was like all good illustrators concerned about the way his work would appear on the finished page; frequently, as in his *Geometria*, his *Life of the Virgin*, and his *Great Passion*, he would dictate the typeface in which the text was to be set.

The technique of copper engraving was first used in the 1470s, and Dürer, together with Hans Holbein, the Younger, working in Basel and then in England, was among the first to master it. Copper engraving allowed the artist to obtain a finer line and more detail than was possible with wood. However, one of its disadvantages was that, because the design was cut out of the plate instead of left in relief, as in woodcutting, copperplates had to be printed separately from the text—the paper, then, had to be pressed into the plate instead of vice versa, and this tended to bring about a separateness between text and illustration.

Although religious subjects had always been freely illustrated, Renaissance humanists were at first reluctant to illustrate the classical works they had been rediscovering—they believed that the results would be vulgar and unworthy. This tradition was flouted by the Venetian printer Aldus Manutius, who in 1499 published one of the most revolutionary illustrated books of all time. His *Hypnerotomachia Poliphili* (*The Dream*

of *Poliphilus*), which told the allegorical love story of Poliphilus and the nymph Polia, brought together the most excellent woodcutting, typography, and printing that was possible in Manutius's day.

Whereas the *Hypnerotomachia* was an expensive book, beautifully produced for a wealthy audience, other Italian printers working in Florence sought to interest, with their Rappresentatione (or plays), those at the opposite end of the social scale. The Rappresentatione were collections of sacred and secular plays set among simple, lively woodcut illustrations and produced by the cheapest means possible. They first appeared between 1550 and 1580, and many of them continued to be reprinted up until the middle of the seventeenth century. These Italian books of plays had a close parallel in British chapbooks, which first became popular in the mid-seventeenth century. The chapbooks were short (either sixteen- or twenty-four-page) booklets of stories and ballads, often inspired by contemporary events. They served a purpose similar to that fulfilled by modern-day paperbacks, magazines, and newspapers, and in fact it was not until newspapers first appeared, in the nineteenth century, that chapbooks died out. Their illustrations were zestful but often crudely executed, designed to make a quick, simple impact.

At a time when social divisions were even more extreme than they are today, early book illustrators were reaching as wide a spectrum of the population as the book illustrators of today, and the function of illustration varied just as greatly. Existing alongside books like the *Hypnerotomachia*, books produced with all of the finest

Caprice

Parallel with the revival of the decorative arts between 1880 and 1900 was the doctrine of aestheticism—mingled with a strong influence of the Japanese style—of which Oscar Wilde was the prophet and the young Aubrey Beardsley the disciple.
Opposite left: Illustration for *The Savoy* By Aubrey Beardsley, 1896.

Opposite right: A drawing in which the movements of the dancer Loïe Fuller celebrate the serpentine line that was much favoured by art nouveau. By Will Bradley, 1895.
Right top: Christmas card. By Alan Cracknell.
Right bottom: Advertising page for the printing of a chapbook. By Will Bradley, 1905.

materials and up-to-date technology and intended to be seen, felt, admired, and collected as works of art in themselves, were the plays and chapbooks, the ephemera of the day, whose function it was simply to make an immediate impression.

While the Germans and Italians were the great innovators in early illustrated books, the French excelled in their Horae (or Books of Hours). These books, which began to appear at the end of the fifteenth century, perpetuated the medieval tradition of illuminated manuscript versions; but whereas those manuscripts had been produced for the educated elite of the church and their wealthy patrons, the Horae were aimed at that segment of the population that was barely literate. The books were usually in a small, easy-to-handle format (about 15 × 8 cm, or 5.9 × 3.2 in) and contained between ten and twenty illustrations as accompaniment to such stories as Christ's Passion and the ordering of the calendar, and to those other subjects traditionally included in Books of Hours. Clearly the main purpose of these illustrations was to educate, and they were as important as the text, if not more so. The text would frequently be cut or else written specially to fit the spaces between the pictures, which carried independent and often lengthy captions explaining their significance. The Books of Hours as produced by Dupré, Vérard, and Geoffroy Tory became more and more elaborate and splendid. They offer an interesting comparison with modern illustrated books, in which, as literacy declines, text has again become secondary.

In contrast to the fifteenth and sixteenth centuries, the seventeenth and eighteenth saw few new developments in illustrative techniques and styles, in part, perhaps, because the written word had by now assumed more importance. These were literate times, and illustration could not say more than was being said by the text.

This argument may, paradoxically, be proved by the phenomenon of emblem books, which had their heyday in the seventeenth century. Emblem books originated in Italy with Alciati's *Emblemata*, first published in 1531. The book went into ninety editions in the sixteenth century alone, was translated into many languages, and started a fashion for more of the same in France, Spain, the Netherlands, and Britain. The books were collections of emblematic pictures, often using the symbols of heraldry, that were accompanied by a text (which was often a poem). Text and illustration both were essential: one could not be understood without the other. Yet few of the illustrations achieved artistic excellence, because the form made impossible demands on the illustrator; the message—the significance of the emblem —was simply all-important, and there was no place for visual creativity.

The Fairy-Tale Element

A portrayal of Little Red Riding Hood according to the illustration tastes of the early twentieth century, in a pamphlet publicizing the book, printed in Belfast. To find the origins of children's illustrations one must go back to the statuette peddlers of previous centuries who, before the advent of modern channels of communication, produced popular images and sold their creations in the street. But the statuette peddlers, like the first illustrators such as Doré, had no thought to facilitating the mental processes of the child by simplifying the sign or by creating more engaging or involved pictures, not even when they produced pictures for fairy tales. It was the designers who came into the limelight about 1900 who made themselves the interpreters and the mediators of more gentle suggestions —such were the aims of the members of the Liberty generation.

Below: An evocative picture for an illustrated book on the magical world of fairies. By Brian Froud for his book *Faeries*, 1978.

Emblem books reflected the same love for extreme and complex imagery that gave rise, simultaneously, to metaphysical poetry. The latter was a far more successful art form, however, because when that imagery was translated into visual terms it often became absurd, which naturally had a disastrous effect on the poem's elevated theme. And to some extent the eighteenth-century reading public considered illustration vulgar, just as the Renaissance humanists had. It seemed unworthy of the great classic works they admired most, such as Shakespearean dramas, and also an attempt, as Charles Lamb said, "to confine the illimitable." This was the age of the novel, and it seemed insulting to both the writer's creativity and the reader's imagination for an artist to portray or pin down his own particular image of a character or scene—it would limit rather than expand the text.

Illustrators fell into ill repute for another reason. It became common in the eighteenth century to reproduce paintings by means of engraving and etching techniques, and engravers therefore came to be seen as plagiarists. The English Royal Academy refused to admit engravers or etchers as members. These illustrators, however, were actually protecting themselves by taking up the new commercial techniques: now they could control the reproduction rights to their works. William Hogarth was the first artist to engrave his own paintings for this reason (unfortunately he did not always do his own work justice, for he was a better painter than an engraver).

Illustration again took a new turn at the end of the eighteenth century, when the Englishman Thomas Bewick revived the art of wood engraving. Instead of using the side-grain of soft woods to make his blocks, as woodcutters had done in the past to make theirs,

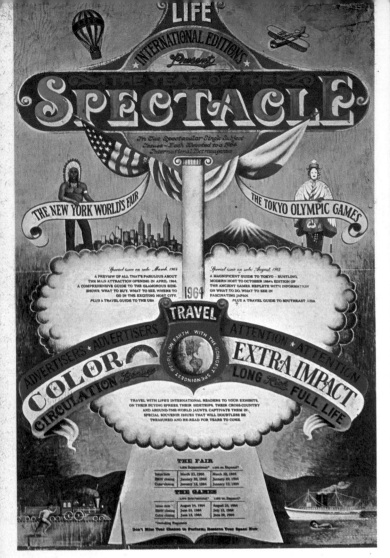

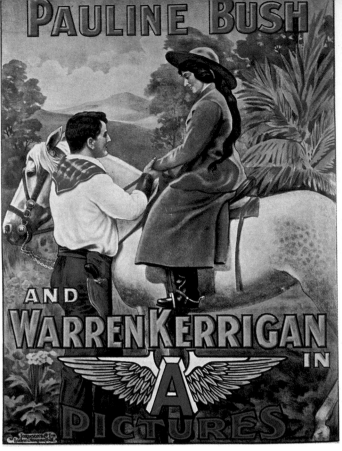

Above and below: Decorative anonymous posters for two 1914 films.

Exceptional Performances

Above: An evocative print. By Paul Davis, one of the modern artists who has often gone back to the stylistic trends of a naive and popular culture and brings to life a delightful nineteenth-century world, 1964.

Bewick used the tough end-grain of boxwood, which enabled him to do more intricate work. He devised a way, using fine parallel lines, of producing a half-tone effect, which had previously been possible only in metal engraving. Bewick was also unique in that he cut his own blocks and supervised the printing pro-cess so as to ensure that justice was done to his designs. The woodcuts, which could be printed again at the same time as the text and therefore tended to be closely related to it, continued as the ultimate mode of illustration until photo-engraving was invented, in the nineteenth century.

While Thomas Bewick was portraying the world around him (his favourite subjects were the landscape of his native Northumbria and the animals and birds that inhabited it), William Blake had been illustrating with words and pictures his otherworldly visions. Blake, while influenced in his design and illustration by the illuminated manuscripts of the Middle Ages, was

The Caricature Poster

first and foremost an individualist, and part of no movement. He had been trained as an engraver, and had illustrated the works of other authors, such as Edward Young's *Night Thoughts* and Thornton's *Virgil*, but it is for his illustrations to his own works—particularly *Songs of Innocence and Experience*—in which there is a unique unity between pictures and text, that he is chiefly remembered.

While at first Blake worked in traditional woodcuts, he later developed a new technique of relief etching, similar to the line-block method used today. The design was drawn onto a copperplate in a liquid impervious to acid, which was used to eat away the background, leaving the design in relief. He also devised an elaborate method of transferring colours onto his basic design using cards painted with tempera, afterward adding a colour wash by hand. From beginning to end he supervised the whole process of reproduction.

The nineteenth century proved to be the golden age of the literary illustrator. It was a time more than any other in which the writers of the day found "their" illustrators, when illustrations and text were at their most complementary. As Philip James pointed out in *English Book Illustration, 1800–1900*, "The etchings of Cruikshank are in perfect harmony with the literary idiom of Dickens (both were Cockneys); Millais and Trollope match each other in exquisite unity; Lewis Carroll's combination of sheer non-sense and sober story telling is reflected in Tenniel's drollery which has the air of reality; and Arthur Hughes and Christina Rossetti blend in the quintessence of Victorian sentiment, sweet but not cloying."

In these examples the illustrator took his inspiration from the text and at the same time added to it another dimension. But the nineteenth century also saw the beginning of a new freedom for the illustrator with the advent of magazines and newspapers. It was through these mediums that the artist was finally able to convey his own personal message—which at that time was often a social or political comment—without reference to any particular text.

In Britain Charles Knight's *Penny Magazine* was founded in 1832, *Punch* in 1841, and *The Illustrated London News* in 1842. In France the daily newspaper *Le Charivari* provided the opportunity for the lithographer and painter Honoré Daumier to caricature the petits bourgeois. He followed his subjects from the tribunal to the auction room, from the Stock Exchange to the hospital, from the city street into their own homes, and with his inexhaustible humour he captured the ridiculous in every situation, the physical and moral weaknesses of each individual. Among the books he illustrated with similar perspicacity were *Les Bohémiens de Paris*, *Emotions Parisiennes*, and *Don Quixote et Sancho Panza*. Daumier's contemporary, Paul Gavarni,

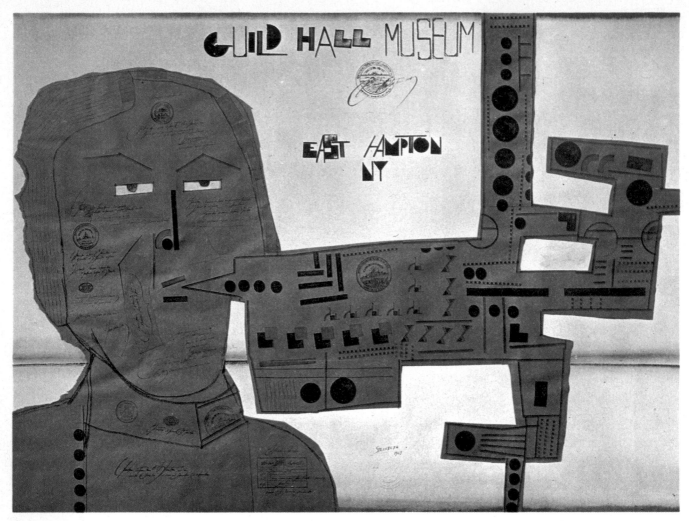

The Calligraphic Use of the Sign

Above: A coded message for art lovers in an exhibition poster. By Saul Steinberg. 1969.

Below left: A complex figurative description for a musical poster. By Akira Uno.

Below centre: Poster for a Ben Shahn exhibition created by utilizing one of his drawings and his signature.

Below right: The folder for a collection of engravings and aphorisms. This is a message intended for a limited public. By Yoshio Hayakawa.

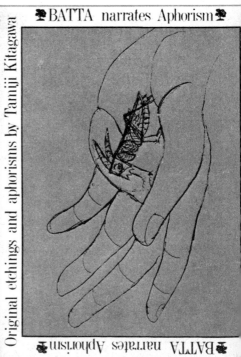

A Cinematographic Style

Below: An acrylic painting on canvas to illustrate a novel. By Giovanni Mulazzani.
Right: Gilbert Stone often employs the perspective laws of anamorphosis in his illustrations, which seem to be projected in cinemascope.

Left: A poster that aims to mythicize the personalities of the Beatles, portraying them in an Olympian setting. By Tadanori Yokoo.
Below: Portraits charged with subtle irony and a delightfully human quality. By Norman Rockwell, who was perhaps the major illustrator of the Roosevelt era and noted for having designed for all the most important American periodicals of his time.

The Dramatic Portrayal

Below: A programme for the Polish Drama Theatre worked out by means of an ambiguity of perception. By Franciszek Starowieyski.

Bottom: In this theatrical poster, heavily stylized cut-out black figures are set against the background according to a proven expressionist technique. By Bob Gill.

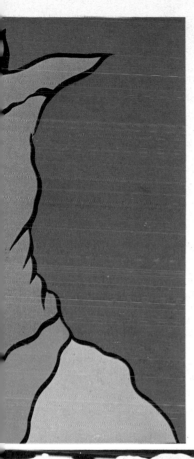

Left: Japanese poster. By Keisuke Nagatomo and Seitaro Kuroda.
Right: The dramatic voice of a blues singer is evoked in this record-sleeve illustration. By Philip Hayes.
Below centre: Theatre programme. By Kiyoshi Awazu and Gan Hosoya.
Below right: The mask of a singer, portrayed as a nightmarish vision, for a Montparnasse performance. By André François.

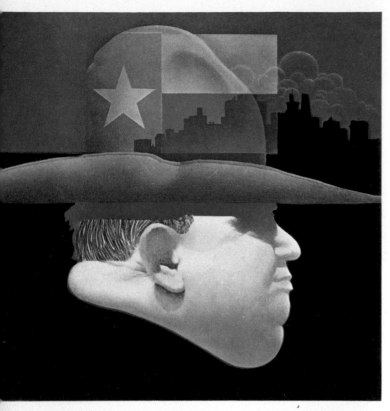

produced equally biting satire with his illustrations for *L'Artiste* and *Les Français Peints par Eux-Mêmes*.

In addition to the new mediums introduced in the nineteenth century, many new developments in printing came to light. Some of the greatest illustrators of the century exploited the new techniques; others reacted against them and attempted to revive more traditional methods. Lithography was invented by Aloys Senefelder in Germany in the 1790s, and his treatise on the subject was published in other European languages ten years later. In this new technique, the image was drawn in an unctuous, ink-repellent substance on an ink-absorbent stone and an inked roller was passed first over the stone and then over the paper. The advantage of this method was that an unlimited number of impressions could be taken, whereas the lifespan of even a copperplate was limited to about four thousand. If lithography is to be economic, however, the whole book—both text and illustrations—must be printed by the same method. The first edition of Edward Lear's *Book of Nonsense*, published in 1846, was one of the few books to be produced in this way in the early days of lithography.

Steel engraving, developed in America, came into use at the beginning of the nineteenth century, when it was employed for printing bank notes; it was first used to render book illustrations in 1823. Steel-engraved plates lasted longer than copper ones, and they made even finer, more detailed work possible. Steel engravings like those done by J. M. W. Turner to illustrate the poems of Byron, Scott, and Milton tended to be on a small scale, including many vignettes. Again, if illustrations had to be printed separately from the text (as did any metal engraving), it was not possible to print large editions cheaply. And this was the age when long print runs—needed to satisfy the tastes of the new middle class created by the Industrial Revolution—were of prime concern to printers.

In 1835 the English printer George Baxter patented a method of colour printing. He printed the basic design from an engraved or lithographed plate, then added colour in the form of oil-based inks using as many as twenty engraved wooden or metal blocks in the process. His particular aim was to reproduce the effect of oil painting, and as he was devoted to the cause of educating popular taste he sold his work at artificially low prices—clearly it was a most expensive method of production. He went bankrupt and was obliged to sell licences to use the method, which came into

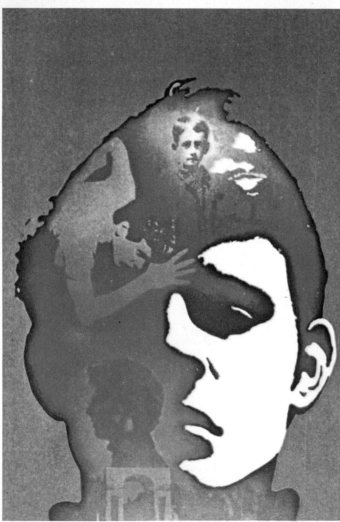

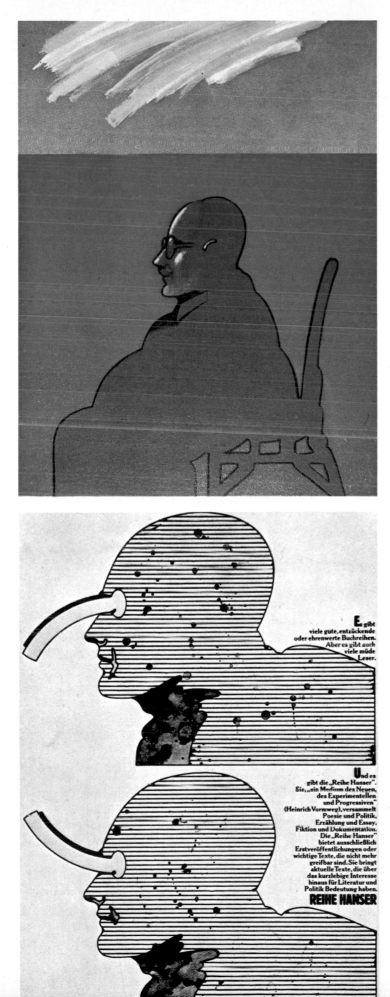

Left: The influence of the principles of irrationality of the Brücke expressionists comes to the surface in this illustration. By Heinz Edelmann, one of the most prestigious designers of the past few decades. Edelmann developed in an editorial climate, gaining experience mainly in the pages of *Twen*. Later, with his heterogeneous and pyrotechnical interpretations, he moved to advertising and the cinema, creating among other works *Yellow Submarine*, considered a masterpiece of graphic design as applied to the cinema. A recognized leader of a particular breed of illustrators who frequently resort to psychoanalytic symbolism—to the dissociation between the body and its mental processes in a dreamlike atmosphere of hysteria— Edelmann is among the major European exponents of dramatic illustrations.
Below: Another Edelmann creation for a magazine. 1970.
Above: A watercolour for a psychology publication. By Josse Goffin.

The sky is often used as background by illustrators, to make fantastic situations more effective.

Below: An illustration for a novel in a free and evocative interpretation of a state of mind. By Férenc Pinter.

Right: Poster celebrating the nonviolent ideals of America's hippies. By Peter Max.

Bottom: Two posters for exhibitions of the work of Jean-Michel Folon. By the artist, whose fantastic graphic components and lyrical palette made him admired throughout the world.

Graphic Dreams

general use after the 1850s. The printer Edmund Evans used it to reproduce the nostalgic, subtly coloured children's-book illustrations of Randolph Caldecott and Kate Greenaway.

During the same period, the process of chromolithography was being developed, and Owen Jones's *Alhambra*, published in 1836, was the first illustrated book using this technique. Jones was a disciple of Noel Humphreys, who also used the process in his 1844 *Illuminated Books of the Middle Ages*. These two illustrators anticipated the work of William Morris in their aim to create a unity between typography and illustration; unlike Morris, however, they made use of all the new printing technology.

In Germany, chromolithography was the method used to produce Heinrich Hoffmann's *Struwwelpeter*, published in 1845. This children's story, illustrated by the author, was enormously popular (it still is being reprinted), and following its highly successful appearance, chromolithography came to be widely used to provide bold, spacious illustrations for children's books. In France, Toulouse-Lautrec took advantage of the new methods of colour printing to produce his bold, clean-lined posters.

The invention of photography was both a stimulus and a challenge to illustrators. Robert Langton's discovery in 1851 of a way to photograph drawings onto wood meant that the artist's original design could be automatically and faithfully reproduced—it could even be enlarged or reduced as required. But it meant, too, that the engraving process was now to become entirely mechanical.

The first photographic line-block, which involved photographing an image onto a prepared metal plate and using acid to remove the surrounding area, was produced in America in the 1870s; on March 4, 1880, the *New York Daily Graphic* reproduced an illustration by this method. Although George Meisenbach of Munich is generally credited with having developed the half-tone screen, which he patented in 1882, *The Illustrated London News* used the technique for the first time in June 1880.

One of the great illustrators of the nineteenth century who welcomed these technological advances was the English black-and-white illustrator Aubrey Beardsley. While the style and content of his work were derived from the past (*Salome*, published in 1894, was inspired by traditional Japanese prints and *The Rape of the Lock*, of 1896, by the engravers of the eighteenth century), he designed specifically for the new photographic line-block process of reproduction.

At the opposite extreme, the nineteenth century produced William Morris. Morris rejected what he saw as the decline in aesthetic standards around him, and set out at the Kelmscott Press to emulate the earliest medieval printers. He insisted on designing every

element of the books he published—paper, print, and binding. He used only woodcut illustrations (and this after the line-block had been invented!), and to complement their heavy black character he used heavy black typefaces. Morris believed that the role of illustration was primarily decorative, and that its narrative function was secondary; thus many of the Kelmscott books had no individual illustrations but they did have extremely ornate title pages; others, including Kelmscott's famous *Chaucer*, were illustrated by the English painter Edward Coley Burne-Jones.

William Morris was a crusader in the cause of craftsmanship, and he sought to influence public taste with the high standards of his designs. Certainly his work had—and continues to have—a considerable effect on the art of illustration, although it did not, ironically enough, reach a mass audience in his own time, since his work was available only to the wealthy.

In Britain in the early part of the twentieth century the influence of William Morris led to a deeper rift between artists working for private presses (the Vale, the Eragny, the Golden Cockerel, and the Nonesuch being some of the most productive among these) and those working for the trade. Charles Ricketts, working first at the Vale Press and then at the Eragny Press, designed his own typefaces and commissioned Lucien Pissarro to produce woodcut illustrations for books like the *Livre de Jade*, which Ricketts printed himself in 1911. Eric Gill wrote, illustrated, and designed type for books published by the Golden Cockerel Press. His most famous illustrations, which were highly decorative engravings, were done for Golden Cockerel editions of *Troilus and Criseyde*, *The Canterbury Tales*, and *The Four Gospels*. The Nonesuch Press, founded by Francis Meynell and Stanley Morison in 1923, differed from the other private presses in that its proprietors took advantage of all the latest techniques. They produced some of the most splendid illustrated books of all, including Milton's *Comus* with Mildred Farrar's colour lino-cuts and the Nonesuch Bible illustrated with engravings by Stephen Gooden. Nevertheless all of these private presses were publishing only limited editions (few of them were economically viable), and to some extent their cause was an artificial one—many of the books they published were no more than excuses for illustrations, their very existence in the twentieth century an anomaly.

The illustrators who chose to work for the trade in the first half of this century had a wider choice of mediums than ever. The most exciting developments in commercial book illustrations were taking place in children's books, and artists who excelled in this field included Arthur Rackham and Edward Ardizzone. Barnett Freedman, Edward Bawden, and Ronald Searle all worked in advertising as well as on books; Anthony Gross and Lynton Lamb produced outstanding illustrations for classic novels. But increasingly the opportunities lay outside the field of books, and were to be found in magazines, newspapers, and advertising.

In France it appears that the work of William Morris had no effect, and there was no such gap between books that were privately or commercially produced. The French illustrated books grew more and more lavish. The greatest artists of the day were proud to work for books, and it was not uncommon for texts to be written to fit their illustrations. Expensive new processes were exploited to the full. Compared with the rather neurotic British attitude toward modern technology, the attitude of the French seems remarkably healthy and uncomplicated. Ambroise Vollard was the most influential of the French art dealers and publishers, commissioning illustrations from Pierre Bonnard, Maurice Denis, Georges Rouault, Marc Chagall, and André Dunoyer de Segonzac. Other artists who produced illustrations for books included Raoul Dufy, Giorgio de Chirico, Henri Matisse, Fernand Léger, Georges Braque, and, of course, Pablo Picasso, who illustrated a large number of books using etchings, wood engravings, aquatints, and lithography.

The history of American illustration begins in the mid-nineteenth century with the versatile Felix Darley. He worked in wood engraving, steel engraving, etching, and lithography, and illustrated such books as Washington Irving's *History of New York*, of 1850, as well as magazines like *Harper's Weekly* and *Every Saturday*. His last important work was an illustrated Shakespeare of 1886.

As in England, a number of illustrated magazines were founded in the 1850s in America. These provided a new medium for many young artists, among whom were Winslow Homer, the celebrated Civil War artist, and Howard Pyle, who is best known for the "bucking bronco" cover he did for the *Saturday Evening Post*. The Wild West image of America was perpetuated, too, by illustrators like Peter Rindisbacher, George Catlin, Frederic Remington, and by Friedrich Kurg and the Swiss-born Karl Bodmer, whose work is best known abroad.

Toward the end of the nineteenth century, American magazines and newspapers pioneered the development of such new reproduction processes as photoengraving, and American illustrators like Edward Penfield and Maxfield Parrish were among the first to exploit them. By the 1920s America had caught up with Europe's Industrial Revolution, and American illustrators, including many European immigrants, were faced with a massive reading public. The popular weekly magazines began to exercise a powerful influence: their large-format covers were a kind of portrait gallery of American life, portraying the American people as they themselves wanted to be seen. Naturally the editors of each magazine tried to establish a characteristic style of

The Metaphysical Silence

Below: The character of Maigret, symbolically portrayed. By Férenc Pinter.
Right: Poster with a neometaphysical atmosphere. By Cassandre, 1932.

Above: A picture for an illustrated book with the flavour of surreal irony. By Roland Topor.
Right: A Magritte-like illustration for a medical publication on mental depression. By Richard Hess.

SAY IT
WITH
TELEFLOWERS

Fantasy and Advertising

Left: Advertisement for long-distance flower giving. Here again is the unmistakable style of Cassandre, who always tried to assert his crepuscular and slightly decadent poetry, expressed in a wholly symbolic lexicon made up of interpenetrating images. 1947.

Bottom: The visualization of one of the aspects of corporate identity of a large organization—the service sector—illustrated by means of a hyperrealistic technique for greater effectiveness. By Pentagram of London.

illustration, which meant that the same artists were used repeatedly (many were given exclusive, long-term contracts). In the case of the weeklies this put the artists under immense pressure, although gradually traditions were established and readers came to recognize and even expect the familiar styles.

The *Saturday Evening Post* covers came to be dominated by the illustrations of J. C. Leyendecker and Norman Rockwell, and were supplemented with the work of other able artists employing a similarly decorative vein of realism to portray native, everyday subject matter. The cover illustrations ranged from John Falter's scenes of American city streets and home life in the Midwest farm belt to Neysa McMein's pretty young girls and Mead Schaeffer's dramatic war and Western paintings. The long list of *Saturday Evening Post* cover artists also included Steve Dohanos, Paul Bransom, Thornton Utz, John E. Sheridan, Richard Sargent, Jack Welsh, John Clymer, John Atherton, and Howard Scott.

Collier's, a rival weekly, followed a somewhat different pattern, leaning toward the more simplified statements of poster art. Edward Penfield was one of its ablest illustrators, with Frederic Dorr Steele and Walter Appleton Clark among others.

These two types of covers flourished side by side on newsstands for years. During this time another general magazine, *Cosmopolitan*, in a smaller format than the others, was printing a seemingly endless series of pretty girls' faces as illustrated by Harrison Fisher. After Fisher retired, Bradford Crandell continued the tradition for another twelve years.

When we look at these three styles after a lapse of several years we see that certain distinguishing qualities stand out. The long *Post* procession adds up to a fascinating and often revealing pageant of everyday American life, while the *Collier's* series is more adventurous in treatment and subject matter. *Cosmopolitan*'s unrelenting faces are simply a bore.

American women's magazines, too, have exercised an enormous influence over illustration. *Woman's Home Companion, Ladies Home Journal, Pictorial Review, Good Housekeeping, Delineator, Harper's Bazaar, Woman's Day, Vogue, Vanity Fair,* and countless others designed for a similar audience give a detailed account not only of fashions in clothes but also of household matters, family life—every aspect of the housewife's dreams and concerns. Again, the cover policy of each publication gives an indication of its viewpoint and contents. *Good Housekeeping* established a conservative, well-contented image with its years of Jessie Wilcox Smith's cozy family-life paintings, their flavour faintly reminiscent of late Victorian times. Later a somewhat different note was struck with Cole Phillip's illustrations, which combined realism and poster

Lucas Service

Lucas Service

Lucas
CAV
Girling
Bryce

Left: Idealization of a natural product, the tomato, turned into a sauce. By Nobuhiko Yabuki.
Bottom: A joyous poster that promotes a soft drink by referring psychologically to an effervescent, ecological background. By John Alcorn.

technique—a patrician faced beauty, for instance, would be rendered with realistically modelled face and hands, while dress, accessories, and background were treated in a flat, posterlike way. *Vogue* and *Harper's Bazaar* naturally emphasized the latest and most extreme fashions, often designed with Parisian flair by French artists. *Vanity Fair* radiated wit and sophistication.

Sometimes smaller magazines like *Sunset*, published in California and distributed in the West, appeared with unusual and excellent cover designs by such artists as Merle Johnson and A. Methfessel. For children, *Boy's Life* tended to follow a kind of junior *Saturday Evening Post* style, while magazines for younger age groups, such as *Story Parade*, *Jack and Jill*, and *Junior Red Cross News*, featured more lighthearted and inventive covers. *Reader's Digest*, the smallest of the "big" magazines, still follows the time-honoured practice of devoting its cover to a list of contents, although painted scenes, usually landscapes, appear on the back so that a picture-hungry public is not entirely deprived of its usual fare.

It was not only a rapid increase in the reading public that stimulated the growth of American magazines; American businesses were buying up the advertising pages, and all concerned profitted through this activity. The illustrations of America's favourite commercial artists were not only to be found just on fiction and features pages anymore—they came to dominate advertising space, too. J. C. Leyendecker's work might be seen on a cover of a magazine and also within its pages in an ad for Interwoven socks; Frederick Gruger divided his skills between fiction and Yuban coffee. Today this is not impossible, but it is highly unlikely: fiction has dwindled, and advertising is in the hands of the photographer.

Some of the early advertising series have survived as classics, such as the paintings done for Steinway and Sons, which included Ernest L. Blumenschein's *Indian Suite*, N. C. Wyeth's *Beethoven and Nature*, and Harvey Dunn's *Schubert Composing the Erlking* and the *Fantastic Symphony by Berlioz*. Franklin Booth produced a handsome series of illustrations for the Estey Organ Company, and Rene Clarke a series of sensitive compositions for Crane's, the paper manufacturer. The great draftsman Henry Raleigh did some of his finest drawings for a Maxwell House coffee series, and Guy Arnoux drew a charming set of pictures for Ovingtons. Bernard Brussel-Smith's remarkable skill as a wood engraver can be seen at its best in his series of advertising illustrations for Merck Sharpe & Dohme, Squibb, and Smith, Kline & French.

Since World War II, America has been flooded by a spate of advertising in an infinite variety of forms: booklets, cue cards, posters, billboards, catalogues,

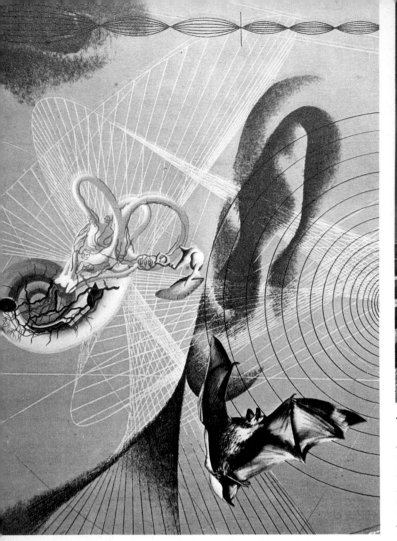

The Scientific Design

Above: The wonders of hearing, sonar, and bionics are combined in an evocative picture for an encyclopedic publication. The illustration is a news-giving item, and its application to the scientific field inevitably remains a case for free interpretation. By Hans Erni.

Above: A surrealistic painting for a booklet, created in a symbolic vein in which the detachment from the egg is portrayed. By Michael Hasted.

Below left: The connection between the system that regulates the brain and the female reproductive organs is depicted in this picture for Wyeth Laboratories. By Alex Gnidziejko.

Below: A double page from an American publication, featuring a spectacular illustration on the properties and characteristics of wood and its rational industrial exploitation. By Jack J. Kunz.

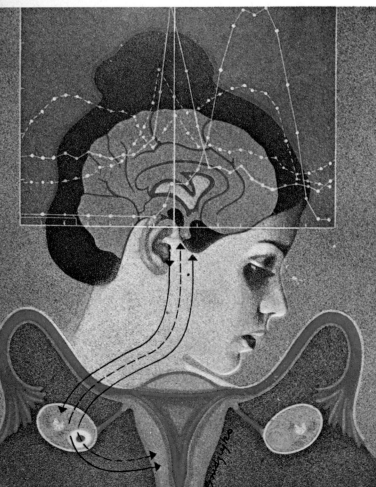

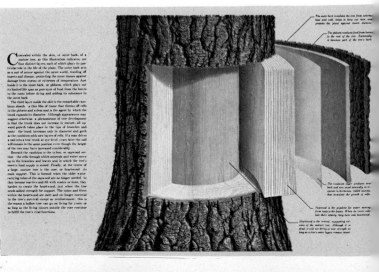

The Visual Tale

Above: Two-page illustration created by the superimposition of images. Illustration by Warner Book; graphic creation by Chet Jezierski.
Right: The members of a musical group projected into an unreal dimension, which helps to increase their worth. By Akira Uno.

Below left: Mixed-technique montage, based on the figure of George Washington and on the birth of America. By Fred Otnes, 1975.
Below right: One of the recollections of the exploits of anarchists and revolutionaries of the nineteenth century. By Flavio Costantini from a book devoted to Ravachol.

Hyperrealism

It is difficult to establish whether some of the more recent trends in illustration have come to the fore in the wake of the latest pictorial currents, or whether it was these pictorial currents that made the illustration techniques their own, as was the case fifteen years before the advent of pop art and advertising.

Right: A romantic painting for *Viva* magazine that sublimates the image, attaining the effect of a blurred photograph. By Merrill Cason.

Below: Divertissement for a cover of the photographic magazine *Zoom.* By Guy Fery.

Below right: Pop record sleeve, a mixture of surrealism and science fiction. By Masamichi Oikawa.

Opposite left: A fantastical interpretation of what is probably America's most famous symbol, in a picture painted for a New York insurance firm. By Doug Johnson.

Opposite, far right: The aggressive image of an American football player; the pure white of his helmet strongly contrasts with the player's face, which has been painted with a spray gun. By Ed Lindlof.

Opposite below: Illustration for a record sleeve. By Robert Giusti, who has for years contributed to the most important American periodicals.

postcards, circulars, window stickers, and packaging.
Fashions in design change from year to year, and new
ones are created with the aid of consumer research.
Advertisers and their illustrators deliberately set out to
show the customer what he wants to see, to portray
the life he wants to lead—or at least, the life they want
him to lead.

One of the major influences on recent American
illustration has been the Push Pin Studios, founded in
New York in the 1960s by Milton Glaser and Seymour
Chwast. The two had studied design and printing
together, and their work in posters and magazine
advertising represented a move away from realistic
portrayal, previously fashionable, toward a more graphic
and more individual style. The Push Pin Show held in
London and Paris in 1970 made a tremendous impression on those in the field, and in its catalogue Jerome
Snyder described the work of Push Pin Studios as "a
graphic language intellectually diverse, articulate and
above all authentic. A language spoken in ever-challeng-
ing ways and consonant with pluralist American
society." The show had an impact on illustrators like
Paul Davis, Edward Sorel, Barry Ziad, John Alcorn,
James McMullan, and Isadore Seltzor, all of whom
subsequently joined Push Pin Studios.

Illustrated books and magazines now look completely
different from the way they appeared in the first half
of the century, and this is due to the widespread use of
lithography. Instead of preparing text and illustration
blocks separately, as in letterpress printing, lithographic
production requires that the whole book be planned in
advance, and executed at one time. Pictures, as a

The Contamination of the Comic Strip

result, tend to be fully integrated with the text instead of grouped together in sections printed on different paper. The illustrated book, in which pictures are as important as the text, has become a whole genre in itself, and a most profitable one.

Illustrators have withstood the challenge from photography. While photographs are able to capture an instant in time, they are not always able to convey information or flavour in the way that the illustrator can. Harold Evans, editor of *The Sunday Times*, stated: "Graphics can let us see the unseeable, the intricacies of surgery, the supposed functions of the anti-ballistic missile system, the big event before it has happened." A diagram can explain what a photograph cannot, such as the key events in a riot or a mine rescue, for instance. Illustrations in books play an important part in providing variety and contrast to photographs.

In the 1960s there was a vogue for using the blown-up photographic image in advertising, particularly in large-scale campaigns that included television commercials. Consequently there was little demand for the skills of the poster designer, and standards dropped. With the economic recession of the 1970s, however, the poster—which is a relatively inexpensive form of advertising—has been revived, and some of the most creative contemporary illustration is now being done in this field.

Opposite, top left: A comic strip for the magazine *Rock & Folk*, treated, in the so-called underground style, with a willfully reluctant gesture toward good draftsmanship. By Lionel Koechlin.

Opposite right: Advertising for a Japanese-made car, achieved with the comic-strip technique. By Takuya Hikita and Nayaho Fujita.

Opposite bottom: Advertisement extolling the qualities of a particular toothpaste. By Ikki Shimada, 1973.

Above left: The sensuality of Guido Crepax's style is recognizable in every detail of the stories illustrated by him and in his constant use of the cinematographic framework, which accentuates the dynamic qualities and enhances the detail.

Above: A completely graphic story, reminiscent of early comic strips, reveals the inexhaustible imagination of its creator. By Saul Steinberg for *The New Yorker.*

Left: Poster for National Library Week created by means of elegant calligraphy, and by the insertion of pictorial elements that contribute to the animation of the scene even though they have no precise, logical association with it. By Peter Max.

Below: Illustration for a story in prose and pictures in a double page from *Penthouse* magazine. By Bob Lawrie.

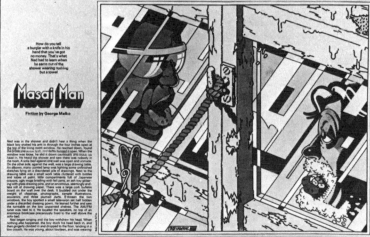

Woman Idealized

The entire history of graphics, from the nineteenth century onward, has been studded with the recurring motif of woman elevated to symbol. In associating with whatever product is being advertised, she sometimes dons the garb of a muse, a fairy, an enchantress, or—more recently—an earth mother, a dispenser of all things, from essential nourishment to sex.

Left: A turn-of-the-century theatre programme, created under the influence of the best traditions of Japanese art. By Manuel Orazi.
Above: Poster for an art exhibition revealing a few affinities with the symbolism spread by the Nabi group in France. By Eugène Grasset.

Opposite, above left: The lively, impressionistic style of Jules Chéret can be seen in this 1889 poster advertising a cigarette paper; the woman, with her haughty pose, seems to be playing the role of Carmen.
Opposite, above right: Here, for the same product, is a style more congenial to art nouveau, although with a gypsy subject. By Alphonse Mucha.
Opposite below: The distinguished middle-class woman reading *Arena* has been drawn with a few essential strokes, but with character; the overall style anticipates a taste that would be popular in the 1920s. By Lucian Bernhard, 1906.

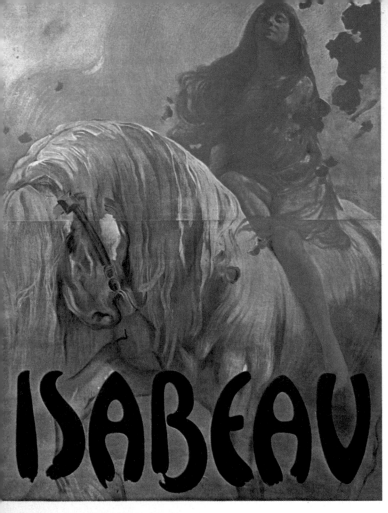

Left: Poster in which several ingredients of early-twentieth-century iconography recur. By Giuseppe Palanti.
Below left: Cover of the fortnightly art periodical *La Revue Blanche*. By Henri de Toulouse-Lautrec, 1895.
Below: One of the many programmes created by the artist for Sarah Bernhardt's theatre. By Alphonse Mucha, 1898.

The Art Deco Influence

Below: A neo-Grecian figure designed by a craftsman of the figurative current in art deco graphics. By Erté, a Russian who worked in Paris and who created theatre sets, costumes, *Vogue* covers, and countless illustrated prints for books, 1925.

Below right: A drawing inspired by the past, created for *McCall's* magazine. By Barry Zaid of the Push Pin Studios.
Bottom left: Advertisement for a television programme, with pictures and typography inspired by the graphic art of Seymour Chwast.
Bottom right: The magical world of Oz, revisted. By James McMullan.

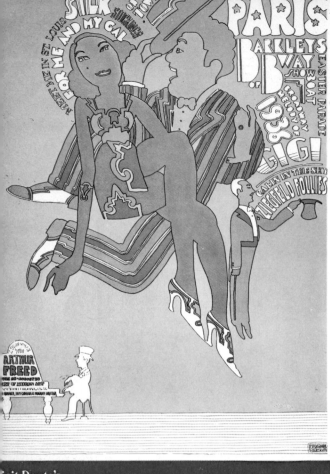

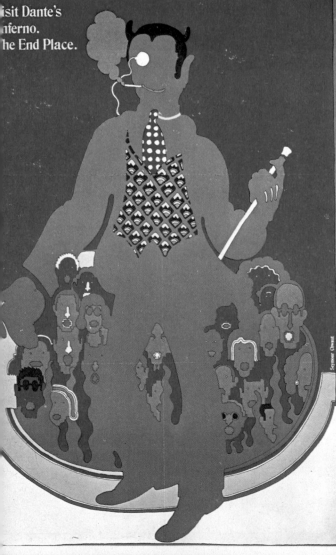

VALENTINE   OLIVETTI

A group of graphic artists and illustrators
working in New York but made up of
different temperaments that stem from
heterogeneous cultural formations has
established a cultured and lively visual
language, going back to pictorial styles of
the past and launching into avant-garde
experiments. These are the members of
the Push Pin Studios, an association
that has embraced ample commitments,
and not just in America.

The Push Pin Studios

Opposite left, above and below: Two amusing pictures by Seymour Chwast. *Opposite, above right:* Poster for Olivetti in which the artist takes up a pictorial motif explored by Piero da Cosimo in the fifteenth century. By Milton Glaser. *Opposite, bottom right:* Record sleeve for jazz musician Thelonius Monk. By Paul Davis.

Right: Exuberance of form and skill in execution are prerogatives of the work of John Alcorn, who has produced countless illustrations, mainly in the editorial field, working in the United States and also, between 1970 and 1976, during his stay in Italy.

The best contemporary illustrators are increasingly independent in their styles and themes. The tendency has been to move away from a literary illustration—one that elucidates a concept already expressed in words—toward a more expressive, more individual work through which the artist may convey his own visual or emotional idea. There are three clearly identifiable styles in contemporary illustration: romanticism, hyperrealism, and "social conscience." The romantic, or fantastic, movement is perhaps a reaction to what some might perceive as the ugliness and gloom of modern life; it can be seen in Brian Froud's enormously popular *Faeries*, in the imitations it has spawned, and in the work of Guy Brillant. Hyperrealist illustrators have been influenced by the work of Salvador Dali, René Magritte, and the dadaists. Their work is powerful and disturbing; it is a reflection as well as the product of decadence. Among the leading exponents of this style are the French illustrator Pierre Peyrolles and the German Gottfried Heinwein. Heinwein's works, his pale, degenerate colours, bear a striking resemblance to the set designs made by Patrice Chéreau for the first full-length performance of Alban Berg's opera *Lulu*, in Paris in March 1979. Other hyperrealists include Julian Allan and Larry Learmonth. The social-conscience illustrators are perhaps the most influential of all. Their work is unrelated to other contemporary art forms: it has its origins in illustration. Its purpose is to criticize contemporary society; very often the technique employed is part of the subject matter—this helps to emphasize the meaning of the picture. Social-conscience illustrators

are at work in London and New York, and although their purposes are similar, their styles are very different. The Englishman Ralph Steadman uses his uncompromising cartoons to expose the absurdity and hypocrisy of modern society. His work has included illustrations for *Rolling Stone* magazine, a cover for *Weekend* magazine on the subject of seal-culling, "The American Dream," and "The Patty Hearst Trial" (included in *European Illustration 76/77*). Other social-conscience illustrators working in London include Russell Mills and Robert Mason.

The New York school of social-conscience illustration is dominated at the moment by the English artist Sue Coe. She uses violent images to convey a violent, shocking message. Her work includes "The Rape of Rosa Velez" (*European Illustration 77/78*) and "Carlos" (*European Illustration 79/80*). Other American social-conscience illustrators use the images of Hollywood and Disneyland to characterize the American way of life, while Saul Steinberg acerbically noted: "The Mickey Mouse face is sexless, neither black nor white, without character or age; for me it represents the junk-food people, the spoilt young ones who have all their experiences inferior as they are handed to them on a plate."

The influence of social-conscience illustration is being felt and seen throughout Europe as well. It is obviously an extraordinarily powerful force, and one in which meaning has displaced the decorative images of the past. It is a sign that the art of illustration is more vigorous than ever before.

8. GRAPHIC ART FROM JULES CHÉRET TO THE PRESENT

The words on the printed page are to be
looked at, not listened to.
EL LISSITZKY

In formulating the historical outline of graphic art —
albeit a broad one with quick references to different
cultural tendencies—the beginning may be established
with the recent birth of the modern advertising poster,
which generally dates from the 1880s.

Certain studies identify the birth of graphic art with
the invention of Gutenberg's printing press in about
1438; others have it coincide with the work of the
medieval amanuenses and compilers of codices and
liturgical books; others push its origin even further
back to the age of Egyptian hieroglyphics or to the
Upper Paleolithic—that is, to the drawings of the Las-
caux Caves in France.

If, however, we are talking about a type of graphic
communication destined to reach a broader audience
than was formerly the case in a time when culture was
expressed in a hierarchical and elevated sense and
restricted to an elite, then we must adhere to a description of more recent events, all occurring within the
context of a society formed and developed under the
influence of the Industrial Revolution, and with a cultural conscience that is wholly urban. Graphic art,
therefore, will be defined as a product multiplied and
supported by an ideological substratum and meant to
spread to wider social strata through commercial
advertising, the dissemination of cultural information
(or information of public interest), and the implementing
of editorial production of various sorts, using the most
recent media devices such as television, the cinema,
and the electronic elaboration of an image.

With the growth and intensification of urban structures
together with breathtaking industrial and commercial
developments, and with the strengthening of a progressive bourgeoisie that did not exist in previous
centuries, demands by communications circuits spring
up that undoubtedly go beyond the internal ones of
a group or tribe. Thanks also to a period during the
last decade of the nineteenth century that was relatively
free of belligerent activities and revolutionary tensions,
even graphic art—as well as related activities, such as

the developments of the decorative arts—enjoyed a
particularly fervid creativity and became charged with
new stimuli and new meanings.

England is the country where the Industrial Revolution
got under way, and where certain fundamental discoveries were made to accelerate the process, such as
Henry Bessemer's invention in 1856 of the blast
furnace for melting steel, which, by replacing iron,
enabled the steel industry to leap forward. A con-
comitant cultural development was bound to
correspond to this productive growth. The debate that
raged around the automobile—the new "monster"
of industrial civilization—began after the first Great
Exhibition, held at London's Crystal Palace in 1851,
backed up by the pioneering engineering feats of Joseph
Paxton.

Reactions were swift to rise up against an industrial
production that was considered generally inferior, as
[...] London. The clumsy imitation of prod-
[...] ufactured by hand, using such
[...] als as cast iron, was frequently cited
[...] st machines. More indignant than ever
toward this state of affairs were two apostles of the
English artistic renaissance, John Ruskin and William
Morris. But for all the ideals that these two figures
romantically strove to uphold in their total negation
of the machine, favouring a return to lifestyles that
were medieval in spirit, a committed and irreversible
innovative process nevertheless evolved which served
to conquer once and for all the eclecticism that all
the arts of the nineteenth century had fallen victim to.
First of all Morris repudiated the "imitation of an
imitation of another imitation," maintaining that art
was the "way in which man expresses the joy in his
work" and insisting that art be created "by the people
for the people." The criticism most often levelled at
Morris is that his tapestries, miniatures, and polychrome
stained-glass windows and books were nothing more
than museum exhibits from their inception and were
accessible only to a rich and aristocratic elite enamoured
of collectibles. At the Kelmscott Press, founded by
Morris in 1890, such contradictory editorial products
as were printed were at once refined objects intended
for a limited audience and the starting point for the
English graphics renewal, which was acknowledged
by the entire modern world. Graphic art in
England flourished principally in books; the stylization
that characterized the whole of applied art which then
flowed into art nouveau found its origins in the Pre-
Raphaelites and in Morris's hand-printed books.

The most popular kind of graphic art comes not from
books but from posters, which according to a middle-
class conception are not only the source of a message

It was through postimpressionists like
Pierre Bonnard and Henri de Toulouse-
Lautrec who at the turn of the century
were drawing closer to graphics, and
specifically to lithography, that the
French affiche evolved; this was one of
the trends that characterized France's art
nouveau, in contrast to the styles of
England's Arts and Crafts movement and
the Vienna Secession. Pictured is a lithograph for *La Revue Blanche*. By Pierre
Bonnard, 1894.

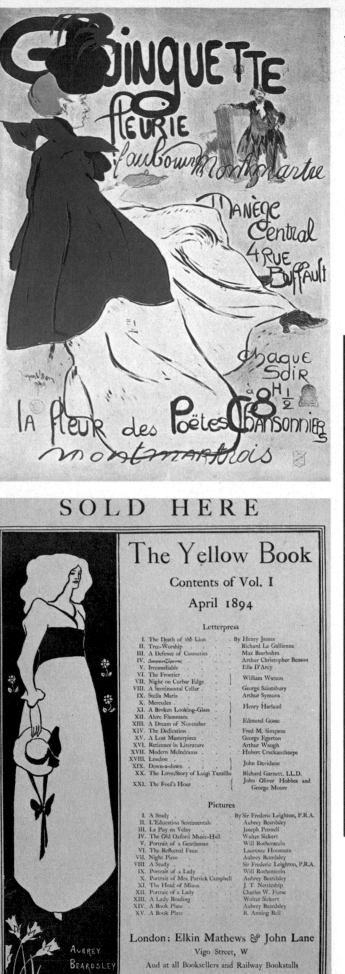

The Birth of Modern Graphics

Left: A billboard intended for the Parisian bohèmes. By Jacques Villon, another master whose work straddled the cultures of nineteenth-century postimpressionism and the avant-garde of the 1910s, 1899.
Right: A picture inspired by the splendour that was Italy in the late Middle Ages. From a book by William Morris, published c. 1890; illustration by Edward Burne-Jones.
Below: In this idyllic, fairy-tale-like poster the sharp personality of the artist is revealed, yet the influence of Aubrey Beardsley is still in evidence. By Will Bradley, 1894.

Left: Advertisement page for *The Yellow Book,* one of the magazines to which Aubrey Beardsley contributed most. His art is always two-dimensional, devoid of light and shade; in giving up corporeity and spatial dimensions for slender, elongated figures, he reveals the influence of the Japanese masters.
Opposite: Cover of the art magazine *Pan,* which fought a number of battles in favour of the new Jugendstil tendencies. By Josef Satler, 1895–96.

CORDIAL
CAMPAR

Left: Poster executed in the floreale style—the Italian version of art nouveau—created for an exhibition held in 1900. By Adolfo Hohenstein.
Above: Poster for a liqueur. By Marcello Dudovich, one of the most famous of the Italian commercial designers; his posters lured countless contemporary consumers with his natural characters and with the extreme legibility of his messages.

Opposite, above left: Cover for *Lippincott's.* By Will Carqueville, 1896.
Opposite, above right: Poster for cooking oil, created according to the strictest canons of the Dutch Nieuwe Kunst school by one of its leading representatives, Jan Toorop. 1895.
Opposite, below left: Poster by Otto Fischer, one of the pioneers of the German artistic poster. 1896.
Opposite, below right: This poster, although made up of syntagms that were well known to the international art nouveau, was the first abstract poster—and probably the first painting that was nonfigurative in an absolute sense. For these reasons it is considered historical. By Henry van de Velde, 1897.

The Secession Style

The two tendencies that were formed in the cultural climate of turn-of-the-century Vienna and the Wagnerschule compared in many respects, yet they contrasted the personalities of Josef Olbrich and Peter Behrens with those of Josef Hoffmann and Koloman Moser.

Right: Peter Behrens's poster for the Darmstadt Künstler Kolonie. 1901. *Far right:* One of Moser's numerous programmes for an exhibition of the Vienna Secession. 1902. The following year Moser and Hoffmann founded the Wiener Werkstätte.

but also an essential completion of an urban decor, one in which streets should be transformed into drawing rooms or art galleries. The poster—made technically possible after lithography was refined, a century after Aloys Senefelder's invention and half a century before the development of chromolithography—found very worthy interpreters among some world-renowned artists working in Paris. Indeed, the Ville Lumière at the turn of the century became the capital of affiche art, as it became for all the other arts, a veritable omphalos of the world. From the top of the Eiffel Tower—a new spatial iconographic sign and a symbol of engineering boldness that was, after the advent of the age of electricity, illuminated by thousands of light bulbs—the society of a carefree belle époque seemed to greet the new century in a spirit of eternal well-being.

The diffusion of the decorative arts, with art nouveau in full flower, shows how the consumption of products that were not strictly speaking utilitarian had reached fairly wide proportions in all levels of the population. The Paris shop Bing and Liberty's of London were centres of great commercial interest. In Nancy, France, in 1898 Émile Gallé, unable to fulfill the magnitude of requests flooding in to him from all over the world, launched a glass factory to back up the craft production of his most prized pieces.

In the field of poster art, Jules Chéret, Henri de Toulouse-Lautrec, Jacques Villon, Pierre Bonnard, and Théophile Alexandre Steinlen were the principal exponents until the 1890s. The style that predominates is a postimpressionist one: the deft and nervous stroke crystallizes feelings, picks up and emphasizes moments of reality, pinpoints the gracious mood of the era's costumes. The milieu represented is almost invariably the lighthearted one of fashionable restaurants, theatres, artistic performances. Although advertising posters were not yet greatly in demand at the turn of the century, Chéret can be considered the father of this art with his vast production of affiches.

In Chéret the poster found a master of organization on several levels, with his rhetorical use of the foreground to emphasize the pictorial motifs, projecting them forward from out of the background, his use of vibrant colors, and his fondness for depicting the nodding or smiling feminine silhouette. After his association with the Chaix printing firm was firmly established, there occurred a technical evolution of the poster, above all in the chromatic presentation and in the possibilities of action on the part of the artist. Chéret put his name to over a thousand posters and was the first to introduce the large format. During those same years and in the ones immediately following, the serpentine line and the other stylistic elements of French art nouveau began to assert themselves and gradually

came to replace the postimpressionist idiom, first with Eugène Grasset and then with the Czech Alphonse Mucha, the fine creator of female figures of Slavic allure and a vaguely gypsylike appearance.

It was in the 1890s that England began to challenge France's supremacy in the field of posters, due precisely to that cultural growth that occurred in all sectors of the decorative arts directly after the Great Exhibition of 1851. It was chiefly the reform and the correct proselytism initiated by Henry Cole, Christopher Dresser, and Owen Jones, the author of the influential manual *Grammar of Ornament* (1856), which enabled art to break away from an exclusive dependence on nature that was in accordance with the canons of conventionality. It was this transition that allowed such graphic artists as Aubrey Beardsley, J. W. Simpson, the Beggarstaff brothers (William Nicholson and James Pryde), Dudley Hardy, and the members of the Glasgow school, particularly Charles Rennie Mackintosh, his wife, Margaret Macdonald, and her sister Mrs. McNair, to develop a preeminently stylized art which soon imposed itself all over the continent. The most advanced point of reference for all late-nineteenth-century English graphic art, however, remains Aubrey Beardsley, who was really connected more with editorial production than with posters and who, at the age of only twenty, knew how to interpret the taste of the age so precisely and with so strong a personality that his very name came to be synonymous with English aestheticism. Animated by a perverse beauty, his figures reveal certain significant values derived from the Japanese graphic art of Utamaro and Hokusai, although nowhere so clearly as in his famous illustrations for Oscar Wilde's *Salome.* As Robert Smutzler wrote, "The asymmetric distribution of weights, the serpentine line, the renouncing of corporeity, space, light and shade, are elements of Japanese importation, despite the direct inspiration being joined to the indirect one, in the sense that Beardsley already leans towards James McNeill Whistler's Japanese-like style."

A direct link with fin de siècle London culture, and with Aubrey Beardsley's art in particular, is discernible in the United States in Will Bradley, who created playbills, posters, ephemeral prints, and the front covers for a small Chicago avant-garde magazine, *The Chap-Book.* Intensely creative, Bradley produced a large number of works, fascinated as he was by type design, printing, and illustrations for children. The city he worked in, Chicago, had a considerable work force and a strong urban development owing to a rapid growth of industrial and commercial activities. While Chicago became the world's first skyscraper capital, there is no link between the steel-and-glass structuralism of the Chicago school's architectural style and Bradley's sharply art nouveau manner, which in the

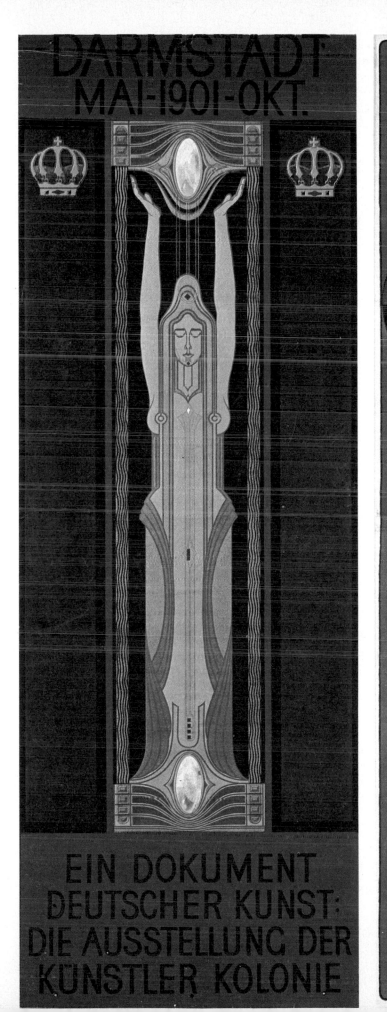

DARMSTADT
MAI-1901-OKT.

EIN DOKUMENT
DEUTSCHER KUNST:
DIE AUSSTELLUNG DER
KÜNSTLER KOLONIE

VER
SACRVM
V.
JAHR

XIII AVSSTELLVNG
D.VEREINIGVNG
BILDENDER KVNST
LER ÖSTERREICHS
SECESSION

GEÖFFNET V.9–7 VHR
EINTRITT 1 KRONE

LITH. v. DRVCK A. BERGER WIEN. VIII/2.

·VER·
·SACRVM·
·IV·JAHR·

IX·AVSSTELLVNG·DER·
·VEREINIGVNG·BILDENDER·
·KÜNSTLER·ÖSTERREICHS·
(SECESSION
GEÖFFNET·VON 9 BIS 7·UHR· EINTRITT·1·K·

LITH·DRVCK A BERGER WIEN 8/3·

Left: Catalogue for the Ninth Exhibition of Painters of the Vienna Secession, organized, like the previous eight, by the magazine *Ver Sacrum*. Illustration by Alfred Roller, 1901.
Opposite, above left: Poster for AEG light bulbs. By Peter Behrens, 1901. Behrens's collaboration with AEG allowed him to touch all those sectors in which he excelled—architecture, design, and graphics—and it probably constitutes the first real instance of art direction as such.
Opposite, below left: An abstract composition publicizing a Secession exhibition, similar to those Sponsored by *Ver Sacrum*. By Adolf Böhm.

poster *The Serpentine Dancer*, inspired by the American dancer Loïe Fuller, is closer to the aestheticizing glass art of New Yorker Louis Comfort Tiffany. In Tiffany's vases, Fuller's dancing, and Bradley's posters there is a common denominator in the shape of the serpentine line, in the flat, light, elegant, tendentiously abstract shape.

The other outstanding figure and major influence in American graphic art is Edward Penfield. Born in New York, Penfield was art editor of *Harper's* magazine from 1890 until 1901. He also worked on front covers and posters for *Collier's* magazine and in 1904 published through Charles Scribner's Sons a series of illustrations of his travels abroad. His style draws on a greater degree of realism than Bradley's, with a two-levelled, two-dimensional portrayal in colours surrounded by drawing, and with a clear and compact use of lettering.

The work of the Scotsman Charles Rennie Mackintosh, and the tendency he revealed to the Glasgow school which demanded a more rigorously geometrical use of art nouveau canons, had a strong influence during this time on another artistic centre of worldwide renown—Vienna. It was in Vienna, in 1902, a year after the English magazine *The Studio* had devoted a monographic issue to him, that Mackintosh's art was made known to the public. Already in 1897 some Viennese artists, in reaction against an imperious academicism, had founded the Vienna Secession, finding their charismatic leader in Gustav Klimt. The Secession soon found its temple in the little country mansion with the gilded dome with laurel leaves, built in 1898 after the design of Josef Olbrich, the most talented among Otto Wagner's ex-pupils. This same period saw the birth of the magazine *Ver Sacrum*, which besides becoming a veritable training school for the members of the Secession also availed itself of contributions from Rainer Maria Rilke, Hermann Bahr, and the young Hugo von Hofmannsthal, and which was, in addition, where the most interesting works of the new graphic directions, of which Kolo Moser was the mouthpiece, were published. In 1903 Moser joined forces with Josef Hoffmann to found the Wiener Werkstätte, which, in the wake of the English Arts and Crafts movement and with an eye on Mackintosh, aimed for a qualitative improvement of production in all sectors, from architecture to household goods, from furnishing to fabric designs, from jewelry to clothing, from bookbinding to graphic activity in general, putting itself for the thirty years between 1903 and 1932 at the service of a wealthy clientele throughout Europe, and spreading its products even across the Atlantic. Hoffmann was the last great art nouveau artist and undoubtedly the supporter of the conquest of a linear tendency, and had created

ALLGEMEINE
ELEKTRICITÄTS
GESELLSCHAFT

A·E·G· METALLFADENLAMPE

ZIRKA EIN WATT PRO KERZE

Right: Programme reproducing a project
created by Josef Olbrich for the Secession's villa, which with its dome of
gilded leaves at once innovated the whole
of European architecture. 1898.

VER·SACRVM

DER·ZEIT·IHRE·KVNST·
DER·KVNST·IHRE·FREIHEIT·

OLBRICH

VIII·
AVSSTELLVNG
DER·VEREINIGVNG
BILDENDER·KVNST
LER·ÖSTERREICHS

SECESSION

GEÖFFNET·9-7·EINTRITT·IX·

LITH·V·BRÜER·A·BERGER·WIEN·VII/8

SECESSION

KVNSTAVSSTELLVNG· D̄
VEREINIGVNG· BILDEN
:DER
KVNSTLER· OESTERREICHS ··

WIEN· WIENZEILE·   VOM ·12·
NOVEMBER· BIS· ENDE· DECEMBER·

LITH·ANST·V·A·BERGER·WIEN·VIII·

Opposite above: Two posters from about 1910 which still bear the cultural influence of both the Munich and Vienna Secession artists. By Ludwig Hohlwein, who was by then an established figure in the world of graphics.

Opposite below: Poster by Julius Klinger, a Viennese who worked for many years in Berlin; he was endowed with a considerable talent for formal synthesis and a sharp sense of humour. 1910.

Above left: Poster by Leonetto Cappiello, an Italian working in Paris, who undoubtedly contributed to the history of the French poster of the 1910s and 1920s with his elegance and his symbolic synthesis, and with the fauvism of his palette. 1910.

Above: End-of-the-century poster. By the Beggarstaff Brothers Studio, of which the Scotsman James Pryde and the Englishman William Nicholson were members.

Left: A powerful picture accompanied by a print with a clear impact. By Lucian Bernhard, who created the so-called Sachplakat (poster about an object), and is considered to be one of the forerunners of modern graphics.

Left: Poster for a theatrical work created in a grotesque vein. By F. Karol, 1904.
Below: Programme for a 1908 art exhibition. By Oskar Kokoschka.
Below left: This altogether exceptional graphic composition, between expressionism and literary symbolism, was created for a 1911 exhibition in Dresden. By Franz von Stuck.

Opposite above: Poster of the Neue Sezession of Berlin, organized by twenty-seven artists who were rejected by the official exhibition of the Berliner Sezession. Painting for the poster by Max Pechstein, 1910.

Opposite below: Two catalogue covers created by means of xylography by Ernst Ludwig Kirchner at different moments of his career, one for an exhibition of the Brücke at Dresden's Arnold Gallery in 1910 (near right), the other for a personal exhibition of his in Bern in 1933 (far right).

The New Four-Dimensional View

Left: One of the prints done at the Weimar Bauhaus for the great exhibition of the summer of 1923, to which both teachers and pupils contributed. The poster is composed with the symbol of the school, a head made up of strictly geometric elements, designed by Oskar Schlemmer. By Fritz Schleifer.

Below: Leaflet publicizing a publication by the Weimar school. Layout by László Moholy-Nagy.

Right: The first cover of the Dutch magazine *De Stijl*, which also gives a visual expression to the theories and principles of neoplastic art. By Vilmos Huszar, 1917.

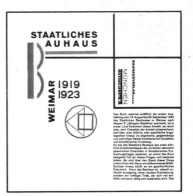

Below left: Cover for an art exhibition catalogue. By Hendrikus Th. Wijdeveld, founder and editor of another Dutch art magazine in opposition to the de Stijl group, *Wendingen;* published for over a decade, it grouped together many architects of the Amsterdamse school.

Below right: A Bauhaus-style poster for the Kunstgewerbe Museum in Zurich. By Peter Renner.

INTERNATIONALE
TENTOONSTELLING
OP FILMGEBIED

ITF

FILM

14 APRIL
15 MEI
1928
GROOTE KONINKLIJKE
BAZAR ZEESTRAAT 82
DEN HAAG

P. ZWART.

AU SS TE LL UN G

EUROPÄI
-SCHES

KUNST-
GEWERBE

herbert bayer bauhaus

6. MÄRZ
15. AUG.

1927

LEIPZIG

GRASSIMUSEUM

Left: Programme for a 1928 film festival at The Hague. By Piet Zwart, in a style that has now become international. *Below:* Cover for a catalogue of 1927. By Herbert Bayer, who was first a pupil and then a teacher at the Bauhaus; he was undoubtedly the major exponent of the graphic principles formulated in Dessau and the best interpreter, in a creative sense, of their evolution in the United States, where he settled permanently after leaving Nazi Germany.

since the early years of the century architectonic dispositions of masses that were rigid and simplified, and where decoration was altogether eliminated or reduced to a geometric function. Indeed, from the early days of the Wiener Werkstätte he had declared: "I am particularly interested in the pure square and the use of black and white as dominant shades, precisely because no such clear elements have ever appeared in previous styles."

In Italy art nouveau was merely imported, and was better known as the Liberty style (from the London manufacturer who was the first to spread the new products), or floreale. It is mainly in the field of architecture that artists of undisputed talent emerged, such as Ernesto Basile, Raimondo d'Aronco, and Giuseppe Sommaruga, at the turn of the century, those whose work in graphics and particularly posters stood out included Adolfo Hohenstein, Leopoldo Metlicoviz, Marcello Dudovich, and Leonetto Cappiello, while in the editorial world such distinguished figures as Adolfo de Carolis, Duilio Cambellotti, Cisari, and Antonio Rubino, the children's illustrator, were seen to excel. It was the graphic artist Cappiello, however, who was the focus of international attention. Working in Paris from 1898 on he inherited the art of Chéret, taking the salient features of the master's work to their extreme with the use of symbolism and chromaticism. Cappiello's original interpretation of the advertising poster instantly sets him apart from other artists; a character will dance against a uniform, frequently black background almost giving the appearance of having been borrowed from the commedia dell'arte or from ancient fables, enlivened by fauve colours and supported by an advertising notion which is even more stimulating, and which he himself defined as an "arabesque idea." In Cappiello's work the flat and tonal use of colour and the contrasting support of the complementary colours are prominent.

Graphic art found popular recognition in Italy even in an indirect sense, through the field of periodical printing, which, although concentrating chiefly on supplying information—on spreading news—is a direct derivation from the culture of the nineteenth-century feuilleton. The Italian public was fascinated in particular by a series of pictures in the magazine *Domenica del Corriere* in which topics were treated in a fairy-tale idiom and painted with heartrending realism by Achille Beltrame.

The situation was altogether different in Germany, where art nouveau was producing directions that were far from homogeneous, even leading at times to opposite tendencies. The two cultural centres on which all German activities pivoted were Munich and Berlin. The magazine *Jugend*, from which Jugendstil derives its name, began publication in Munich in 1896, with the emphasis on news, rarely attaining a high formal

295

Above: This poster by Herbert Bayer for a German exhibition in Paris indicates where his art, which already tended to break away from rigid constructivist canons, was heading: toward the creation of his own surrealist dreams.
Below: A Bauhaus advertisement created for a Jena cooperative society. By Alfred Arndt, 1923.

Above: Two examples of neoplastic layout, the most effective way to visualize every concept contained in the text. Each piece of text, in order to be read, must be observed with the same attention given to the image. Created by László Moholy-Nagy for his essay "Dynamik der Gross-stadt," 1922.

abcdefghi
jklmnopqr
stuvwxyz
a   d d

Above: The Universal typeface. Designed by Herbert Bayer in Dessau in 1925.
Opposite left: Composite technique, dubbed fotoplastik, used for making posters. Devised by László Moholy-Nagy.
Opposite right: Collage by John Heartfield, one of the inventors of the photomontage technique and the creator of a fierce political satire against German National Socialism and its proponents.

level. In Berlin the luxurious and large-format magazine *Pan* was published, to which Friedrich Nietzsche, Fernand Khnopff, Maurice Maeterlinck, Henry van de Velde, Hugo von Hofmannsthal, Arnold Böcklin, and many other famous figures contributed from time to time.

The two currents directly derived from Jugendstil are, on the one hand, that trend which, sustained by the Sachlichkeit ideology, led directly to the Werkbund, and, on the other, the trend of the significant albeit brief season of early expressionism, which was descended from the more symbolist components of Jugendstil, the nihilist rebellion, and Nietzschean thought. The renewal in the field of German graphic art and the stylistic quest were expressed above all in the pages of the Munich magazine *Simplicissimus*, which dealt with the problems of contemporary society in a satirical and polemical vein. The leading mind of the group was Thomas Theodor Heine, who, besides being one of the major German poster artists of the early twentieth century, was one of the founders of, and for several decades a major contributor to, *Simplicissimus*. His "Bulldog" poster, a symbol of aggressive satire, made him famous. It is one of the classic German posters, in which all the elements of a specific poster art are fused: an intense concentration of content, a powerful visual recall, the essential quality of the draw-

ing, the use of simple and chromatically attractive surfaces—a pleasing harmony of individual parts in a declared poster unity.

In Berlin at the turn of the century Lucian Bernhard, Julius Klinger, Julius Gipkens, Ernst Deutsch, and Hans Rudi Erdt were working with success, as was Otto Fischer in Dresden. The name of Lucian Bernhard is associated with a particular kind of graphic art, one which was born of the demands of the poster and which tends to make itself noticed in the environment of the modern city even in the midst of intense traffic. Its message is strictly informative and is realized exclusively through the object being advertised and with a text which is often reduced to the mere name of the company; the whole is strongly characterized and upheld by vivid colouring. The objective of this type of graphic rendering is to transform the object in question and the name distinguishing it into a single mnemonic symbol, according both to a precise advertising ideology in support of marketing and to an unequivocal expression of the concept of Sachlichkeit.

Working chiefly in Munich at that time was perhaps the most famous among German graphic artists, Ludwig Hohlwein, who produced thousands of graphic creations. Each theme approached by him is taken to a formal stylization—albeit within the framework of a realistic representation—which tends toward geometry,

1. КАЖДЫЙ ПРОГУЛ

2. РАДОСТЬ ВРАГУ,

3. А ГЕРОЙ ТРУДА —

4. ДЛЯ БУРЖУЕВ УДАР.

НАРКОМПРОС РОСТА N°858

Left and above: Two cartoons praising
the revolution of the proletariat. By
Vladimir Mayakovski, c. 1910.
Below left: Two double pages made up
entirely of typographical elements. By
El Lissitzky for Mayakovski's *Reading
Aloud.* As Lissitzky himself said: "My
pages relate to the poetry in a way similar
to a piano accompanying a violin."

Centre top: Cover for *Isms in Art*, edited
by El Lissitzky and Hans Arp. 1925.
Centre bottom: A page from *Mecano*, a
dada magazine published in Switzerland
during the 1920s to which Lissitzky and
Theo van Doesburg, among others,
contributed.
Below: Constructivist poster with clear
references to revolutionary values. By
El Lissitzky.

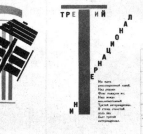

the accomplishment of tonal levels, the determination of light and shade vibrating on a neutral background. Its strong personality makes this an isolated artistic phenomenon occurring outside of any particular school or group; beyond the advertising meaning that is an obvious function of his posters, they represent an era and chronicle a world in which the high German bourgeoisie of the 1920s can be recognized.

In the decade preceding World War I—that is, about 1905—some Munich artists gave birth to the expressionist movement, which placed itself in a position antithetical to naturalism. In the ideology of this movement, the vision of reality is forced through deformation—which strengthens its expression—in a process of psychic order, everything is contemplated with a dramatic embitterment and pathos that refer back to Nietzsche and the symbolism of Böcklin. The principal exponent of this trend was Herwarth Walden, editor of *Der Sturm*. The artists who gathered in the Brücke tried, in an irrational and romantic gesture, to escape from a society fiercely bound by bourgeois conventions by seeking refuge in art. Erich Heckel, Ernst Ludwig Kirchner, Max Pechstein, and Oskar Kokoschka, exploiting techniques congenial to the mode of expression, such as xylography, drew numerous posters, particularly for art exhibitions, showing that they could arouse a spiritual impulse even through this medium. In 1911 another expressionist group, the Blaue Reiter, led by Vasili Kandinski and Franz Marc, recovered and infused into the artist's quest that popular iconography derived from fairy tales and the imagery of preceding centuries.

In the German field in the early years of this century a strong architectonic component was at work that, having Jugendstil as its starting point, led to a formal process of rationalization culminating in the modern movement. Besides the Munich group, of which Hermann Obrist, August Endell, and Otto Eckmann were the chief exponents, we should consider the structural work of Henry van de Velde, who, although he exemplified the Belgian trend in art nouveau, decided to move in 1899 to Germany to work, after the enthusiastic approval he had received there. In 1906 he won a teaching post in the grand duchy of Weimar-Saxony, where he sowed the seeds for the future Bauhaus movement.

Peter Behrens, like van de Velde, also went into architecture, having passed through the pictorial and graphic experience. In 1901 Behrens took part in forming the artists' colony on the Mathildenhöhe in Darmstadt (designed by and built under the direction of Josef Olbrich), where he created his own house as well as a few graphic projects for the official inauguration. When the Deutscher Werkbund was founded in 1907, Behrens was one of its principal artists and staunchest supporters. The Werkbund, grouping together

The Other Avant-Garde

After the establishment, between 1910 and 1920, of historical avant-garde trends in all areas of the arts—from futurism to cubism, from dada to expressionism, from de Stijl to constructivism—there was a rappel à l'ordre and a decided return to the themes of classicism. This continued until the mid-1920s, when the phenomenon of art deco exploded; it encompassed all the previous tendencies, recovering above all some of the values of cubism and early abstract art.
Below left: A propaganda card for the Italian Fascist combat troops. 1937.
Below right: Poster by Marcello Nizzoli. 1931.
Opposite above: Poster advertising an international photographic exhibition. By G. Trump. 1930.
Opposite, bottom left: Illustration by Jean Dupas. 1930.
Opposite, bottom right: Advertisement for Borsalino. By Marcello Dudovich, 1930.

21 APRILE XV

FEDERAZIONE DEI FASCI DI COMBATTIMENTO DI MILANO

"CAMPARI„ l'aperitivo

differing artistic currents that were not joined by a coherent ideological creed, nevertheless found common denominators in its professed faith in quality, in its strong tendencies toward concreteness and objectivity, and in its adherence to the spirit of Sachlichkeit, which had been fluttering through Germany for some years. The main figures inspiring them were artistic craftsmen associated with the English Arts and Crafts movement, such as William Morris and his disciple C. R. Ashbee. The Werkbund members were in opposition to all commercial abuse and they believed in protecting the moral questions with which art must involve itself.

Because it included exponents from all sectors, the Werkbund could control the activity of German industry (and, when required, limit its harmfulness) under the aesthetic profile of production. In a speech in honour of the foundation, Fritz Schumacher held that the specific duty of the Werkbund was "to overcome the alienation between material executor and inventor, attempting to fill the gap that arises between them." As already mentioned, the man who more than anyone else made his own artistic activity harmonize with that of the Werkbund was undoubtedly Peter Behrens. Under the direction of Walter Rathenau, an enlightened and progressive industrialist who was successor to the founder of the AEG—one of the big German combines—Behrens was assigned to a job unprecedented in the history of design, that of devising everything for this company—logotype, shops, advertising, objects for manufacture (for example, arc lamps, electric kettles), typefaces for the various publications, the factories (the famous turbine factory in Berlin of 1909 was one of his projects), the living quarters for the workers' families, even the sailing club—thus making himself known as the first real art director's consultant in a colossal work of corporate identity.

Thus, for the first time, the aim of communication shifted from the aristocratic level, where it had been contained almost exclusively within artistic circles, to a more popular level, which involved, even if only marginally, the working classes. The prevailing spirit was not Morris's desire to return to craftsmanship

Right: Poster for the *Revue Nègre*. By Paul Colin. In about 1925 even graphic art joined forces with syncopated music, jazz, and—particularly in Paris—American styles, and the result was a runaway success.

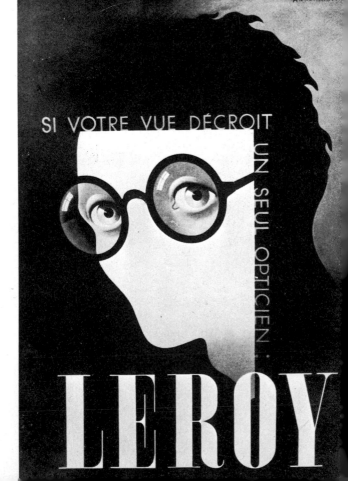

Above: One of Adolphe Mouron Cassandre's more famous posters, created in 1927 for the French railways. In the vast expanses of these compositions an atmosphere of crepuscular stillness may be discerned, one which can be related to the metaphysical paintings of Giorgio de Chirico.
Right: Poster for an optician; an interesting effect is obtained by means of the contrasts between black and white and between the detail of the eyes and the absence of other somatic traits in the drawing. By Cassandre.

Opposite, above left: Another poster by Cassandre that concentrates in symbolic form a few essential elements of the concept to be advertised; this style can be placed between Amédée Ozenfant's purism and the analytical cubism that preceded it by several years.
Opposite, above right: A poster by Severo Pozzati (Sepo), who, working in Paris from 1920 onward, fitted congenially into the group of graphic-art innovators.
Opposite bottom: Poster advertising the the services of railway restaurant cars, which were very popular at the time. By Alexeieff, 1928.

Opposite, above left: One of the tourist posters created by Herbert Matter in 1936, which together with the posters of Herdeg constitute the beginning of modern Swiss graphic art.
Opposite right, above and below: Two very different graphic works by Max Bill,

both from 1931. The poster for a ballet performance (top) is redolent with dadaist references, while the one for an art exhibition already belongs to the formal, geometric strength which Bill would assert after the war, particularly through his teaching at the Hochschule für Gestaltung in Ulm.

but rather Ashbee's notion that "modern civilization rests on machinery, and no system for the encouragement or the endowment of the arts can be sound that does not recognize this."

In 1907, the year in which the Deutscher Werkbund was founded, Picasso painted *Les Demoiselles d'Avignon*, the work that symbolically marked the beginning of a new era in the field of art. The ties that bound art to nature were definitively broken; cubism contested and disintegrated perspective, a technique, established in the Renaissance, which provoked in man a three-dimensional vision of the world. Cubism in France and futurism in Italy, although derived from very different schools (the first from Cézanne's structuralism, the other from European symbolism, mediated by Gaetano Previati), reached the similar conclusion of introducing into the picture the concept of simultaneity, which led—perhaps unconsciously—to the artistic portrayal of a scientific discovery of enormous portent that was made at the beginning of the century. After Einstein's theory of relativity was made known in 1905, the Russian mathematician Hermann Minkowski in 1908 was the first to conceive of the world in four dimensions. In the artistic field, Minkowski's model influenced the pictorial and subsequently the architectonic expression of the fourth dimension.

During this time the revolutionary artistic technique of the cinema began to take shape, which was particularly linked to the space-time concept. From the first abstract paintings, about 1911, by Vasili Kandinski, Frantisek Kupka, and a few others, there was to be seen a progressive disintegration of subject, which led to new theorizings by the various groups which come together under the label of the historical avant-garde. As regards graphic art, two main points of focus are fundamental: in 1913 Kazimir Malevich painted a geometric composition with a single black square on a white background, from which the ultramodern trends of constructivism, suprematism, and neoplasticism were developed; a year later Filippo Tommaso Marinetti composed one of his famous manifestos, *Parole in Libertà*, in which he emphasized explosive meanings, visualizing noises through typography and showing a new way of visually interpreting literary products, which a few years later would be taken up by the dadaists, the surrealists, and by Guillaume Apollinaire in his famous *Calligrammes* (1918). These compositions finally freed the page from the neoclassical shackles of traditional typography.

During World War I, those European artistic centres that were already well known to the old and new cultures—London, Berlin, Munich, and Paris—were joined by the two neutral nations Switzerland and the Netherlands, soon to be transformed into important

Above: Advertising composition in which some of the pictorial tendencies of the 1920s are discernible. By E. McKnight Kauffer, 1924. With great taste and an advanced culture, the American-born

Kauffer created many posters for the city of London.
Below: Cinema poster. By Paul Rand, another American designer who gained international recognition, 1950.

polos of artistic attraction. Tristan Tzara founded dadaism in 1917 in Zurich, where many political refugees had made their home, and in the Netherlands the vital aesthetic activity was centred in Amsterdam, Rotterdam, and Leiden.

Unlike the Italian futurists, who enthusiastically sang the praises of the machine and confused the sound of cannons with industrial progress, seeing war as revolution, the dadaists saw themselves as anarchical, nihilist forces, rejecting any intercourse with bourgeois culture and so very swiftly reaching a fierce desecration of its most intrinsic values. Dadaism, like nature—as the dadaists themselves said—has no meaning. All their periodicals—*Merz, Club Dada, 391, Mécano, Der Dada*—expressed themselves from the viewpoint of attitudes, in a fashion similar to the futurist publications, and with the possible exception of *Der Dada*, they exalted the printing elements to the maximum. In *Der Dada*, founded in Berlin in 1919 by Raoul Hausmann, John Heartfield, and Georg Grosz, the technique of photomontage was introduced for the first time. As a new technical instrument, photomontage served graphic art with a renewed and expressive pictorial tendency. Several figurative expressions were also developed by Francis Picabia and Man Ray.

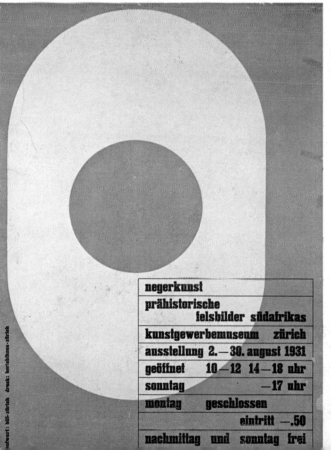

The Semantic Sign

francuska komedia filmowa nagrodzona w CANNES
ZABAWA W MASAKRĘ
scenariusz i reżyseria ALAIN JESSUA
w rolach głównych JEAN PIERRE CASSEL
CLAUDINE AUGER MICHEL DUCHAUSSOY
ELEONORE HIRT produkcja réné thevenet

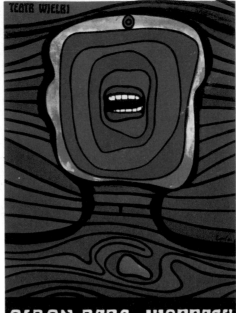

TEATR WIELKI

ALBAN BERG WOZZECK

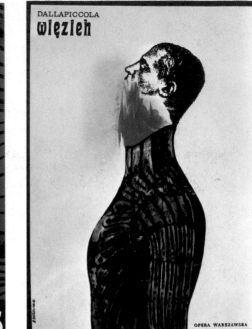

DALLAPICCOLA
więzień

OPERA WARSZAWSKA

In the posters by the Polish masters a great synthesis in the figurative expression is ever-present.

Above left: By Franciszek Starowieyski, native of Kracow, who won numerous awards and mentions in various international exhibitions on the poster.

Above centre: By Jan Lenica, a versatile artist who worked in France and West Germany and is the author of writings on the poster and the plastic arts.

Above right: By Roman Cieslewicz, who among all the Polish artists epitomized the better tendencies of Central European graphic art.

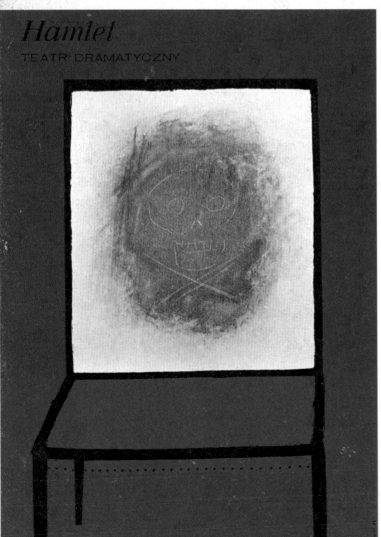

Hamlet
TEATR DRAMATYCZNY

USS Nautilus

GENERAL DYNAMIC

Opposite, below left: A poster of unmistakable dramatic lyricism and exceptional resolution of composition. By
Henryk Tomaszewsky, 1962.

Opposite, below right: Poster for the
U.S.S. *Nautilus* atomic submarine project.
By Erik Nitsche, 1955.

Below: Raymond Savignac, who carries
on the tradition of commercial design,
always comes up with a pleasant surprise
in each new poster.

In the Netherlands, the magazine *De Stijl* was
founded in Leiden in December 1917 by Theo van
Doesburg, to which for some years Piet Mondrian also
contributed important theoretical writings. The cover,
designed by Vilmos Huszar, is quite significant, giving
an indication of the future dogma and poetics of the
group. It consisted of a composition with geometric
levels, spaced out as though they were intersected by
vertical and horizontal lines, as a negative. The for-
mulation of *De Stijl*'s visual language rested precisely
on the rigid juxtaposition of horizontal and vertical
lines, on the right angle, and on the layers of colour,
through which a vision of universal harmony, against
all subjectivism, was attained.

But the magazine that was most representative of
official culture and Dutch architecture was *Wendingen*,
founded in 1918 and directed by Hendrikus Th. Wijdeveld. The graphic art expressed in the magazine is of
great interest; a single issue reveals the influence
of H. P. Berlage and Frank Lloyd Wright as well as
the decorative slant of the Far East, already present
in the Dutch Nieuwe Kunst and in the studies of
de Groot. Because of its preoccupation with artistic
themes, the group that revolved around the magazine
was unfairly labelled as reactionary, whereas the vast
architectonic output they presented (of which Michel
de Klerk is the most talented interpreter) and the themes
of the numerous monographs they dealt with are more
than worthy of consideration.

During the Russian Revolution of 1917, the progressive
artists of that country enthusiastically offered their
services to revolutionary propaganda, with the declared
intention of contributing to the transformation of the
world. During the four or five years that followed the
Revolution an even keener battle was fought to effect
changes in the social and cultural life; art schools all
over the country were reformed, new museums were
built, and artistic performances were organized in which

The Descendants of the Bauhaus

The generation of German and Swiss graphic artists that received its training from the Dessau workshops, mainly during the years between 1926 and 1928, and whose masters were Herbert Bayer, Joost Schmidt, and László Moholy-Nagy, subsequently organized their knowledge and developed a tradition which is with us today.

Left: Cover and inside page of *Die Neue Haas Grotesk.* Layout by Josef Müller-Brockmann, 1960.

Below: Experimental piece within the field of type design, in a double page from the publication *Neue Grafik.* 1959.

Above: A grid, or rough drawing on a square-page format, after the editorial tendencies of the German schools.

Below: Sample page from the paper of the Ulm Hochschule für Gestaltung, published from 1958 until the closing of the school.

Below, centre and right: Pages from Emil Ruder's manual on typographical layout.

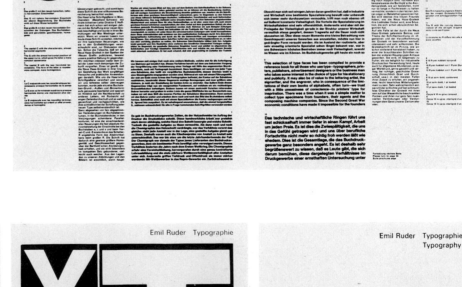

painters, actors, and musicians took part. In 1918 a school for arts and technology, known as Vchutemas, was founded in Moscow. In 1919 Vladimir Tatlin devised his dynamic *Monument to the Third International*, a symbol of the new constructivism.

One of the artists who most greatly contributed to the graphic renewal of revolutionary art and, more generally, to the whole period of historical avant-garde, was undoubtedly El Lissitzky. In 1920 Marc Chagall invited him to teach at the School of Fine Arts in Vitebsk, together with Malevich. In the following year Lissitzky was in charge of directing the interiors project studio at Moscow's Vchutemas, where the central figure was Alexander Rodchenko. Lissitzky divided his time between the studio and several trips abroad, returning home full of experiences, enriched by functional researches and contacts with the European avant-garde.

In Berlin in 1922 he met Walter Gropius, Theo van Doesburg, and László Moholy-Nagy, with whom he formed links. He contributed to a number of magazines, including *Der Gegenstand/Objekt, De Stijl, Ma,* and *Broom.* From 1919 he undertook a complex research programme, of which the central reference points remain the poster *Hit the Whites with the Red Wedge* (1919) and a book in the style of a thumb-index in which he interpreted Vladimir Mayakovski's futurist poetry. Lissitzky wrote of it: "This book is made up only with the case material. My pages relate to the poetry in a way similar to a piano accompanying a violin. As thought and sound form a united imagination for the poet, namely poetry, so I have wanted to create a unity equivalent to poetry and typographical elements." Furthermore, a series of painted works known as *Proun* marked his shift from the field of painting to

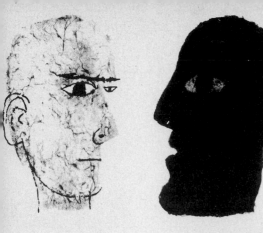

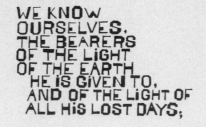

Above: A typical message pronounced by Ben Shahn by means of the editorial medium, featuring angular drawing, pregnant with meanings, and a calligraphic script that is both humanitarian and poetic, 1964.

Right: This unusual cinema poster seen as pure graphic expression was memorable for a period much longer than was usual for any traditional pictorial signboards, precisely because of its high symbolic value. By Saul Bass, 1955.

Far right: Advertisement for a design exhibition of 1951. By Otl Aicher.

Above: Logo of the magazine *Avant-Garde*. Designed by Herb Lubalin with the letters of a typographical system of his own invention.

Left: A few ingredients from the graphic bag of Herb Lubalin, used in the pages of a cultural magazine that appeared in 1968. Lubalin was one of the major talents of graphic design, particularly in the field of typographical drawing.

ANDY WARHOL March 15th through April 3rd, 1965

Right: The portrait of Liz Taylor in one of Andy Warhol's famous series, which undoubtedly enjoyed a relation and a mutual influence with international graphics and advertising, 1965.
Centre: Pamphlet for an exhibition of the work of Roy Lichtenstein, which draws expressive and technical values from the comic strip, revamping their language with new, richer connotations.
Bottom: Che Guevara portrayed in a Cuban poster; the technique employed is one of mythical representation peculiar to the great mural paintings.

that of constructing architectonic space, as had happened with Kazimir Malevich and the Dutch de Stijl group. After 1928 Lissitzky settled almost exclusively in Russia and devoted himself to intense propaganda work for the state, introducing the experience of photography more and more into his work and emphasizing ever more strongly in graphic composition the presence of realistic elements, even within the rhetorical drive of the propaganda.

The relations and affinities between Lissitzky, Doesburg, and Moholy-Nagy, in acting as a formative core for the production of ideas, became a determining force in about 1923 in the development of Bauhaus graphics. The School of Applied Arts and Crafts founded by Henry van de Velde in Weimar in 1906 flourished for about a decade, until the outbreak of war; being Belgian, van de Velde was obliged to abandon that area, which had become enemy territory for him. With the setting up of the first republican and democratic state in Germany, the Weimar Republic, the school was reactivated in 1919 with totally new criteria, embracing Weimar's Institute of Fine Arts as well under the one name of Staatliches Bauhaus Weimar. Called upon to direct the new institute was Walter Gropius, who had already distinguished himself at Werkbund exhibitions in the years between 1911 and 1914, having worked in Peter Behrens's studio. From Vienna Gropius brought with him Johannes Itten, the man to whom he believed he could entrust didactic and preparatory tasks of great importance. Itten, however, introduced into his courses not only the psychological techniques applicable to the theory of colour but also a series of philosophical, therapeutic practices of a mystical and individualistic kind, closer to esoteric doctrines than to the rationalism later recognized by the school. Then, with the presence of Doesburg in Weimar from 1921 to 1922, two opposing factions sprang up which rapidly came to blows; Itten finally had to resign, and Doesburg left Weimar for Paris. Itten's course was restructured by one of the school's ex-pupils, Josef Albers, and by the newcomer Moholy-Nagy. Although he had to direct the metal laboratory and not the printing one—which had not as yet been set up—Moholy-Nagy created with Gropius the layout and some jackets of the *Bauhausbücher*, which began publication in 1925 (the year the school moved to its new base at Dessau). His way of interpreting graphics, the language-script relationship, and the spatial portrayal of the text and the picture gave the page new meaning, albeit by consciously violating certain fundamental rules of writing, such as the elimination of capital letters in nouns, peculiar to German, which provoked a strong reaction from the public. Moholy-Nagy, as Hans M. Wingler maintains, was also able to make a clear distinction between the autonomous portrayal, typical of

Roy Lichtenstein · September 28 - October 24, 1963 · Leo Castelli 4 E. 77 N.Y.

Directions for the Future?

After the great season of graphic design, which probably enjoyed its halcyon days during the 1960s and the early 1970s, a new set of figurative trends has asserted itself recently, along with a particular interest in illustration. The directions and the new names that are coming to the fore in this field seem to acquire their identity either through the currents of a heightened realism or else through a grotesque design evocative of nightmares.

Left: A black panther that recalls the naive art of Henri Rousseau. By Paul Davis. *Below*: Illustration for the Exxon Corporation publication *Information, Please*. By Roger Hane, 1972.

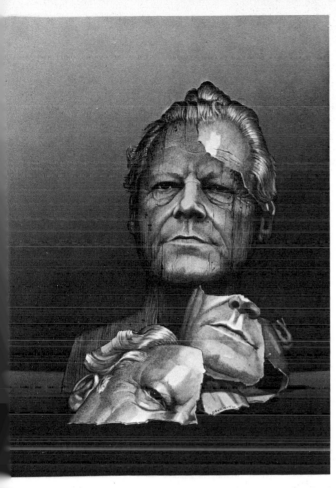

Above left: Illustration for the periodical *Konkret* for an article on the fall of Willy Brandt. By Hermann Dagwitz, 1977.
Below, left: Painting that recalls the German realism expressed in the films of Pabst. By Gottfried Heinwein.

Above: Magazine illustration for *Weekend Magazine* for a Canadian survey on seal hunting. By Sue Coe, 1978.
Below: Bonnie and Clyde from the *Radio Times* feature "The American Dream." By Ralph Steadman.

the painterly approach, and the illustration, a task he reserved for photography. He was one of the initiators of photography without a camera, and his theses provided a spur for more in-depth studies both within and outside the Bauhaus.

The other two graphics figures who were among the most important to emerge from the Bauhaus were Joost Schmidt and Herbert Bayer, who both progressed via the curriculum from students to masters. They were the chief creators of the various Bauhaus-style prints, in which constructivist, suprematist, and neoplastic tendencies were defined and codified. Bayer in particular, creator of certain typeface designs, was concerned with removing personal values from the printing composition in order to lead it into a state of pure rationalism. One of his writings from the Dessau period reads: "Functional advertising graphics should above all draw inspiration from the laws of psychology and philosophy. Advertising today is handled almost exclusively on an emotional level."

After the Bauhaus moved to Berlin in 1931 and after its final suppression by the Nazis in 1933, many teachers or ex-teachers left Germany and settled for the most part in the United States, where the ideas and the convictions formed in the Dessau melting pot were taken up and spread all over the world through numerous publications and the introduction of new courses and institutes, such as the New Bauhaus, of 1937, and the Institute of Design, of 1938, both in Chicago and under the directorship of Moholy-Nagy. In 1938 Bayer, too, emigrated to America, where he wielded a great influence on the development of exhibition techniques and advertising graphics. At this point, graphic art—in the sense of graphic design—had established its foundations, and so international were the principles governing it that it spoke a universal language.

The generation that followed the Bauhaus masters continued along the way that had been paved for it, while specifying its techniques to a greater degree and adhering to them in a highly professional way. These techniques included a greater mastery of the art of photography (discovered relatively late in the field of graphics and advertising), the definition of new layout grids, and the specific study of a more perceptive reading of the printed letter. Those who spring most readily to mind are mainly Swiss, from Herbert Matter (who subsequently moved to the United States) to Walter Herdeg, Hans Neuburg, and Max Bill (who in 1952 founded the Hochschule für Gestaltung at Ulm) to Carlo Vivarelli, Josef Müller-Brockmann, and Max Huber (who has worked in Italy since 1946). Others include Ladislav Sutnar, Jan Tschichold, Gyorgy Kepes, Walter Dexel, and Paul Rand, as well as the Italians Giovanni Pintori, Albe Steiner, and Franco Grignani. The work of all these artists was founded on quality

and strictness of form, concepts they passed on to the generation of graphic designers working from the end of the 1950s onward.

Obviously the historical development has not been as linear as these brief notes suggest, but it has often had a sinusoidal progression, particularly during the years surrounding World War I. It was the war, in fact, that abruptly interrupted the activity of the avant-garde artistic world, leading back particularly in Italy and France to a restoration of traditional values, to a rappel à l'ordre—perhaps more through psychological conditioning than from any objective need. The neoclassical nostalgia for metaphysics, expressed during those years in the paintings of Giorgio de Chirico, had paved the way for a kind of art that looked to the past. In Italy, even those literary and artistic periodicals that carried the most weight at the time advertised the break with the avant-garde, idealizing instead the stylistic values of tradition, from the earliest primitive painters to Giotto and the artists of the Renaissance. This was the case with the twentieth-century Milanese group. In Vienna, the artists who centred round Hoffmann and the Wiener Werkstätte from 1914 onward gradually abandoned the staunch canons of geometricism, a peculiarity that had been a trademark of their art, in order to return to art deco and to a kind of neo-Biedermeier inspired by Dagobert Peche. In France, a toned-down form of modernism tended to absorb all the fashions that came into the limelight, and in an ironic and cheerful vision the phraseology of the cubist language combined the symbolism of the academic repertoire, the fashions of Poiret, the Russian ballet, African sculpture, Robert Delaunay's coloured disks, the stars' paillettes, and the spurting fountains. This was all confused in an essence of artificiality which would later produce new figurative genres. The apotheosis of all this took place against the background of the great Exhibition des Arts Décoratifs held in Paris in 1925, which defined a particular style, that of art deco.

The most representative artists of French art deco, besides the Russian Erté—who worked more within the environment of theatrical costumes and sets, furnishings, and editorial graphics, contributing largely to *Vogue*—are George Lepape, Adolphe Mouron Cassandre, Jean Carlu, and Paul Colin. In Italy, those whose work stood out in the genre included Mario Sironi, Marcello Nizzoli, and Severo Pozzati (Sepo), who worked in Paris. Among all these, however, the artist who achieved a celebrated reputation for this type of culture was Cassandre, who, taking up some elements of the postcubism of Georges Braque and Fernand Léger, the purism of Amédée Ozenfant, and the spaces and silences of metaphysics, created some unparalleled posters, such as those for the Compagnie des Wagons Lits. Cassandre emphasized on the surface the gravity of two-dimensional figures in highly stylized forms. He made a noteworthy contribution to the theatre, designing numerous important sets.

Experiences similar to Cassandre's were developed in England by the American E. McKnight Kauffer, although in a way which tended more toward postcubo-futurism. His posters for the *Daily Herald*, in 1920, for the museums in London in 1922, and, later, for the London underground and for Shell, are characterized by the cubist division of surfaces and the dynamism of the forms.

These artists pointed out other untried paths—ones often quite different from those traced by functional art as described above—which enabled many other graphic artists from all over the world to develop a more fantastic and creative vein. This is what happened with Raymond Savignac and Herbert Leupin, for instance, who developed affiche art in a more traditional sense, underlining it with a current of gentle irony.

Savignac, who worked with Cassandre, is identified only through some of the master's posters, such as those the two created for Dubonnet and Nicolas.

In the years following World War II a strong development of the advertisement took place, along with the powerful growth of international agencies, while during the past decade we have witnessed a marked recovery of figurative art through illustration, and a greatly decreased use of abstract forms.

With the growing development of the editorial world, particularly within the fields of illustrated periodicals and children's books—and in illustrated books in general—as well as a strong production of animated designs for television, the graphic artist's profession has within half a century passed progressively from an activity reserved for only a very few artists to what approaches a cultural industry.

BIBLIOGRAPHY

The Sign and Symbol

Achille Bertarelli. *Le Stampe Popolari Italiane*. Milan, 1974.
Roger Cook. *The Tree of Life: Images of the Cosmos*. London, 1974.
Paolo Graziosi. *Palaeolithic Art*. London, 1960.
C. G. Jung. *Man and His Symbols*. New York, 1968.
Warren Kenton. *Astrology: The Celestial Mirror*. London, 1974.
Madhu Khanna and Ajit Mookerjee. *The Tantric Way*. London, 1976.
Francis King. *Magic: The Western Tradition*. London, 1975.
Stanislas Klossowski de Rola. *Alchemy*. London, 1975.
John Mitchell. *The Earth Spirit: Its Ways, Shrines, and Mysteries*. London, 1975.
Erwin Panofsky. *Studies in Iconology*. New York, 1939.
Jill Purce. *The Mystic Spiral: Journey of the Soul*. London, 1974.

The Sociology of Communication

José Aranguren. *Human Communication*. London, 1967.
Jean Baudrillard. *La Société de Consommation: Ses Mythes, ses Structures*. Paris, 1974.
Peter L. Berger and Thomas Luckmann. *The Social Construction of Reality*. Garden City, N.Y., 1966.
John Carter and Percy H. Muir, eds. *Printing and the Mind of Man*. London, 1967.
Gian Paolo Ceserani. *I Persuasori Disarmati*. Bari, 1975.
Max Gallo. *The Poster in History*. London, 1974.
Laurence Leamer. *The Paper Revolutionaries: The Rise of the Underground Press*. New York, 1972.
Peter Max. *Poster Book*. New York, 1970.
Marshall McLuhan. *The Gutenberg Galaxy*. Toronto, 1962.
———. *Understanding Media: The Extension of Man*. New York, 1964.
———. *War and Peace in the Global Village*. New York, 1968.
Marshall McLuhan and Quentin Fiore. *The Medium Is the Massage: An Inventory of Effects*. Toronto, 1967.
Mario de Micheli. *Manifesti Rivoluzionari*. Milan, 1973.
Vance Packard. *The Hidden Persuaders*. New York, 1958.
Lamberto Pignotti. *Fra Parola e Immagine: Arte e Comunicazione nella Società di Massa*. Padua, 1972.
Lamberto Pignotti and Egidio Mucci. *Maschio e Femmina: La Donna Inventata dalla Pubblicità*. Florence, 1978.
Arturo Carlo Quintavalle. *Pubblicità: Modello, Sistema, Storia*. Milan, 1977.
Jasia Reichardt. *Cybernetic Serendipity*. London, 1968.
Attilio Rossi. *I Manifesti*. Milan, 1966.
Dino Villani. *Storia del Manifesto Pubblicitario*. Milan, 1964.
Robert C. Williams. *Artists in Revolution*. Bloomington, Indiana, 1977.
Gary Yanker. *Pop Art: Over 1000 Contemporary Political Posters*. London, 1972.

Art Direction and Advertising

Giuseppe Campa, ed. *Pubblicità e Consumi in Italia*. Milan, 1976.
S. Watson Dunn. *Advertising: Its Role in Modern Marketing*. New York, 1961.
Umberto Eco. *La Struttura Assente*. Milan, 1968.
Stuart Ewen. *Captains of Consciousness: Advertising and the Social Roots of the Consumer Culture*. New York, 1976.
Giampaolo Fabris. *La Comunicazione Pubblicitaria*. Milan, 1968.
Leslie E. Gill. *Advertising and Psychology*. New York, 1953.
George Lois and Bill Pitts. *The Art of Advertising: George Lois on Mass Communication*. New York, 1977.
Pierre Martineau. *Motivation in Advertising: Motives That Make People Buy*. London, 1957.
S. Prakash Sethi. *Advocacy Advertising and Large Corporations*. Lexington, Mass., 1977.

Graphics and Visual Perception

Sven Tito Achen. *Symbols Around Us*. New York, 1978.
Dawn Ades. *Photomontage*. London, 1976.
Rudolf Arnheim. *Art and Visual Perception: A Psychology of the Creative Eye*. Berkeley, 1954.
John Berger. *Ways of Seeing*. London, 1972.
Sergio Bersi and Carlo Ricci. *Linguaggi e Progetto*. Bologna, 1976.
Giovanni Brunazzi. *Enciclopedia della Stampa*. 12 vols. Turin, 1969.
John W. Cataldo. *Graphic Design & Visual Communications*. Scranton, Penn., 1966.
Gillo Dorfles. *Simbolo, Comunicazione, Consumo*. Turin, 1962.
Anton Ehrenzweig. *The Hidden Order of Art*. London, 1970.
Germano Facetti and Alan Fletcher. *Identity Kits*. London, 1971.
Alan Fletcher, Colin Forbes, and Bob Gill. *Graphic Design: Visual Comparisons*. London, 1963.
Milton Glaser. *Graphic Design*. New York, 1973.

E. H. Gombrich. *Art and Illusion: A Study in the Psychology of Pictorial Representation*. Oxford, 1960.
Peter Gorb, ed. *Pentagram*. London, 1978.
R. L. Gregory. *Eye and Brain: The Psychology of Seeing*. London, 1966.
Armin Hofmann. *Methodik der Form- und Bildgestaltung*. Teufen, 1965.
James Hogg, ed. *Psychology and the Visual Arts*. London, 1969.
Giancarlo Iliprandi. *Linguaggio Grafico*. 3 vols. Milan, 1964–73.
Gyorgy Kepes. *Language of Vision*. Chicago, 1944.
Gyorgy Kepes, ed. *Module, Proportion, Symmetry, Rhythm*. New York, 1966.
———. *The Language of Vision*. London, 1969.
Wolfgang Köhler. *Gestalt Psychology*. New York, 1947.
Lucy Lippard, ed. *Dadas on Art*. Englewood Cliffs, N.J. 1971.
Attilio Marcolli. *Teoria di Campo*. Florence, 1971.
Enzo Mari. *Funzione della Ricerca Estetica*. Milan, 1970.
Massin. *Letter and Image*. New York, 1970.
Bruno Munari. *Arte come Mestiere*. Bari, 1966.
———. *Design e Comunicazione Visiva*. Bari, 1968.
———. *Artista e Designer*. Bari, 1971.
———. *Codice Ovvio*. Turin, 1971.
Wally Olins. *The Corporate Personality*. London, 1978.
Franco Maria Ricci and Corinna Ferrari. *Top Symbols and Trademarks of the World*. 7 vols. Milan, 1973.
Emil Ruder, *Typography: A Manual of Design*. New York, 1967.
Maurice de Sausmarez. *Basic Design: The Dynamics of Visual Form*. London, 1964.
Herbert Spencer. *Pioneers of Modern Typography*. London, 1969.
Peter Wildbur. *Trademarks*. London, 1966.

Graphics and the Environment

Philippe Boudon. *Lived-In Architecture*. London, 1975.
Theo Crosby. *How to Play the Environment Game*. London, 1973.
Norman Mailer, Mervyn Kurlansky, and John Narr. *The Faith of Graffiti*. New York, 1974.
Tom Porter and Byron Mikellides. *Colour for Architecture*. London, 1976.

Illustration in Advertising and Publicity

Daivd Bland. *A History of Book Illustration*. 2nd ed., rev. Berkeley, 1969.
———. *The Illustration of Books*. 3rd ed., rev. London, 1962.
Harold Evans. *Pictures on a Page*. London, 1978.
Philip James. *English Book Illustration, 1800–1900*. Middlesex, 1947.
Henry C. Pitz. *200 Years of American Illustration*. New York, 1977.
R. Margaret Slythe. *The Art of Illustration, 1750–1900*. London, 1970.
Rolf Söderberg. *French Book Illustration, 1880–1905*. Translated by Roger Tanner. Stockholm, 1977.
Geoffrey Wakeman. *Victorian Book Illustration: The Technical Revolution*. Newton Abbot, Devon, 1973.

History

John Barnicoat. *A Concise History of Posters: 1870–1970*. London, 1972.
Terry Bishop, ed. *Design History: Fad or Function?* London, 1978.
Mildred Constantine, ed. *Word and Image: Posters from the Collection of the Museum of Modern Art*. New York, 1968.
Graphic Design of the World. 7 vols. Tokyo, 1974–76.
Josef Müller-Brockmann. *A History of Visual Communication*. New York, 1971.
Hellmut Rademacher. *Masters of German Poster Art*. New York, 1966.
Philippe Schuwer. *Histoire de la Publicité*. Lausanne, 1965.
Jacques Viénot. *Cappiello*. Edited by Jack Rennert. New York, 1977.
Maximilien Vox. *Plakate A. M. Cassandre*. Saint Gall, 1948.
Robert C. Williams. *Artists in Revolution: Portraits of the Russian Avant-Garde, 1905–1925*. Bloomington, Ind., 1978.
Hans M. Wingler. *Das Bauhaus*. Cambridge, Mass., 1969.

Magazines and Annuals

Annual. Art Directors Club, Milan.
Annual. Art Directors Club, New York.
Annual of Advertising Art in Japan. Art Directors Club, Tokyo.
Das Plakat. Berlin, 1910–1921.
Design and Art Direction. London.
European Illustration. London.
Graphis. Zurich.
Gebrauchsgraphik. Berlin.
Illustrators: Annual of American Illustration. New York.
Modern Publicity. London.
Penrose Annual: Review of the Graphic Art. London.
Pubblicità in Italia. Milan.

INDEX
Page numbers in *italics* indicate references to illustrations.

Scarfone, Ernest 116
Schaeffer, Mead 266
Scherr, Max 33, 55
Schiavo, Elso 137
Schleifer, Fritz 294
Schlemmer, Oskar 142; 69, 294
Schmid, Max 176
Schmidt, Joost 308, 314; 69
Schönhaus, Sioma 180
Schroeder, Kathe 158
Schulthess, Emil 84
Schumacher, Fritz 300
Scott, Howard 266
Searle, Ronald 204
Seltzer, Isadore 271
Senefelder, Aloys 260, 286
Shahn, Ben 33; 32, 38, 39, 256, 310
Shapur, Fredun 199
Shaumann, Peter 128
Sheridan, John E. 266
Shigeta, Ryoichi 242
Shimudu, Ikki 272
Shimomoto, Yoshikatsu 40
Shinoda, Yu 202
Show 56
Shulton's Art Department 194
Siano, Jerry 105
Signal 46, 53
Silano 59
Simplicissimus 51, 297
Simpson, J. W. 286
Sironi, Mario 314
Sirowitz, Len 112, 128
Sloan, John 248
Smith, Jessie Wilcox 266
Smoke House Associates 235
Smutzler, Robert 286
Snyder, Jerome 271
Sogno di Polifilo, Il 18
Sokolsky, Melvin 129
Sorel, Edward 271
Soroos, Peter 212
Sozzi, Ennio 94
Spagnol, Mario 64
Starowieyski, Franciszek 72, 258, 306
Stauffacher, Barbara 207
Steadman, Ralph 279; 313
Steele, Frederic Dorr 266

Steinberg, Saul 247, 279; 70, 256, 273
Steiner, Albe 314; 52, 155
Steiner, Henry 75, 183
Steinlen, Théophile Alexandre 286
Stern, Bert 56
Stettler, Wayne 181
Stevens, Martin 107
Stöcklin, Niklaus 117
Stone, Gilbert 257
Storch, Otto 57
Strand, Kerry 158
Straxov, A. 42
Stuck, Franz von 292
Studio Boggeri 103
Sugiura, Kohei 21, 47, 71, 74
Sugiura, Shunsaku 181
Sunday Times Magazine 272; 54, 55
Sutnar, Ladislav 314
Suzuki, Hachiro 111
Suzuki, Seiji 106
Swierzy, Waldmar 78

Takahashi, Kinkichi 37
Takanashi, Yutaka 111
Tanaka, Ikko 62, 141, 148
Tapley, William 204
Tatsumi, Shiro 56
Taubin, William 85
Teige, Karl 147
television 88, 92–111, 272, 281
Terence Donovan & Partners 88
Terrazas, Eduardo 138
Testa, Armando 81
Tobo, Tomoyuki 233
Tomaszewsky, Henryk 306
Toorop, Jan 285
Topor, Roland 265
Toscani, Oliviero 100, 101
Toulouse-Lautrec, Henri de 187, 263, 281, 286; 50, 255, 276
Tovaglia, Pino 138, 139, 151, 152, 154
Trapp, Willy 90
Traube, Herbert W. 158
Treasure Chest, The 20
Trepkowski, Tadeusz 48
Très Riches Heures du Duc de Berry, Les 11

Trionfo Ermetico 14
Troisi, Alfredo 122, 153
Troller, Fred 176
Trump, G. 301
Tscherney, George 170, 177
Tschichold, Jan 314; Elementare Typographie 147
Tsuchiya, Koichi 129, 137
Turner, Peter 57
Twen 261; 57
Twitchell, Kent 225

Uematu, Kuniomi 40
Ungerer, Tomi 44, 52, 127
Unimark International 152
Uno, Akira 146, 256, 269
Urbaniec, Maciej 78, 79
Utz, Thornton 266

Vale Press 264
Van Bladel, Ida 184
Van de Velde, Henry 297, 299, 311; 285
Vanity Fair 266, 267
Vasarely, Victor 139; 213
Ver Sacrum 288
Victor Hutz 90
Vienna Secession 238, 286, 288, 291
Vignelli, Massimo 153
Villon, Jacques 286; 282
Viva 270
Vivarelli, Carlo 314
Vogue 266, 267, 277, 314; 60, 61
Voyage de Nicolas Klimius dans le monde souterrain 18

Wada, Makoto 43
Wagner, Frank 177
Wagner, Otto 288; 238
Wakabayashi, Hiro 58, 59, 60
Wakui, Yoshio 189
Walden, Herwarth 299
Walker, Wallace 192
Walter Landor Associates 177, 178
Ward, Jack 105
Warhol, Andy 311
Webb, Peter 89
Webb, Sidney 65

Weekend 279; 313
Weiblen, Hans Peter 175
Weiss, Len 130
Wellmer, Gerhard 209
Wells, Mary 245
Welsh, Jack 266
Wendingen 294, 307
Wertheimer, Max 133, 135
Whelan, Paul 137
Whitney, John: Permutations 158; 161
Wiegand, Bob 233
Wiener, Norbert: Cybernetics 158; The Human Use of Human Beings 158
Wiener Werkstätte 286, 288, 295, 314
Wijdeveld, Hendrikus Th. 307; 294
Willet, John: Art in a City 231
Wilson, Wes 144
Wilvers, Robert 111
Wolf, Henry 56, 112
Wolfe, Tom 153
Wolff, Michael 191, 194
Wyman, Lance 138

Yabuki, Nobuhiko 267
Yamaguchi, Harumi 106
Yamamoto, Ryoichi 189
Yamashiro, Ryuichi 62, 70
Yokoo, Tadanori 71, 74, 185, 202, 233, 257, 263
Yokosuka, Noriaki 59, 125
Yokoyama, Kumiko 169, 176
Yokozawa, Takakazu 40
Yoshida, Tadao 88, 111, 129
Yoshida, Taiho 146

Zald, Barry 271; 277
Zaletsky, Roy 116
Zamercznick, Wojciech 71
Zan, Lou 107
Zanuso, Marco 188
Zenoni, Giorgio 240
Zieff, Howard 92, 112, 116
Ziegler, Zdenek 38
Zoom 57, 270
Zwart, Piet 295

CREDITS

In the following references the first number, in roman type, indicates the page. The following number, in italic type, identifies the position of the illustration on the page, from left to right and top to bottom.

ABC, 18, 2
Michiaki Abe, 142, 2, 3; 178, 5; 278, 4
Abitare, 63, 2, 4
© ADAGP, 2
Adi, 138, 2, 3; 199, 1
Adver, 101
John Alcorn, 267, 2; 279
Alka-Seltzer, 108, 5
American Illustrators, 260; 268, 3; 269, 1; 270, 1; 273, 2
American Showcase, Inc., 156, 1
Shigeo Anzai, 202, 1
Kyoko Arai, 168, 6; 176, 3
The Art of Advertising, 86; 93; 97, 4; 98, 2; 99
Art Directors Club, Germany, 127, 2
Art Directors Club, Milan, 88, 5; 90, 2
Art Directors Club, New York, 104, 1; 107, 1; 116, 4; 128, 1; 130, 1, 2, 3; 259, 1; 273, 2
Art Directors Club, Tokyo, 165, 2
Asahi Breweries Co., Ltd., 94, 4
Avant-Garde Media, Inc., 310, 4, 5, 6
Kiyoshi Awazu, 218, 1
A-Z, Milan, 149, 1, 2, 3
Bauhausbücher, 296, 2
Herbert Bayer, 295, 2
B Communication, 107, 3
Benson & Hedges, 126; 127, 3

Berg International Éditeurs, 19, 3
Raccolta delle Stampe Bertarelli, 16, 1, 2, 18, 1, 27, 4; 29, 1, 2, 3, 4, 5, 7
Better Vision Institute, 128, 2
Adam & Charles Black, Ltd., 66, 1, 2
Boffi Arredamenti, 110, 1
Braun, 111, 4
George Braziller, Inc., 310, 1
British Museum, 164, 1
Busnelli, 110, 2
Canada Dry Corporation, 124, 2
Casabella, 63, 1, 3
Mimmo Castellano, 157, 1
CBS, 113, 1, 2
CDC Dubonnet, 96, 6
Chaihuadjareon, Paylon/Thailand, 166, 1, 2; 167, 3
Baron Ciagà, 240, 4
Conde Nast Publications, Inc., 57, 1; 60, 1, 3; 61, 1, 2
Constable, 31, 2
Container Corporation of America, 125, 3; 171, 3, 5; 178, 6
Continental, 129, 3, 4
Corgi, 65, 3
Flavio Costantini, 269, 4
Alan Cracknell, 251, 1
Guido Crepax, 273, 1
Wim Crouwel, 156, 3

Paul Davis, 312, 1
De Beers Consolidated Mines, Ltd., 105, 2
Robert Delpire Éditeur, 28, 1
Design and Art Direction, 88, 3; 89, 2; 94, 1; 97, 3; 131
Design Group Italia, 179, 1; 181, 4
Doi Assoc., 208
Studio Dumont, 20, 5; 21, 1
Verlag M. DuMont, 29, 6
Eastman Chemical, Inc., 116; 3
Heinz Edelman, 261, 1
Editoriale Domus, 62, 3, 4, 238, 2
Emme Edizioni, 66, 3, 4
Eros Magazine, Inc., 56, 1, 2
European Illustration, 118, 1; 119, 1; 159, 2; 248, 2, 3; 252, 1; 257, 1; 261, 2; 263, 2; 265, 3; 270, 2; 272, 1; 273, 4; 313
Fabbri Editori, 238, 1
Fischer, 64, 4, 5; 65, 5
French Government Tourist Office, 85, 2
Shigeo Fukuda, 219, 2; 242, 3; 243, 3
Fuji Xerox Co., Ltd., 111, 3
Yukio Futagawa, 207
Roger Gain, 209, 2
Éditions Gallimard, 148, 5, 6
Abram Games, 35, 1, 3

J. F. Gaudineau, 240, 1, 2
Gebrauchsgraphik, 137, 1
Gelli, Ex-Libris Italiani (Hoepli, 1930), 23
General Wine and Spirits Company, 97, 2
Eric Gill, 156, 2
Gillette, 111, 1
Die Glückliche Hand (René Simmen), 30, 2
Group-Parme, 229
Haas'schen Schriftgiesserei, 308, 1, 2
The Hague, 25, 2
Hanuman in Art and Mythology (Aryan and Prakashan), 20, 6
Hiromu Hara, 165, 4
Harcourt, Brace and Company, 67, 1, 2
Harlech Television, 153, 2
Hartford Publications, Inc., 56, 3
Harvey Probber Furniture Co., Ltd., 110, 3
Heartfield Archive and Getrud Heartfield, 40, 2
Richard Hess, 265, 4
Hochschule für Gestaltung, Ulm, 308, 5
Armin Hofmann, 136, 1, 2
Haensel Holzminden, 95, 1
L'Homme Face à la Maladie (Le Livre

Besides the above citations, the authors wish to thank the following institutions, publishers, and individuals:

Air France; Alan Aldridge; Kickisaburo Anzai; Masuteru Aoba; Katsumi Asaba; Setsu Asakura; Saul Bass and Associates, Inc.; Herbert Bayer; Dorothy Beall, Bijutsu Shuppansha; Pieter Brattinga; Linda Brockbank; Bungeishunjusha, Ltd.; Bunka Shuppankyoku; Canon Col, Ltd.; Chichibunomiya Museum; Seymour Chwast; Paul Colin; John Cox; Daido Woollen Co.; Hilary Davis; de Jong Co., Ltd.; Dick Elfers; Tamotsu Ejima; Humphrey Evans; Janina Fijalkowska; Alan Fletcher; Hideki Fujii; Shigeo Fukuda; General Dynamics; Milton Glaser; Francis Glibbery; Graphic Design Associates; Terrence Griffin; Shukuro Habara; Yoshio Hasegawa; Werner Hauser; Yoshio Hayakawa; Seiichi Hayashi; F. H. K. Heurion; Shigemi Hijikata; Gan Hosoya; Max Huber; Shichiro Imatake; Eiko Ishioka; Yoshio Itabashi; Kenji Ito; Kenji Iwasaki; Japan Travel Bureau; Japan National Railways; Japan Design Center; JUN Co., Ltd.; Yusaku Kamekura; Takahisa Kamijo; Akio Kanda; Mitsuo Katsui; Masaru Katsumie; Shigeo Katsuoka; Yosuke Kawamura; Minsho Kawasaki; Julien Key; Kiyoshi Kibe; Tsunehisa Kimura; Kinketsu Department Store; Kuni Kizawa; Hiroshi Kojitani; Olga Kokoschka; Keisuke Konishi; Hiroshi Konno; Takashi Kono; Kukriniksy; Hisami Kunitake; Kuprejanov; Teruyuki Kunito; Yoji Kuri; Akira Kurita; Kenichi Kuriyagawa; Seitaro Kuroda; Jun Kusakari; Giichi Kusuhara; Lora Lamm; Jan Lenica; Light Publicity, Ltd.; Lion Dentifrice Co., Ltd.; Herb Lubalin; Lufthansa; Hiroshi Manabe; Tadashi Masuda; Makoto Matsunaga; Meiji Confectionery Co., Ltd.; Takushi Mizuno; Morinaga Confectionery Co., Ltd.; Tetsuo Miyahara; Morinaga Confectionery Co., Ltd.; Joseph Müller-Brockmann; Musashino University of Art; Muzeum Naradowe; Tadahito Nadamoto; Kazumasa Nagai; Keisuke Nagatomo; Masayoshi Nakajo; Makoto Nakamura; Nikka Whisky Distilling; Nippon Kogaku Co., Ltd.; Isao Nishijima; Tadahisa Nishio; Eric Nitsche; Marcello Nizzoli; Hisamitsu Noguchi; Hiroshi Ochi; Ayumi Ohashi; Tadashi Ohashi; Masamichi Oikawa; Hiroshi Ota; André Pasture; Giovanni Pintori; Q. P. Corporation; Paul Rand; Jacques Richez; Nomi Rowe; Toshio Saeki; Saito Process; Masatomo Sakaguchi; Shigetaka Sawada; Nicole Segre; Seibu Department Store; Seibundo Shinkosha; Norman Shapiro; Toru Shigenari; Ikki Shimoda; Shiseido Co., Ltd.; Shizenkan, Ltd.; G. K. Shuppansha; Rippu Shobo; Jack Skeel; Herbert Spencer; Heinz Spielmann; Yutaka Sugita; Hohei Sugiura; Suntory Co., Ltd.; Swissair; Jun Tabohashi; Kinkichi Takahashi; Haruo Takino; Keiichi Tanaami; Shiro Tatsumi; Tokyo Photo Arugas; Toyata; Toyobo Co.; George Tscherny; Kenichi Ueda; Kuniomi Uematsu; Tadao Ujihara; Akira Uno; Van Jacket, Inc.; Nobuhiko Yabuki; Harumi Yamaguchi; Yamaha Hatsudoki Co., Ltd.; Ayao Yamana; Ryuichi Yamashiro; Yuzo Yamashita; Hiroshi Yamazaki; Shizuki Yoshikawa; Reikichi Yura; Makoto Wada; Aijiro Wakita